SISTERS in CAPTIVITY

Other military history books by Colin Burgess

The Diggers of Colditz (with Jack Champ)
Prisoners of War (with Hugh Clarke and Russell Braddon)
Barbed Wire and Bamboo (with Hugh Clarke)
Freedom or Death
(republished as *Australia's Greatest Escapes*)
Australia's Dambusters: Flying into Hell with 617 Squadron
Destination Buchenwald
Bush Parker: An Australian Battle of Britain Pilot in Colditz

SISTERS in CAPTIVITY

Sister Betty Jeffrey OAM
and the courageous story of
Australian Army nurses in Sumatra, 1942–1945

Colin Burgess

**SIMON &
SCHUSTER**

London · New York · Sydney · Toronto · New Delhi

SISTERS IN CAPTIVITY: SISTER BETTY JEFFREY OAM AND
THE COURAGEOUS STORY OF AUSTRALIAN ARMY NURSES
IN SUMATRA, 1942–1945
First published in Australia in 2023 by
Simon & Schuster (Australia) Pty Limited
Suite 19A, Level 1, Building C, 450 Miller Street, Cammeray, NSW 2062

10 9 8 7 6 5 4 3 2 1

Sydney New York London Toronto New Delhi
Visit our website at www.simonandschuster.com.au

A catalogue record for this
book is available from the
National Library of Australia

ISBN: 9781761109089

Cover design: Luke Causby / Blue Cork
Cover images: Australian Nurses Memorial Centre (Betty Jeffrey);
Australian War Memorial P03315.007 (group photo)
Typeset by Midland Typesetters, Australia
Printed and bound in Australia by Griffin Press

The paper this book is printed on is certified against the
Forest Stewardship Council® Standards. Griffin Press holds
chain of custody certification SCS-COC-001185. FSC®
promotes environmentally responsible, socially beneficial
and economically viable management of the world's forests.

CONTENTS

To the heroic nurses who lived this story
but never made it home

They endured the worst together: Sisters Vivian Bullwinkel (left) and Betty Jeffrey of the Australian Army Nursing Service at a 1950 dedication ceremony to the fallen servicemen and women of World War II.

INTRODUCTION AND ACKNOWLEDGEMENTS

BY ANY DEFINITION, BETTY JEFFREY was an extraordinary woman and a dedicated nursing sister, always finding within herself the determination and strength to carry on. Her life would change dramatically as a prisoner of the Japanese during the latter three years of World War II. Together with her fellow nurses, many of whom would not survive captivity, she had to endure deprivation, disease and near starvation while physically weak and exhausted, often discouraged, and experiencing lost hours to a deep melancholy under cruel, primitive conditions. Selfless, devoted and caring, she would always lift herself up and attempt to raise the spirits of those around her whenever life under this shared captivity in disgusting, squalid conditions was at its lowest ebb. She saw it as her personal duty: encouraging, helping and even laughing with those with whom she shared those drab, endless days. This despite existing for more than three years in the ever-present knowledge that any Sumatran sunrise as a prisoner of a merciless enemy could so easily be her last.

As discussed at length in this book, the treatment meted out by

Japanese captors on our Australian nurses was reprehensible and inhumane. Betty's words, and those of others who endured those nightmare years, often make for distressing reading, but she did not attempt to exaggerate or gloss over the facts and personal experiences of brutality, starvation, beatings, the filthy overcrowded camps, an almost total lack of hygiene and privacy, enforced heavy labour, the heartless withholding of food and medicine, and an unforgivable lack of compassion or care by their captors for the sick and wounded.

Recalling memories of her years spent as a Japanese prisoner of war would remain a vivid and painful exercise for the rest of Betty's life, and she generally refused to talk to the media about them. Once, when she had completed a rare interview with the *Age* newspaper in 1998, her parting quip was: 'Of course, you know I will have nightmares tonight.'

Betty's defiance and tenacity in keeping a secret diary throughout most of her internment, which if found could have led to her immediate execution, speaks so highly about this amazing, obstinate woman. Not only did she keep a diary, but she drew some remarkable sketches capturing daily life in the camps and it's a privilege to include five of those in this book, which have been placed throughout the chapters. I feel incredibly privileged to be telling her remarkable story.

While contemplating a main title for this book, I came across a saying that I felt perfectly reflected the indomitable courage, defiance, strength and compassion of Sister Agnes Betty Jeffrey and her young colleagues in the Australian Army Nursing Service (AANS) during the Second World War. That saying was, 'Fall down seven times, stand up eight'. Unfortunately, it happens to be an old Japanese expression, and I had to agree with Betty's great-niece Emily Malone, who thoughtfully put paid to the suggestion:

As you can appreciate, she never forgot what her captors did to her, the nurses and the women and children in camp . . . despite visiting Japan and taking steps to forgive those who treated her so poorly, she never forgot. Anything Japanese was a stark reminder for her of the war years.

So that proposed title – despite all it might have conveyed about the resilience of the nurses central to this story – was discarded for something more appropriate.

Like so many Australians in the mid-1950s, I had never heard of Betty Jeffrey until my family began to gather around our radio once a week and listen in silence to a dramatic, 52-part serial called 'White Coolies', adapted from the diary notes secretly written and kept by Sister Jeffrey during her three-and-a-half years as a prisoner of the Japanese in Sumatra. As the first episode is listed as airing on 10 August 1955, I would have been just eight years old, but I can never forget that compelling introductory music and the voice of a young Gordon Chater as he intoned the opening lines. It was also when I first recall hearing such amazing media personalities as Ruth Cracknell, June Salter and Queenie Ashton speaking their lead roles as week by week this enthralling saga unfolded, growing ever more intense and unmissable.

In the opening episode, we listened to a wonderful tribute to the nurses involved in this powerful, real-life story, spoken by Colonel Annie Moriah Sage, CBE, RRC, formerly Matron-in-Chief of the Royal Australian Army Nursing Corps, and a person Betty Jeffrey would always hold in the highest regard. Here is what Matron Sage stated in her introductory monologue, an abridged version of the foreword she had written the previous year for Betty's classic 1954 book:

This is the truth about women who fought in the last war. Yes, I mean fought, for they did fight, just as surely as the sailor with his submarines and guns, the soldier with rifle and tank, and the airman with his bombs and machine guns. But for these women it was a different kind of war; they fought against anything that threatened to destroy life. What they suffered physically was almost inhuman, but only women can fully appreciate their terrible mental anguish, and the constant, dreadful fear of what the Nipponese could and might do to them.

This is not fiction, but truth. A truth that should be heard and remembered, not only for the fine example of courage and bravery it tells, but also for the grand humour, resourcefulness and ability to keep morale at the highest possible level.

The longer the war progressed, the greater grew my admiration for them. I will never cease to love them all.

In high school, like so many of my youthful male peers, I could hardly wait to get my hands on some of the remarkable true-life books about the Second World War from our school or local library, with a particular interest in books on the prisoner of war experience – *The Colditz Story*, *The Wooden Horse*, *Reach for the Sky*, *The Great Escape* and *The Naked Island* among them. I also found and purchased a treasured paperback copy of *White Coolies* in a second-hand book store in Sydney. In 1979, on a whim, I decided to write to Betty Jeffrey at her home in East Malvern, Victoria, to express my long-held admiration, and in her kind response she remarked: 'I am happy that you still enjoy your yellowing, dog-eared copy of *White Coolies* – that serial was endless! It "got" me in too!'

As the years passed, I fulfilled a youthful pledge to write some books dealing with the Australian POW experience, which I felt was a sadly neglected facet of the war. To my joy (and perhaps not a little astonishment!), these were published in both Australia and the United Kingdom. It therefore came as a very welcome surprise in 2018 when I was contacted by Simon & Schuster in Sydney, asking if I would like to participate in publishing new and updated editions of my POW books from many years ago. I was delighted to oblige, and since then they have published four of these books.

However, as a result my literary cupboard was bereft of any further war stories and, when I was asked if I might have any ideas for a book dealing with any human aspect of Australians at war, I suggested a book on the late, much-admired Sister Betty Jeffrey. This struck an immediate chord with their editorial team, so I contacted the Australian Nurses Memorial Centre (ANMC) on St Kilda Road, Melbourne.

The ANMC had enjoyed a long and fruitful association with Betty Jeffrey, who was instrumental in its beginning and development, and where she was the first administrator. I subsequently received a very encouraging response from the current centre manager, Elizabeth (Liz) Allwood, who put me in touch with Emily Malone, Betty's great-niece. Emily is an honorary life member of the ANMC and a member of the centre's History and Heritage Committee. After checking with other family members, Emily gave me a provisional go-ahead, which meant the research and writing could begin.

'As a family we all believe a Betty Jeffrey biography needs to remain true to who she was as a person, her accomplishments and life experiences,' Emily wrote.

We are all incredibly proud of her (me especially) but we are biased of course! There is something about the word 'strength' that I have always thought of when reminiscing about Aunty Bett. It is a word I use when I speak about her to others. I have always said that it was her inner strength, incredibly close friendships with the nurses and fabulous sense of humour that was the reason she survived a shipwreck, two-and-a-half days in the water and three-and-a-half years as a POW.

Betty Jeffrey would reluctantly retire from her position with the ANMC due to a recurring illness suffered in the mid-1950s, but she steadfastly continued to represent former prisoners of war and nurses. In 1987 she received the OAM (Order of Australia Medal) for her ongoing and selfless commitment to ex-servicemen and -women.

We lost Betty Jeffrey on 13 September 2000 at the grand age of 92, leaving behind her a mighty legacy of caring, devotion and compassion. She truly was a shining example to all nurses throughout her life – during internment and beyond – a magnificent Australian, and an inspiration to us all.

There are many to whom I owe some particular thanks for their kind and thorough assistance with this book and I must single out the tremendous support and encouragement offered to me right from the start by Betty's great-niece Emily Malone. Despite a heavy workload of her own, she gave me her time and some valuable insights into her great-aunt's life and legacy. In Melbourne, she also organised a weekend gathering at the centre of family members and some other people who had known and worked with Betty, which gave me two wonderful days of interviews, as well as information and photo gathering. Thank you for this, Emily, and the reflections given by your parents Robert and Jane Malone, and other family members Sara Renshaw, Tim and Elaine Gale and Antony Jeffrey. I also extend my sincere thanks to Ann Sprague, Diane Whitehead, Arlene Bennett, Helen Pickering, Sue Sherson and John Bullwinkel for taking me further into Betty Jeffrey's life and legacy.

I would like to acknowledge the use of interviews and notes from several of the nurses over the years who returned home safely from captivity, but who have since left us. These memories have been included in whole or part in this book to support the remarkable story of Sister Betty Jeffrey. The source subjects (under their wartime surnames) include Sisters Vivian Bullwinkel, Iole Harper, Jessie Simons, Wilma Oram, Kath Blake, Florence Trotter, Christian Oxley, Veronica Clancy, Pat Darling, Nesta James and Sylvia Muir.

One special thanks and acknowledgement must go to Brian Ashton, who put me in touch with his sister Jill. In 2003, Jill privately published the secret diary kept by her aunt, Sister Carrie Jean Ashton (she preferred to be called Jean), throughout her early war duties, capture and imprisonment – those ghastly years she shared with Betty Jeffrey and the other AANS nurses. The diary was painstakingly copied and typed from the original by Jean's sister-in-law, Joyce Ashton. I am grateful to Jill Ashton for allowing me access to a copy of this diary, which greatly aided in reconstructing some of the events mentioned by – or even missed reporting by – Betty Jeffrey. I also appreciated the assistance of David Man from the Muntok Memorial Peace Museum website, historian Gillian Ednie, Janet Buick at the Stonnington History Centre in Malvern, Victoria, William Dale and Joy Derham of the Ex-Prisoners of War and Relatives Association (Victoria), and special appreciation to

Clive Baker, who read an early draft of the manuscript and assisted with some expert editing suggestions.

Another recent publication offering further background is *The Poinciana Tree*, a lightly fictionalised recreation of the author's life and family – particularly that of his mother Aimée – brilliantly written by celebrated arts manager Antony Jeffrey AM, whose father Alan was an older brother of Betty Jeffrey.

Through the invaluable resource of the National Library of Australia's Trove website (https:/trove.nla.com.au) I was able to review newspaper articles contemporary with the periods covered in the book which revealed anecdotal material that would otherwise have been incredibly difficult to locate. These newspapers include the Perth *Daily News* and *Sunday News*, the *West Australian*, the *Australian Women's Mirror*, the *Sydney Morning Herald*, the Sydney *Sun*, the Adelaide *Advertiser*, the Melbourne *Advocate*, *The Age*, the Melbourne *Herald*, the Melbourne *Argus*, the Newcastle *Sun*, the Burnie (Tasmania) *Advocate*, the Riverina *Herald*, the Albury *Morning Mail*, the Armidale *Express* and the Townsville *Daily Bulletin*.

White Coolies and other books, articles and interviews given by the Australian nurses during and immediately after the war reflect the often hostile feelings of these women towards their Japanese captors, and they continually referred to them as 'Japs'. This abbreviated version of the word 'Japanese' is today regarded as a derogatory term, but its use in many quotes within this book will need to be tolerated by the reader. Different times, different expressions. There were other less-than-flattering contemporary descriptions of the Japanese people as a whole, and particularly certain individuals, but these instances have been side-stepped in the narrative, rather than cause offence to anyone. Similarly, the word 'coolie' is not in common use today; it is a term once applied to local Asian workers who laboured hard for low wages while living in substandard conditions.

With the passage of so many years, it proved difficult in just a handful of cases to properly acknowledge the source of some photographs and illustrations used in this book. Should anyone care to contact me through the publishers we will give due accreditation in any subsequent editions.

Different accounts of this story in other publications often use alternative spellings of some translated place names, such as Banka/ Bangka, Muntok/Mentok and Loebok Linggau/Loeboek Linggau/ Lubuklinggau, but in all instances I have relied on the spelling used in *White Coolies*. Also in keeping with the entries in Betty Jeffrey's diary, it was decided to retain imperial measurements such as feet and yards, although in certain instances the metric equivalent has been added.

In conclusion, I would like to acknowledge an amazing team of people at Simon & Schuster (Sydney) who have made the publishing experience – often so gruelling at times – into a true pleasure. It is incredibly rewarding to be working with such talented, professional and helpful people as Managing Editor Michelle Swainson, Editor Rosie Outred, Luke Causby (cover art) and my wonderfully diligent copyeditor Mark Evans, whose keen eye for fact and faults helped make my manuscript even more authoritative, while unearthing many of my grammatical errors and rectifying ill-chosen punctuation. Thank you all for your friendship, ongoing support and encouragement throughout.

Colin Burgess, New South Wales, Australia

2023

Reunion in the grounds of Charitas Hospital, Palembang, 1979: Betty Jeffrey and Dame Margot Turner sing 'The Captives Hymn' with the surviving nuns and Sister Catharinia *(third from right, back row)*.

FOREWORD

LAVINIA WARNER IS A BRITISH writer and producer – creator of many highly successful television programmes. These include the documentary Women in Captivity *(1979), and the powerful BBC TV series* Tenko *(1981–1985), which told of women internees in a Japanese prison camp. Today she is CEO of Warner Sisters, the independent production company she founded.*

Never having actually met Colin Burgess, the author of this excellent book, I am fascinated to learn from his Introduction that 1979 had been an important year for both of us in terms of contacting the heroine of *White Coolies*, Betty Jeffrey. Colin wrote her a 'fan letter' expressing his long-held admiration, and, almost simultaneously, I was phoning her long-distance to ask if she would fly to Indonesia and be part of my documentary about a women's wartime prison camp in Sumatra. Thank goodness she said yes – it was the beginning of an important friendship for me.

Women in Captivity was for BBC's Omnibus, and ABC Australia had made a contribution to the budget. In addition to filming women survivors in the UK, we were taking Betty Jeffrey, Dame Margot Turner, and Dutch nun Sister Catharinia back to the actual locations of their imprisonment. Being nurses, Margot and Betty had struck up a good friendship in camp and this bond was immediately rekindled 37 years later. Sister Catharinia had become close to them too, and was still travelling in Indonesia for her religious Order. We only had nine days to chart over three years of their captivity and, given the heat, travel and pressure of time, it was a gruelling shoot even for me and the small film crew, never mind for women in their 70s. Sumatra was a developing Indonesian country with all the chaos and growing pains that entailed. For example, ours was the best hotel in the capital of Palembang, but it was only half-built, which meant that where our bedrooms had been allocated (up on the 3rd floor), the corridor ended in a huge gaping hole open to the elements. The women were courageous and wonderful company; they were absolute naturals in front of the camera and cemented their good friendship with humour as well as deep emotion when the memories came flooding back. Betty's fortitude mirrored her strength in camp, and certainly motivated us to keep up with the schedule.

We covered the locations and main stages of their harrowing story – the forced evacuation from Singapore and their subsequent shipwreck was recounted from the mangrove swamps of coastal Sumatra. The early days of their internment was shot in the actual remains of the bungalows and garages where Betty described how, 37 years ago 'to the day', the Japanese had packed in 300 women who tried to organise themselves in the face of dwindling rations and some frightening situations. Then, as they moved camps and numbers grew to 600, we charted the worsening conditions as they existed on less and less food, and got very sick. The only time we saw Betty drained physically and emotionally was when we filmed at a railway station and she climbed into a cattle truck similar to ones they had endured on the hellish journey to their next camp. However, she rallied in time for our portrayal of that last camp. We had found a rubber plantation which resembled the remote one they had been forced into, and Betty's descriptions of the horrendous conditions were vivid and heart-rending . . . 'Everyone was ill. Everyone was starving. Everyone had only one cup of rice a day . . . A little group of our nurses were the grave-diggers, and two of them would go through the (makeshift) hospital every morning and just count how many were going to die that day. We were losing about three or four people a day and the nurses would just go out and dig that many graves, because as soon as they died, we straightaway had to put them in very rough coffins and bury them.' Lost to the world, the 600 became 300, and due to the absence of any medical supplies, even that number would have been depleted had it not been for the few remaining nurses' exemplary care.

One of the big highlights of the filming for me had in fact been back in Palembang. It seemed astonishing that the Charitas Hospital, run by Dutch nuns before and during the war, was still standing and still run by nuns. Sister Catharinia had gathered five of the original nuns who had helped nurse some of the sickest prisoners and, in the early days, got messages out to men in a nearby camp. There was an emotional reunion, and then Betty asked if they could all sing 'The Captives Hymn' together. This hymn, written by a gifted missionary in camp, had been sung every Sunday, even in the last location when everyone had become so weak. It was incredibly moving listening to the sweetness of unaccompanied female voices, and I could imagine not only those terrifying days in camp, but the sisterhood that transcended it.

I suddenly felt an overwhelming need to get the story of these camps out to a much bigger audience. While the crew were packing up their gear, I rushed back to the half-made hotel before all the others, climbed up to my room and instantly jotted down several pages of an idea for a drama series about a fictional group of women in a camp (inspired by those women I'd met and those I'd read about from other camps). It was as if my pen was possessed. I couldn't stop until I had loosely sketched out a possible treatment. When I eventually went downstairs to get a coffee, I saw Betty there on her own, still quietly contemplating that afternoon's moving events. I told her what I felt and what I'd just attempted to write, and she immediately encouraged me to keep going with the idea. So Betty was the first to hear about what was later called *Tenko* and was my first supporter. We just couldn't believe that the nuns were still there, and that small miracles still came out of shocking misery. I've never forgotten that afternoon, nor Betty's significant part in it.

The bond we forged during the filming trip continued for years afterwards in a long correspondence. I still have lots of her letters, often up to five pages, written on that blue, flimsy airmail paper, and still full of her warmth and wisdom. She wrote to me when she received the AO medal in 1987 for her huge part in setting up the Australian Nurses Memorial Centre and her subsequent brilliant work for it. I felt so proud to know her but was so very sad to have never seen her again before she died in 2000.

FOREWORD

In 2013, a group of us organised a concert to commemorate the vocal orchestra that had been created in camp to raise spirits when the sickness began to take its toll. Betty had been a member of that unique orchestra. We also heard the 'The Captives Hymn' sung again, and once more it evoked huge emotion. It was the first concert of its kind in England, and when I got a tap on my shoulder at the party afterwards and was introduced to Betty's lovely great-niece, Emily, it was as if my friendship with her aunt had come full circle.

The story of Betty Jeffrey and the other women prisoners in Sumatra bridges the gap between history and current reality. We live once more in a time of world conflict, and are constantly seeing images of female victims, from the huge refugee camps in Syria to the Ukrainian women and children forced to leave their homes. Comparisons with earlier wars are still valid, and stories of former captives like Betty Jeffrey are just as relevant today. Betty's life experience and achievements, her spirit and courage, can continue to provide hope for future change.

This book is a highly readable testament to a life that is a continuing inspiration.

Lavinia Warner,
2023

1

BEGINNING A LIFE
OF DEDICATION

IT WAS THE FIRST DAY of April 1979 and the significance of the date was not lost on 70-year-old Betty Jeffrey as she slowly looked around, taking in everything. Being so close to the equator, she was constantly reminded of the endless humidity and unpredictable weather of the area, when a tropical rainstorm could lash the ground with very little warning. But today there was no evident threat in the thick clouds massed above as she stood quietly, sheltered from the sun beneath a broad-brimmed hat, contemplating her surroundings while standing on the pavement of a narrow, bustling street in the Talang Semoet district of Palembang, now the capital city of the Indonesian province. Noisy motorbikes zipped impatiently past her, often carrying more than one person and all manner of goods in bulging, colourful bags and baskets.

Memories both good and bad came flooding back. On that very same date 37 years earlier – 1 April 1942 – she had stood in dismay and bewilderment in that very same place, under the watchful eyes of a detachment of armed but otherwise listless Japanese guards.

She recalled wearing scrounged and ill-fitting clothing, surrounded by an anxious throng of Dutch women and children, as well as 31 of her Australian Army Nursing Service (AANS) colleagues – those who had managed to survive a recent, harrowing disaster. They were all clutching their meagre belongings and gazing sorrowfully at a squalid cluster of three-room Dutch houses, ten homes in all. They would come to know this place of internment as the Irenelaan camp, named for the Dutch child princess Irene, born just weeks before the outbreak of war. Ironically, the name had been chosen because it translates as 'peace'.

At first, everyone believed this was merely a temporary, overnight stop on their way to a much larger prison camp, but they were in for a surprise. The houses had been taken over by victory-emboldened Japanese forces as they swarmed across the island of Sumatra a few months earlier, and were now intended as the accommodation section of the much larger Irenelaan camp, ready to house a mixed bag of around 300 Dutch, English, Australian and Eurasian prisoners. As well as the Australian nurses, there were nurses of other nationalities, nuns, doctors, teachers, and the families of administrators and planters. It would prove to be far from temporary accommodation; they were destined to spend the next 17 months crammed into the purgatory of this primitive place.

As poignant memories of that day in 1942 washed over Betty Jeffrey, she took particular interest in two of the ten age-weathered houses before her: numbers 7 and 8. Her unit, the 2/10th Army General Hospital (AGH), had been housed in No. 7, while the remaining Australian nurses from the 2/13th AGH and 2/4th Casualty Clearing Station (CCS) were assigned to No. 8. The overcrowded internment camp was desperately short of food and other essential supplies and amenities; the women had to sleep on rough concrete shelves without blankets, and the only means of obtaining water for drinking and washing came from a stone well and two small taps, which were always in high demand. There was absolutely no privacy when using outside toilet facilities or quickly bathing with mere handfuls of water, and their meals mostly consisted of discoloured, contaminated rice, in which small creatures – living and dead – were a common inclusion.

As these and other vivid recollections came rushing back to Betty, she shuddered. The disturbing ghosts of the past were being revisited after she and Dame Margot Turner, formerly of Queen Alexandra's Imperial Military Nursing Service – who once shared those dismal years with her – had travelled back to Palembang at the invitation of a BBC crew, who were filming an Omnibus documentary featuring the two women, called *Women in Captivity*. Earlier that day they had stood on the sun-baked platform of Palembang's Kertapati railway station, scene of so much unforgettable sadness, recalling in front of the cameras for British television writer and producer Lavinia Warner the events and people from those years as prisoners of a callous enemy.

At one stage, Betty was asked what sensations her return to Palembang brought back to her. There were so many: fear, uncertainty, remoteness, hostility, helplessness. After musing for a few moments, she quietly responded, 'I feel . . .' (a momentary pause) 'as if I'd never left the blasted place!'

The history of the Australian Army Nursing Services is a noble and admirable one, populated over many decades by dedicated, brave, caring and compassionate women. As far back as May 1899, the Army Nursing Service was first established in New South Wales. Around sixty Australian nurses subsequently served with the colonial contingents, shipped across to South Africa during the Boer War, which lasted from 1899 to 1902. Some of that number were attached to the New South Wales Army Nursing Service Reserve (ANSR), long recognised as the first military nursing organisation in Australia.

Only one nurse is known to have been lost as a direct result of serving in that war: Sister Frances Emma (Fanny) Hines was one of ten nurses from Victoria sent to South Africa while attached to the state's 3rd Bushman's Contingent. On 7 August 1900, ill and overworked, she died in remote Enkeldoorn, Bulawayo. As her colleague Sister Julia Anderson wrote in a letter home: 'She died of an attack of pneumonia contracted in devotion to duty. She was quite alone, with as many as twenty-six patients at one time, no possibility of assistance, or relief and without sufficient nourishment.' Frances was laid to rest in Bulawayo cemetery with full military honours, and a marble cross commissioned by the Victorian Nurses and Bushmen's Contingent was erected on her grave.

On 1 July 1902, the Australian Army Nursing Service was created as a reserve auxiliary to the Australian Army Medical Corps (AAMC), providing a body of personnel trained and available in the event of any national emergency or war. A Lady Superintendent was then appointed and made responsible for nursing services in each military district. Two years later, the position of Matron-in-Chief was established, with a responsibility for administering the service and acting as adviser to the Director General Medical Services on nursing matters.

During the First World War, nurses were recruited from established nursing services as well as volunteers from the civilian profession, serving as an integral part of the 1st Australian Imperial Force (AIF) at field and base hospitals in Australia; then overseas in Egypt and Lemnos during the Gallipoli campaign; in England, France and Belgium in support of the Western Front; and in Greece, Salonika, Palestine, Mesopotamia and India. Many of them were decorated, with eight receiving the Military Medal for bravery. These women had worked in difficult and often terrifying circumstances, caring for sick and wounded patients in military clinics and casualty clearing stations, of necessity situated near battlefield front lines, as well as on ships and trains.

Someone who never forgot the courage and dedication of the nurses during the First World War was Lieutenant Harold Williams, wounded at the ferocious battle of Mont St Quentin–Péronne in northern France in September 1918. Following his treatment in a casualty clearing station at Daours, he expressed his complete admiration for the nurses' work:

In large marquees, nurses, pale and weary beyond words, hurried about. That these women worked their long hours among such surroundings without collapsing spoke volumes for their will-power and sense of duty. The place reeked with the odours of blood, antiseptic dressings, and unwashed bodies . . . They saw soldiers in their most pitiful state – wounded, blood-stained, dirty, reeking of blood and filth.

At the end of the war the AANS returned to reserve status. At least 2139 nurses had served abroad between 1914 and 1919 and a further 423 worked in military hospitals across Australia. A total of 28 nurses had lost their lives while on active service, or as a direct result of illness or injuries suffered during the conflict.

Following the outbreak of World War II in 1939, the AANS was once again placed on active service and its nurses were enlisted for service overseas with the 2nd AIF. For the greater part of the war they would be the only female service personnel to serve outside Australian territory. It would also mark the first – and only – occasion when Australian nurses became prisoners of war. Sister Betty Jeffrey from Tasmania would become one of those held in extended captivity by the Japanese in Sumatra.

Agnes Betty Jeffrey was born in New Town, 3 kilometres north of Hobart, Tasmania, on 14 May 1908. Although named after her paternal grandmother Agnes (*née* Kelly), she never really took to that name, preferring instead to be called Betty or Bett. When born, she was the second-youngest in a family of six, with two older brothers, Alan Noel and William Reginald, two older sisters, Marjorie Joyce and Frances Amy, and later became an older sister to Gwenyth Mary.

Like Betty – and with the exception of older brother Alan – most of her family decided not to embrace their given names and adopted ones by which they would be known for the rest of their lives. In this way, William preferred to be called Rex, Marjorie became Jo, and Frances decided that she liked being called Mickey. Betty's younger sister Gwenyth Mary grew up as just Mary.

Mary would complete the family of William and Amelia Matilda (*née* Cooley) Jeffrey, who were married in the historic St John's Church, New Town, on 8 September 1896. Even they had pet names within the Jeffrey family, affectionately referred to as either Will and Mill, or Willie and Millie. In fact their children always called them by those names, very rarely referring to them as 'Mum and Dad'.

The Jeffrey family and its many branches have enjoyed a long and certainly varied association with Tasmania since her grandfather William Jeffrey arrived there from Scotland. One person of particular interest in that family history was Betty's maternal great-grandfather Thomas Todd Cooley, born in Little Gaddesden, Hertfordshire, in 1806. Thomas first found himself in trouble with the law at the age of fifteen, appearing at London's Old Bailey on 27 February 1822 charged with the theft of an umbrella. He was acquitted of this charge, but his second appearance at the Old Bailey on 14 May 1823, along with Thomas Connor, was far more dramatic; both were charged with the theft of silver from a Harley Street banker. They were found guilty and sentenced to be hanged, although their sentences were commuted to transportation for life to what was then called Van Diemen's Land, later Tasmania. The convict ship *Chapman* transported them, departing England on 6 April 1824, and fifteen weeks later deposited the men in Hobart Town.

Twelve years after his arrival in Hobart, and still regarded as a convict, Thomas required permission from the Colonial Secretary's Office to marry Scottish-born Margaret Paterson Aberdeen, a free settler. This was given and they tied the knot on 30 May 1836, just four days before the birth of their first child, Sarah Morris Cooley. Another of their six subsequent children was Charles Morris Cooley, who would marry Frances Jones. In turn their daughter, Amelia Matilda (Amy) Cooley, married Betty's father, William Jeffrey.

In 1841, among his many other pursuits, Thomas Cooley had purchased the Horse and Jockey Hotel in Moonah and renamed it Cooleys Hotel. The hotel has since had a long association with the Cooley family, handed down through different family members over the decades and undergoing a number of renovations. The present-day Cooleys Hotel still stands on its original site at 45 Main Road, Moonah.

Betty's father William had joined the post office as an accounts clerk and was listed in official documents as a civil servant. He worked hard and became a senior accountant and later manager at the General Post Office (GPO) in Hobart. The children loved growing up in New Town, although one special treat they looked forward to every Christmas was when the family would travel just 5 miles south of Hobart along the D'Entrecasteaux Channel and spend several weeks of sheer enjoyment swimming, fishing and relaxing at the quiet seaside suburb of Kingston, formerly known as Brown's River. It was here that Betty developed her deep love of swimming, and particularly long-distance swimming.

Betty was destined to spend only the first twelve years of her life and education in New Town. As her father rose through the ranks he frequently had to transfer interstate in order to set up new accounting methods at various branches, which meant the Jeffrey family was constantly on the move, and the children had to attend a number of schools in Tasmania, Queensland and South Australia, where he spent some time as the GPO's chief accountant in Adelaide.

Eventually, in 1911, the family settled down in their own home at 130 Darling Road, their first home in East Malvern, Victoria. Betty loved the area so much that East Malvern would become her home suburb after the Second World War, and for the rest of her life.

Over the next three years Betty attended Tooronga Road State School in East Malvern (now Malvern Primary School). Betty's niece

Sara Renshaw laughingly admitted that Betty would often display a keen if misguided entrepreneurial talent as a child, on one occasion setting up a stall on a street corner and trying to sell ice cream cones to her school friends. Unfortunately these were quite inedible cone-shaped scrolls of thick paper with a suitable-looking filling of whipped-up Lux washing flakes.

Betty continued her education at Warwick Girls School, also in East Malvern, one of Melbourne's first private girls' schools. According to the Malvern Historical Society, the school had over 200 boarders and day pupils from kindergarten to leaving honours, with the younger grades including boys. It also pioneered open-air classrooms, had a laboratory, a library and extensive sports grounds. All four Jeffrey girls went to the school and Betty once recalled for a reporter, 'The fees were about seven pounds a term. I know my father got a discount because there were four of us.'

Ada Turner was the school principal, and her sister Ivy was housemistress. Betty lovingly recalled the scones that Ivy used to make for their morning tea, saying, 'The scones cost a penny and were dripping with butter. Miss Ivy would come out with a big dish laden with hot scones. They were piping hot, right out of the oven and beautiful in winter. In the summer we had home-made fruity ice blocks.' As well as such goodies, many of the girls took a little bucolic pleasure in the peaceful sight of Daisy, the school's cow, happily grazing on a vacant block of land opposite the school.

On a more serious note, Betty had often heard from her parents some remarkable stories of the bravery of nurses tending wounded troops on the front line during the war, which appealed to her keen sense of adventure. One day, when Betty was about twelve, her Aunt Effie paid the family a visit at the East Malvern home they now occupied, 'Lynburn' in Beaver Street. As she recalled many years later during an interview,

> When I was a little girl an auntie of ours visited from Tasmania and I didn't want to see her, so I went up the gum tree on the nature strip. She found me and made me go inside with her. And you know how aunties are; they don't know what to say to little girls. So she just said, 'What do you want to do when you grow up?' I floored her by saying, 'I want to be a war nurse!' No war around and I was going to be a war nurse!

Through hard classroom work and study Betty was able to achieve her Intermediate Certificate and decided to remain at Warwick school, passing her Leaving Certificate two years later in 1926. While at high school she had excelled at several sports, particularly tennis and hockey, and was competitive in both athletics and swimming – the latter sport being one in which she demonstrated solid but unfulfilled Olympic potential, excelling in long-distance swimming events. Running also seemed to come naturally to her and she would often be seen running around the nearby Central Park. There were many occasions when her mother would organise for her to pick up a meat order at the local butcher during her school lunch break and run it home before racing back to school ahead of the bell denoting the end of lunch.

In 1925, her studies at an end, Betty happily took over the role of the school's sports mistress. In an end-of-school-year summary in the Melbourne *Age* newspaper dated 15 December 1927, it was reported that, 'Miss Jeffrey, who has been sports mistress for the past two years, will be very much missed.'

For a time after leaving Warwick school she worked as a part-time sports mistress at another girls' school in North Adelaide before taking on a course in typing and shorthand, which resulted in finding full-time work as a stenographer for a firm of accountants.

Despite settling into a good, steady job, Betty found little satisfaction in turning up each weekday for such monotonous office work, and there was always a lingering desire to consider nursing as a career option. Perhaps one early inspiration for this may have been her Aunt Eliza, who was a trained midwife. However, she kept putting off making any decision on nursing for some years, due to her father's job, which still entailed travelling to different parts of Australia with his family.

In 1931, Betty moved to Brisbane, where she lived with her two older brothers, Alan (a well-known Brisbane accountant) and William (an electrical salesman who preferred to be called Rex), in a good-sized apartment with city views over the Brisbane river at Kangaroo Point. She was now employed by a music firm in their pianola music rolls library, sending these rolls all over Queensland. Later, she would find employment with the same firm of accountants she had worked for in Adelaide.

During one break from work, Betty took the opportunity to visit her parents and other sisters in Melbourne. On the return journey, she sailed back to Brisbane aboard the Adelaide Steamship Company ship MV *Manunda*. Later converted to a hospital ship, the vessel was fitted with modern passenger-friendly twin diesel engines and prior to World War II was engaged in transporting interstate passengers and cargo between Sydney, Fremantle, Melbourne and Cairns. The next time Betty set foot aboard *Manunda* would be in 1945, but under vastly different circumstances.

While sailing up Australia's east coast, Betty became quite seasick and mostly remained in her cabin until the last day, when she ventured to the dining room for a light breakfast and was seated with a group of young women. One of them was similarly-aged Aimée Francis, originally from Coolgardie in Western Australia, who was a nurse under training at Melbourne's Alfred Hospital. She was travelling to Brisbane to visit her brother Owen, who was desperately ill with diabetes in Brisbane General Hospital, where she had arranged to stay in the nurses' quarters.

Relaxing in a deckchair by the pool, Aimée had been impressed by Betty's smooth, strong stoke work as she swam without slowing from one end to the other, with a deft turn as she touched each wall. Over dinner that night she asked Betty if she had tried out for the Olympics, but her new friend was suitably modest, saying that she might have done, but needed to have gone into serious training at least a year before, when she was runner-up in the Victorian free-style 200 metres event.

The two young women hit it off straight away and struck up a friendship. When the ship docked at Brisbane, Betty's brother Alan was there to pick her up in his beloved new car, Dora the Dodge, and he was openly delighted when Betty insisted that her new young friend join them for a meal once she had seen her brother in hospital. Wanting to help, and through a high-up contact in the medical profession, Alan arranged for Owen to be transferred to the Mater Hospital, where he would receive more specialised care for his diabetes and was soon well on the way to recovery. Meanwhile, Alan and Aimée had begun dating, and to Betty's delight the romance blossomed.

*

During her time living and working in a clerical position in Brisbane, which she found quite stimulating and enjoyable, Betty was involved in an unfortunate incident while driving out of New Farm early Sunday morning on 3 September 1933. As she made her way along Thompson Street, a young boy – without looking for traffic coming up behind him – began to cross the road directly in front of her. She braked and swerved to avoid the six-year-old, but ended up hitting him. He was injured and had to be taken by ambulance and admitted to the Children's Hospital. It shook Betty to the core, but everyone agreed it was simply an unfortunate accident, and could have been far worse had she not reacted quickly.

Five weeks after the accident, Betty was able to forget about it for a while when she travelled down to Sydney for the wedding of her older sister Frances to Dr Charles ('Breezy') Gale, a medical specialist from Geelong. Her parents still moved around Australia on work-related assignments and were then living in Mosman, on the Lower North Shore in Sydney. Five weeks ahead of the wedding, Frances (also known as Mick) had sailed down to Sydney aboard the passenger and mail steamer SS *Orungal* to make early preparations. The wedding was held at St Philip's Church in Church Hill, Sydney, on 12 October 1933. William Jeffrey gave away his daughter with a fond kiss, while Betty and her younger sister Mary acted as bridesmaids, and brother Alan was one of the groomsmen. The wedding reception was held at the Hotel Australia, following which the bride and bridegroom left for their honeymoon, touring around New South Wales before heading to Geelong, where they would make their home.

Soon after her return to Brisbane, Betty thought the accident involving the young boy, as awful as it had been at the time, was behind her. Not so the boy's father, who decided to sue her for damages, claiming she had been negligent in failing to keep a proper lookout while in charge of her car. The matter was taken before the Supreme Court the following March, where a jury found that Betty had done all she could to avoid the accident and the boy's own actions had contributed to his being injured. They did award the father £94 to cover hospital costs, but not the £750 he had requested in his suit.

Quite ironically, in light of Betty's later career, the boy's father had previously served in Egypt as a private with the 15th Field Ambulance and later the 1st AGH (Army General Hospital). It was an incident that Betty never seemed to want to talk about in her later years, and even her nieces and nephews were surprised to learn of the accident during the gathering of background information for this book, saying she had never mentioned it to anyone.

There was another wedding to attend in July 1935, when her brother Alan married his nurse fiancée Aimée Francis. On this occasion the marriage ceremony took place within the glorious 19th-century Chapel of St Peter at Melbourne Grammar School, where Alan had been educated. This time Betty – who had introduced the happy couple to each other – was the sole bridesmaid.

In recently reflecting on his parents Alan and Aimée, Antony Jeffrey believes that his mother loved becoming a part of the Jeffrey family. He recalled,

Aimée, my mother, adored the whole family. Partly because she yearned for that closeness that she had lost in her own family, partly because my father was the eldest child and admired hugely by all his sisters, but I think mostly because she felt they were the epitome of a loving family, close and supportive of each other, loving of and loved by their parents and because they laughed a lot and never took life too seriously. As the tallest, most athletic, cleverest and certainly funniest and most fun-loving of the sisters, Betty always held their utmost admiration, though Jo, as the eldest sister, asserted ultimate authority and always held her siblings to account, though usually with a smile or a giggle.

Rex had already decided to move back down to Melbourne to live, so the newlyweds now occupied the spacious apartment at Kangaroo Point. They soon fell into a happy routine every second Friday, according to their son Antony Jeffrey, when Alan would come home at lunchtime and they would drive down to Surfers Paradise for the weekend in his green 1937 Ford V8 Pilot. He was building a holiday house called 'Breffney' at Broadwater, which was finally nearing completion. The name may have come from a mythical, medieval overkingdom, or even a village in Gaelic Ireland, and seems to have resulted from a distant Irish forebear of Alan's. He just liked the name.

As work on the cottage progressed, there was some happy news, as Antony recalled:

Before long to their mutual enjoyment she became pregnant, but the weekends at the beach didn't slacken. Alan worked tirelessly to create a garden around the house enclosed on all sides by the bird-filled native bush. A narrow exit to the sandy track at the front led straight to the sandhills, the roar of the surf and the deserted beach in both directions.

Betty and Rex would travel to Surfers whenever time permitted, helping where they could to complete the cottage, and Betty in particular had fallen for the unspoiled beauty and peacefulness of the area. Post-war, she would spend several months a year staying with a friend on the Gold Coast, often accompanied by her sisters, never tiring of the simple pleasures associated with strolling barefoot along the spectacular, warm golden beaches.

Meanwhile, earlier conversations with Aimée about nursing had influenced Betty to look at applying for similar training at the Alfred Hospital, a leading tertiary teaching hospital in Melbourne where Aimée had received her initial instruction. Finally, she applied and was accepted for training at the Alfred in 1937, aged 29, graduating with her General Nursing Certificate two years on. She then said she was proud to receive her graduation badge and be addressed as 'Sister'. The path into a career in nursing had long been desired and nurtured, as she recalled many years later:

We were always moving. It was a wonderful experience for us young people [and] we made so many friends: Tasmania, Adelaide, to Brisbane and Melbourne. That's why I was so late starting my nursing training. I was having such a good time, I kept putting it off. And then I thought, 'You must do it!' And I did: at the Alfred. Down here in Melbourne, and I loved every day of it. Then I went straight from training into the army.

Aware that war might be looming, Betty signed up with the army reserve the same year she graduated, knowing that if war did break out, nurses would be needed. 'I thought, if there's going to be a war, I'll be in it!' she added. The following year she received her Midwifery Certificate at the Royal Women's Hospital in the Melbourne suburb of Parkville.

Betty would probably have gone on to become a fine civilian nurse, but war intervened and she was keen to be of front-line service to her country and profession. In 1940, she worked for a time as a staff nurse at the 108th Army General Hospital in Ballarat before deciding to enlist in the Australian Army Nursing Service, excited not only by the opportunity to travel, but eager and unafraid to use her nursing experience to aid in the war effort.

On 9 April 1941, Betty filled out her enlistment papers at the AANS Depot in William Street, Melbourne, and received the Army identification number VX53059. After completing her attestation papers she was posted to Darley Military Camp, west of Melbourne, where she helped set up a camp hospital along with five other nurses.

Betty was subsequently notified of her posting to the 2/10th Australian General Hospital, then based at Malacca, in the southern part of the Malay Peninsula. The unit had arrived in Singapore on the *Queen Mary* in February 1941. At this stage of the conflict there wasn't any sign of war erupting in the Pacific, so it seemed to be a relatively safe place for the nurses to work. Being fit and healthy and with no immediate responsibilities at home, Betty felt that going overseas and representing her country was exciting and something she wanted to do. Only those between the ages of 25 and 35 were permitted to go – no one younger or older – but almost certainly there were many others beyond that requirement who somehow managed to be included.

On 19 May 1941, having turned 33 some five days earlier and now promoted to Senior Nurse, Betty joined her nursing colleagues at Port Melbourne as they embarked on the 410-foot HMAT *Zealandia*, which would be escorted to Singapore via Fremantle by the light cruiser HMAS *Sydney*. Built in Clydesdale, Scotland, in 1910, pre-war the *Zealandia* had been a cargo ship and international passenger liner. It saw service as a troopship in both world wars until it was sunk during Japanese air raids on Darwin on 19 February 1942.

On this occasion, the *Zealandia* was carrying 754 troops and nurses and arrived in Singapore on 9 June 1941 following an uneventful voyage from Fremantle. The nurses were immediately transported in a modern air-conditioned train north-west to Malacca, where they would join the 2/10th AGH, already set up and working there under Principal Matron Olive Paschke. Once there, they were allocated quarters within the grounds of the British Colonial Service Hospital, which they jokingly referred to as the White Elephant.

Jessie Blanch, also of the 2/10th AGH, had arrived in an earlier contingent of nurses from Australia and they could hardly believe the peaceful tropical environment after all the news about the fighting in Europe and the Middle East. It took a while for them to become accustomed to the hotel-like attention they received in their quarters, as well as the friendly stares of the locals as they moved around the town of Malacca. While there, 'Blanchie' (as she was known) kept a daily diary of her experiences. She wrote:

> Our view is beautiful from the balcony, which is on the fourth floor. Our hospital is just opposite – five stories [*sic*], nice and cool looking too. We are living under ideal conditions. *Amah*s [maidservants] to do our washing, make our beds, etc., even get our shoes cleaned.

The army hospital – a former school for Chinese children – was located within a reasonably new section of the civil hospital buildings. In addition to treating patients suffering from dengue fever and malaria, as well as all manner of normal injuries and illnesses, the hospital work was not arduous, but they were also assisting Matron Paschke to convert the old school building into a fully functional 200-bed hospital.

For relaxation on their days off, the nurses could visit the town of Malacca. Here they were able to exchange their Australian pounds into the local dollar-based currency, shop around and have clothes made. They would also play tennis, swim, play bridge, see films at the local cinema and attend dances and concerts. Life seemed both pleasant and interesting – for them it was a whole world away from the war and even life back in Australia.

The nurses would often catch the air-conditioned train down to Singapore, 100 miles distant and a six-hour journey. Once there, they would spend a lot of their time relaxing at the Swimming Club on Tanjong Rhu Road, where service personnel were allowed free membership. The ladies' accommodation occupied the ground floor of the massive club, while the upper storey housed a 6500-square-foot dance floor, a restaurant, an air-conditioned steak bar and lounge, a ladies' lounge, reading and writing rooms, a billiards room, the main kitchen and the club's offices. They could spend many happy hours sunbaking beneath beach umbrellas spread around a huge pool, then enjoy a sumptuous meal and drinks served by immaculately dressed waiters. Amid such opulence, the European war seemed very far away, but war would soon catch up with them.

Sister Florence Trotter of the 2/10th AGH was mortified when her mother sent her a cutting from the *Australian Women's Weekly*, which inferred that the Australian nurses in Malacca were living a life of overseas luxury. As she recalls, the article mentioned wild orchids growing outside the hospital gates,

and of course we used to go and pick them and put them in our rooms, and here's this write-up in the *Women's Weekly* saying Australian nurses live like film stars. Orchids in their bedrooms, or mess huts. Orchids everywhere and they said they have servants to do their washing and all this sort of thing. Well of course in that heat and everything, and the way you work, all our starched collars and cuffs, until Matron got permission for us to have them cut . . . off, you had to have someone to do those sort of things, you know, it was just the normal thing. They did all the hospital washing. They had these *amah*s that came in of a morning and just swept your room and did your washing and ironing and it was ready for you when you went back on duty again. Because a stiff starched veil doesn't last very long in the hot tropics. Anyway, they made a big story of it – living like film stars. I laughed about it.

In September 1941, another contingent of nurses from the 2/13th and the 2/4th Casualty Clearing Station (CCS) joined them in Malacca, where they stayed until early October, when their services were required in Singapore. One of those newly arrived nurses was Sister Jessie Simons, who had earlier enjoyed the sights and sounds of Singapore harbour when their ship, the AHS *Wanganella*, was berthing. Despite the war raging elsewhere, life seemed to be simply carrying on in its customary, hectic way in and around Singapore, with vessels of all sizes cramming the harbour and the regular hustle and bustle on the dockside. As Sister Simons recalled,

Once ashore, we were amazed to find that there was no urgent need for us. Our main job for a while was relieving other nurses on duty at the main army hospital, 2/10 AGH established at Malacca, about 100 miles north of Singapore.

She said that she 'felt more like a tourist than a member of an army unit'.

Sister Simons further stated that the nurses had treated very few patients in Singapore, so many of them were temporarily attached to other facilities, while others spent much of their time training in the treatment of tropical diseases and modern military surgical practices. Then, over two days from 21 November 1941, the 2/13th relocated from the hospitals in Singapore to a large, newly built medical facility (intended as a mental hospital) at Tampoi, 4 miles from Johor Bahru and just across the strait from Singapore Island.

Then, amid growing unease across the peninsula, the Australian nurses were informed that all leave was immediately cancelled until further notice. All too soon, life for them would take a dramatic and tragic turn for the worse. Many were destined never to return home.

2

THE FALL OF SINGAPORE

By 13 February 1942, Singapore, the once-peaceful island at the southern end of the Malay Peninsula, was in its death throes. Hordes of Japanese fighters and bombers flew continuously and unopposed over the city, blazing away at random targets, while the streets were chaotic and congested with military traffic and about a million defenceless citizens. Mortar shells and bombs rained down on the terrified city, which burned beneath a thick black canopy of smoke from flaming oil tanks and buildings, obscuring the sun. Dust-covered, bloodied bodies of men, women and children were strewn amid the mounds of rubble, the smell of death lingered everywhere, while fire-gutted buildings toppled and crashed into the streets without warning, adding to the grim human toll.

Before the Japanese invasion, there were 140 Australian nurses serving in the Malayan region. They were basically divided into three groups: Betty Jeffrey's 2/10th AGH had taken on a ten-month position in Malacca, the 2/13th AGH was based in Tampin, while the third group, the 2/4th CCS, was positioned in Kluang, central Johor.

These nursing units had been placed there as the higher authorities believed at the time that any Japanese frontal assault would take place on Singapore and that the wounded could be sent to and tended at these more remote centres.

The unexpected Japanese invasion of Malaya and Singapore was launched from bases in French Indochina and began with the first amphibious landing of troops at Kota Bharu in northern Malaya on 8 December 1941. This took place literally within hours of the unexpected air attack on Pearl Harbor, some 6800 miles away. Unlike the Americans, who were caught completely unprepared for such an all-out attack, British commanders in Malaya and Singapore had been made aware for a number of weeks that Japanese forces might be assembling ready to launch an assault. Despite this, they had put few countermeasures in place, apart from positioning the naval fleet at Singapore on full alert, meanwhile maintaining an overly optimistic confidence that they could easily repel any Japanese offensive.

When the attack did come, the steamroll advance of the Japanese 25th Army under the command of General Tomoyuki Yamashita hit hard, rapidly sweeping through the jungle and mangrove swamps of the Malay Peninsula. The Allies were up against a formidable foe. The enemy's thrust south was both swift and savage, with British troop resistance too thinly spread and unprepared. For Yamashita, speed was of the essence, never allowing the British or Allied forces time to re-group or form defensive lines.

Overstretched defensive positions had been hastily formed at Jitra in the north Malayan state of Kedah by the 11th Indian Division, but this would quickly prove a massive weakness in preventing the Japanese advance. British military leaders had severely underestimated the determination of the Japanese troops and using poorly trained Indian army units to confront them would prove calamitous. There was no sense of military communication between the weak and elitist English officers and the ill-equipped Indian troops under their command, who knew practically nothing of jungle warfare. Within two days of the first Japanese attack at Jitra, the Indian division had abandoned their front-line defensive positions, leaving behind them massive amounts of artillery, ammunition, weapons and armoured vehicles, and – much to the delight of Japanese commanders – large quantities of precious and badly-needed fuel.

Brutality was widely practised, especially by Yamashita's ferocious Imperial Guards Division. As they attacked through the peninsula, Japanese troops were ordered to take no prisoners, as this would only hamper their advance. In fact, a pamphlet issued to them prior to the amphibious landing read: 'When you encounter the enemy after landing, think of yourself as an avenger coming face to face at last with his father's murderer. Here is a man whose death will lighten your heart.'

Within just four days, the thin British front line had been fully broken, forcing a rapid retreat to the south. Japanese aircraft were simultaneously attacking RAF airfields in Singapore, with raids carried out to neutralise the Tengah and Seletar air bases, destroying all aeroplanes on the ground before they could be flown or removed to shelter, which meant they could not be used to support the ground troops. As one unnamed airman later reported:

Most of the Malayan – and Singapore – aerodromes were built on a peace-time plan. They caught the cooling breezes. The living and administrative quarters were out in the open. When war broke out they caught the concentrated strafing of Japanese aircraft. Life was pleasant in the weeks before war was declared in the East, with native servants to perform the menial tasks. We forgot that the aeroplanes were obsolete and too few to be of any real value in a war with Japan. As aerodromes were evacuated down the peninsula on the way to Singapore the unpreparedness struck home. We contacted the soldiers, who showed almost open contempt at the inadequacy of the air support. The lack of naval and air support or protection was enabling the Japanese to land large forces behind the army, forcing it to retreat. And when the troops were all on the island in the last few days before the surrender, with all aerodromes under heavy shell-fire, the role of the Air Force was almost passive.

There was some initial hope that a number of British warships positioned in Singapore, headed by the battleship HMS *Prince of Wales* and the ageing battle cruiser HMS *Repulse*, could help ward off and repel the Japanese landings. Ordered into battle, the two warships left Singapore Naval Base accompanied by four destroyers, including HMAS *Vampire*. They raced up the Malay coast on 8 December to where commanders had been informed the landings were taking place off Singora and Kota Bharu on the far north-east coast. But this deployment would turn into yet another disaster for British morale.

Japanese spotter planes were everywhere and it did not take them long to see the warships moving up the South China Sea and relay their exact position back to base. Admiral Sir Tom Phillips, in overall command of the British fleet, was on board the battleship *Prince of Wales*, and he realised that his two vessels were now highly vulnerable. He ordered both ships to turn around. But it was all too late; on 10 December, with no fighter planes available to beat off enemy aircraft, Japanese torpedo bombers flew completely unopposed at the two ships off the Malayan coast. Following sustained attacks, the *Prince of Wales* and *Repulse* were mortally hit. By early afternoon both had vanished beneath the waves.

Their job done, the Japanese pilots turned back to base while the crews of the destroyer escorts in the vicinity desperately tried to rescue as many survivors as possible from the sunken vessels. In all, over a thousand crewmen from the two ships were rescued, but another 840 were lost to fire, explosions, or had drowned. Admiral Phillips died when HMS *Prince of Wales* sank off Kuantan following the air attack. He and Captain John Leach chose to go down with the ship.

With no effective naval resistance to stop them, this defeat now opened the way for Japanese troops to land unhindered along the Malayan coastline. As British Prime Minister Winston Churchill later noted in his memoirs about that fateful day: 'I put the telephone down. I was thankful to be alone. In all the war I never received a more direct shock.'

Within just eight weeks, Japanese forces had occupied much of Malaya and were pressing forward towards the island of Singapore, then Britain's major base in the Pacific, which had long been regarded as unassailable due to its formidable seaward defences. At first, the people there did not believe the Japanese would get very far. Unfortunately they had not figured on the Japanese unleashing a land advance down through the Malay Peninsula, leaving the island nation inadequately defended and highly vulnerable. The city precincts were already coming under random bombing attacks.

Australians sent to Singapore as part of the 8th Division, AIF, had been caught somewhat unawares by the Japanese thrust. When they disembarked from *Queen Mary* some months before on 18 February 1941 (the luxury liner had been converted into a troopship), they were not slow in expressing their disappointment that they had been sent to languish in this peaceful paradise while other Australian soldiers were deeply involved in the real action, up against the Germans in Libya and Egypt. Volunteers to a man, they were willing to fight, and fight hard, and resented being sent to guard tin mines and rubber and pineapple plantations. Now they were engaged in desperately trying to halt a ferocious onslaught as unstoppable Japanese enemy forces swept through and took over Malayan territory at an alarming rate.

By 20 December, the Malayan island of Penang, once an important trading hub in the Straits of Malacca, had fallen to enemy forces, with graphic accounts of the blitz on the island given by refugees arriving in Singapore. Sweeping over Penang Island in mass formations, Japanese aircraft had relentlessly bombed, machine-gunned and set fire to the island's Chinatown. Hundreds of innocent citizens who had blissfully ignored the warning sirens and failed to take shelter fell to streams of bullets sprayed and ricocheting along the narrow streets. The first enemy planes had appeared earlier, on 9 December, but these were mostly conducting reconnaissance exercises and did not drop any bombs. Two days later an alert was sounded early in the morning, following which 27 enemy planes flew over the island from the direction of the mainland, circled, then dive-bombed the town and shot up the streets, causing the locals to flee in terror, with dozens killed. After the first raid, refugees thronged along the roads out of town, heading for hopeful safety in the island's hills and coastal villages. The air attacks continued the next day, once again with heavy loss of civilian life in the normally crowded Chinatown area.

Towards the end of December 1941, the Malayan capital of Kuala Lumpur was being evacuated. Already, most of the European women and children had fled south to Singapore, with many already desperately trying to organise any sort of passage to India or Australia. With Japanese forces steadily forcing British and Allied resistance further south, it became imperative for the remaining 43 nurses and three physiotherapists of 2/10th AGH to evacuate from the Malacca Army Hospital and redeploy to Johor Bahru, where they would link up with 2/13th AGH and 2/4th CCS before being transported with their patients to southern Singapore. The evacuation was carried out ward by ward – a task heavily dependent on the organising ability and planning of Matron Paschke. Only twelve hours after the transfer of the last patients and nurses from Malacca, the enemy had stormed into the town.

On Saturday, 24 January, Betty and several other nurses were assigned the task of setting up an emergency, temporary 300-bed hospital facility in the St Patrick's Boys' School, located on East Coast Road, Katong, on Singapore's east coast, some six miles from the centre of the city. This would allow the nurses still in Malaya to evacuate south and take up residence in the converted school. They poured all their energy into this task and managed to accomplish it within just two days, even increasing the bed capacity to 600. Soon hundreds of wounded defenders and citizens were being rushed in and treated around the clock, despite a desperate shortage of surgical and other equipment. The staff were later able to expand the hospital even more by moving into a neighbouring guest house, and as the casualty list grew they were also able to take over nearby houses that the owners had abandoned, allowing them to treat rapidly increasing numbers of injured.

As Betty reflected after the war, 'Here we worked, under continuous daylight bombing raids, while the situation grew more tense daily.' The courage and dedication of all the nurses and medical staff under such horrific conditions was nothing short of magnificent, with sleep all but impossible, surviving on brief exhausted naps as the bombing and shelling continued. Curiously enough, the nurses could almost set their watches by the first raid of each day, which invariably began at ten o'clock.

All too soon the Japanese forces had reached Johor in the southern region of Malaya, with a thrust into Singapore their next objective. By this time the three Army General Hospital units had been safely evacuated south to Singapore city. General Sir Archibald Wavell, commander of British forces in Malaya, ordered his troops to hold Johor at any cost until reinforcements could be transported up from the south and a counterattack launched. He knew it was imperative that the Japanese advance be halted there, for the grim reality was that if Johor was lost, Singapore could also fall, posing an immediate threat to the entire Dutch East Indies. However, those hoped-for reinforcements would all arrive too late; the remaining British troops were evacuated south and, with precious little resistance now available, Johor quickly fell to the Japanese.

On 29 January 1942, Lieutenant General Arthur Percival, head of Malaya Command, ordered the 30,000 British troops still remaining in Malaya to retreat to Singapore. Two days later, British engineers blew up and demolished a wide section of the causeway linking Malaya and Singapore in a frantic bid to halt the Japanese advance, leaving the whole of Malaya devoid of defenders. This strategy would only cause a temporary delay to the inevitable; less than two weeks later Japanese engineers had constructed a girder bridge over the gap in the causeway and hordes of troops – two divisions in all – began their inexorable drive towards Singapore on 5 February, shooting or bayoneting anyone they encountered, service personnel and civilians alike.

The resilience and fighting spirit of the Australians in the face of such overwhelming odds has been well – and rightly – documented. They were in a desperate battle against an enemy fully trained in jungle tactics and warfare. Despite being so heavily disadvantaged, the Australians still managed to mount effective counter-offensives and carry out well-planned ambushes, inflicting massive losses on Yamashita's rapidly tiring troops. Had the Australian defensive line been intact and numerically stronger, the result of the offensive may well have been quite different. Unfortunately, the line was thin on numbers and the only supporting troops were those of a fast dwindling Indian army, exhausted and demoralised after days of being forced into continual retreat by the relentless Japanese forces, meanwhile suffering scores of casualties. It was an unsustainable situation despite the valour and sheer guts of the defenders, and the line would soon be breached in several places, allowing Japanese forces to pour through, and Singapore would soon fall.

As war and chaos erupted all around them, medical and other staff working at the Alexandra Military Hospital west of Singapore city remained resolute and continued to care for the steadily increasing number of wounded soldiers and civilians, believing that like all hospitals it would be protected as a sanctuary by the Red Cross. But the Japanese cared little for the strictures of the Geneva Convention or the sanctity of the Red Cross.

With the enemy now intent on advancing into Singapore, the AGH nurses were divided into two groups serving two temporary hospitals; one half would position themselves at the St Patrick's Boys' School in Katong, while the rest were sent to clear up the abandoned Oldham Hall Mission Boarding School for boys in the northern suburbs of Singapore city. As Betty later reflected:

On first inspection [there did] not seem any possibilities of turning the old wooden building into a hospital, but what did Matron [Paschke] do? 'We'll have all this rubbish out of here, this wall down, that wall down, half that wall away from there – and upstairs there are more walls and rubbish.' In two days the place was a spot-lessly clean 200-bed hospital with room for many more.

The work was completed by 13 January, but it would soon be filled by around 700 beds to cope with the ceaseless influx of wounded.

On 6 February, Major General Gordon Bennett, commander of the 8th Australian Division, reported:

Today the enemy dropped 15 shells on the 2/10 AGH. The nurses were cool and courageous throughout the shelling, neglecting their own safety, to protect their patients. The nurses are the nearest thing to angels I can imagine. They devote themselves whole-heartedly to their heavy task, frequently working over the 24 hours to deal with a rush of casualties.

Singapore's blackest day came two days later on 8 February, when the stunning news came through that Japanese forces were storming into the city by land and sea. Absolute carnage and mayhem was about to be unleashed on the population by the invaders. Elsewhere that same day, Japanese troops also entered and seized the crown colony of Hong Kong with relative ease, capturing over 12,000 members of the British and Canadian garrison forces.

On the evening of 10 February, enemy tanks and battle-weary invaders began moving into the outskirts of Bukit Timah village. Three days later, all the British and local nurses remaining at the nearby Alexandra Hospital were ordered to pack up their cases and be ready to evacuate in the next few minutes. Many of those being evacuated had tears in their eyes and pleaded to be allowed to stay, even if the hospital fell into Japanese hands, as they needed to care for their patients.

British Principal Matron Violet Jones (killed the following day in the sinking of the evacuation vessel SS *Kuala*) explained that the order was explicit; a message had apparently been received from Hong Kong giving graphic details of murderous assaults being carried out there by occupying Japanese soldiers. On 19 December, they had slaughtered several unarmed members of the Royal Army Medical Corps (RAMC) working at the Salesian Mission at Shau Kei Wan. Then, on Christmas Day, at a temporary front-line hospital set up at St Stephen's College, they had carried out a bloody rampage, murdering and maiming patients and gang-raping nursing sisters who had elected to remain there, before mutilating and executing them in cold blood.

Although still reluctant, the Alexandra nurses yielded to the command to withdraw, moving out just after two o'clock that after-noon. They felt deeply for the defenceless orderlies and 900 patients they had been forced to leave behind as they prepared to be evacuated from the island. Meanwhile a large red cross had been prominently laid out on the lawn of the Alexandra Hospital and smaller red crosses were hung from the windows.

The following morning marauding pilots paid little heed to the Red Cross signs. As the hospital was unfortunate enough to be situated close to an ammunition depot and oil tanks, the Japanese reasoned they had an excuse to bomb the hospital as well. That afternoon, amid the shelling in the area, Japanese troops from the 18th Division were seen converging on the hospital, at which Captain Bartlett of the RAMC bravely walked out carrying a white flag, with a red cross prominently displayed on his white armband. He pointed to this and called out 'Hospital!' It had no effect; he was shot at, but fortunately the bullet missed and he dived back into the hospital just as a grenade exploded nearby.

Shortly after, and contrary to the traditional neutrality of the hospital, a number of Indian soldiers positioned themselves on the hospital's rooftop and began shooting at Japanese troops below before fleeing the building as their fire was returned. Around 100 incensed Japanese soldiers then rushed into the hospital, rampaging through the surgical and medical wards and operating theatres, indiscriminately shooting and bayoneting the totally helpless doctors, patients and orderlies – even a padre. They only paused in the massacre to loot the corpses.

They could not kill everyone and the Indian snipers were long gone, so the soldiers rounded up and herded around 200 shocked survivors out of the hospital, tied them in pairs, and forced them to walk to a row of three tiny outhouses a few hundred yards down the road. Once they had been shoved inside the small buildings, with more than sixty crammed in each, the doors and windows were nailed shut and they were forced to remain there overnight in the stifling, unventilated heat, with no space to sit or lie down. Many of the badly wounded died where they stood.

The carnage was not at an end. The next morning some Japanese soldiers came back and told the prisoners in each outbuilding that they would receive a water ration, if they sent out two men at a time to fetch it in pails. Under this pretext, they bayoneted the men who volunteered once they had been marched outside, and those still within the outhouses could hear the terrified cries and screams of the hapless victims. British doctor Captain William Young, RAMC, later stated that: 'Every time the door was opened and the two next victims were taken out, those left could see the [Japanese] wiping the blood from their bayonets.' Eventually the soldiers were required elsewhere and moved off, having slaughtered approximately 100 innocent prisoners.

It is believed the orders for these atrocities came from Colonel Masanobu Tsuji, and the killing of unarmed and defenceless prisoners was just a precursor of what was to come on the island nation. After the capture of Singapore, Tsuji would assist in planning the systematic slaying of thousands of innocent Malayan Chinese that his regime deemed to be hostile to Japan. Civil servants, teachers and lawyers were among those captured, driven to secluded beaches and bayoneted or shot dead.

Meanwhile, that same day, exhausted soldiers of the AIF had formed a tightening perimeter around the Tanglin area in the north of the city. They were prepared to resist and fight on, despite knowing that the Japanese were swarming onto the island in overwhelming numbers. Meanwhile the water mains had been smashed by shellfire and bombs, and it became apparent that the island's water supply could not last more than another twenty-four hours.

On 15 February 1942, all British resistance came to a dramatic end. At 8.30 pm that Sunday evening, just as dusk was falling, an Australian gunner in the 2/10th Field Regiment cheered when the order was given to prepare to advance. 'About bloody time!' he shouted. But as the trucks and guns began to move, an eerie silence fell over the perimeter. There was no gunfire and no aircraft flew overhead. It was then that a British Army staff car approached with its headlights blazing, which would ordinarily have presented an easy, fat target for an enemy fighter plane, but the skies remained clear. Nevertheless the Australian gunners waved their arms and yelled in dismay and anger, telling the officers to douse their lights. When the car stopped, an English voice boomed out, addressing the assembled soldiers. They could not comprehend the words they heard next: 'It's all over, chaps!'

The men would soon find out that the British commander, Lieutenant-General Arthur Percival, General Officer Commanding (GOC) Malaya, had decided earlier that day there was no option but to surrender all his troops in the face of overwhelming Japanese forces and aggression. A British surrender party led by General Percival subsequently arrived at Lieutenant-General Tomoyuki Yamashita's headquarters at the seized Ford Motor factory in Bukit Timah at 5.15 pm. Following the signing of the surrender papers, British and Allied troops were ordered to lay down their arms and surrender. All the guns fell silent at 8.30 pm, and 'fortress Singapore' had fallen.

When the troops heard that a surrender had been negotiated and they were to surrender to their enemy, they were both shocked and aggrieved, crying out in pure rage at this unexpected treachery by their leaders after months of now useless combat and the loss of so many of their fellow soldiers. Others, totally exhausted, lay down to sleep after being awake for most of the past few days and nights. Disbelief and disgust slowly gave way to a bitter acknowledgement of ignoble defeat. To a man they had been prepared to fight on, to be wounded or even die, but few of them had foreseen the decision that had been made and forced on them by their leaders. For the first time, the weary soldiers came to the unbelievable realisation that they could now become prisoners of war.

Altogether, General Percival surrendered around 130,000 British, Australian, Indian and Malayan troops – the largest surrender in British combat history. That number included 18,490 Australian servicemen. Over the next three-and-a-half years, nearly 8000 of these men would die from disease or malnutrition as prisoners of the Japanese, while many would be brutally executed for attempting to escape, or for the most trivial of offences.

Meanwhile, shortly after completing all formalities regarding the surrender, Major General Gordon Bennett, in his position as commander of the 8th Australian Division, was determined to formulate an escape plan and not become a high-ranking prisoner of the Japanese. After making preliminary arrangements and having all secret papers destroyed, he handed over command to his artillery commander, Brigadier Cecil Callaghan, his next-senior officer. He later wrote that the atmosphere around his headquarters was depressing as he made his goodbyes to those who had served so admirably with him.

Our hopes and optimistic ambitions had been shattered. Every officer and every man had given the best they had in them in this fight . . . Everyone was stunned by the decision to surrender. All knew for many days that there was no other alternative. Nevertheless the end came as a shock. Their war was over. Their hopes and ambitions were shattered. They were to become prisoners of the despised Japanese. They were to submit to the ignominious position of spending the rest of the war behind barbed wire – at the mercy of the Japanese, who had a very bad reputation for the way in which they treated their prisoners . . . Proud men accept such servility with bad grace.

I, personally, had made this decision [to escape] some time previously, having decided that I would not fall into Japanese hands. My decision was fortified by the resolve that I must at all costs return to Australia to tell our people the story of our conflict with the Japanese, to warn them of the danger to Australia, and to advise them of the best means of defeating the Japanese tactics.

Then, along with two of his staff, Lieutenant Gordon Walker, his aide-de-camp, and Major Charles Moses, he took the opportunity of escaping from Singapore by sea, just two hours after the surrender of Singapore.

As Bennett and Moses waited patiently on a deserted waterfront, Captain Walker swam out to a group of empty sampans lashed together, cut one free and rowed it to a small jetty, where the three men tossed in their packs and clambered aboard. Just as they were paddling away they saw eight men from the Malay Volunteer Forces waving to them and calling out. Bennett couldn't desert these brave men, so he ordered the sampan to be turned around to pick them up. There were now eleven evaders on board. After a long and futile search for a larger vessel, they finally came across a seaworthy *tongkang* – a type of junk – with seven British soldiers on board and several boxes of anti-aircraft shells in the hold (which they would later throw overboard). The Chinese owner of the boat was reluctant to take them to Sumatra, but a deal was finally negotiated and they set sail. They managed to slip past minefields and the silent guns of Japanese-occupied Blakang Mati and headed south.

Five days later, as they moved agonisingly slowly south down the coast of Sumatra on 19 February, Bennett's party was able to hail a much faster vessel and transferred to the *Tern*, a 30-foot launch once operated by the Singapore Harbour Board which had been commandeered and used as an escape vessel by a group of servicemen. The *Tern* eventually took them to the island of Singkep, where they loaded up on provisions and then made their way through the Berhala Strait, and several days later, on 21 February, they reached the town of Djambi, which was still under Dutch administration. As the petrol dumps there had been set ablaze so they wouldn't fall into Japanese hands, there was no fuel for the *Tern* and the rest of the journey had to be completed by ground transport.

They finally arrived in Padang on the coast of West Sumatra, where British officers of Malaya Command had organised a flying boat to pick up a number of service personnel. At dawn on 25 February, the Qantas Catalina landed in the water offshore and flew Bennett and his party to Batavia (now Jakarta), and from there he secured a ride in another flying boat with Moses and Walker to Broome in Western Australia.

General Bennett eventually arrived in Melbourne on 2 March. Although praised for reporting back on the lost defence of Singapore, with valuable information on methods of fighting the Japanese, he was also publicly denounced for leaving his troops to surrender. The following month, further inflaming his detractors, he was controversially promoted to lieutenant general and placed in charge of the 3rd Australian Corps in Perth, although he would never hold a field command again.

Meanwhile, back in Singapore, the ferocious pounding the city had taken from bombs and repeated shelling had resulted in hundreds of bloated bodies piling up on the streets, the pavements and in the monsoon drains. The stench was overpowering and swarms of flies were buzzing around the rotting corpses. The once-peaceful days of colonial rule were over, the bitter defeat leaving chaos in its wake.

Just three days before the general surrender, in view of the gravity of the situation, the 65 Australian nurses remaining in Singapore city had been ordered to pack up and be prepared to leave immediately. Matron Paschke quelled any arguments, stating that these were explicit orders and they had to be obeyed. The consequences, if anyone stayed on, were too horrid to contemplate once the Japanese, with their history of wartime rape and murder, flooded into the hospitals. In a state of anxiety and confusion, they were driven through the tumult to the ruined harbour precincts and hustled aboard an overcrowded evacuation ship, leaving behind a nation in despair. They not only prayed for the people of Singapore, but for a safe voyage back home to their loved ones in Australia.

Instead, that day marked the beginning of a nightmare journey into the hell of captivity under the Japanese.

3

THE *VYNER BROOKE* TRAGEDY

BY 11 FEBRUARY 1942, the fall of Singapore to Japanese forces was both inevitable and imminent. That day, Captain Herbert Geldard, an Australian-born liaison officer with Malaya Command, received instructions to confer with the navy regarding an immediate evacuation of the remaining members of the Australian Nursing Service from Singapore by any available ship. This followed urgent meetings in late January between Colonel Alfred Derham, the Australian 8th Division's senior medical officer, and Major General Gordon Bennett, commander of the 8th Division, during which Derham formally requested the evacuation of all Australian nurses from the Malaya theatre of operations. He expressed fears for their safety in light of strongly rumoured Japanese atrocities the previous month in Hong Kong.

Initially, General Bennett rejected the request, believing such a move might badly affect the morale of his troops, but as relentless Japanese forces moved in, Bennett and General Percival met on 9 February and reluctantly agreed to authorise the evacuation of all remaining Australian nurses from Singapore. At this stage there were 130 nurses, all from the 2/10th, 2/13th AGH and the 2/4th CCS, tending to wounded service personnel in and around Singapore.

On receiving his instructions, Captain Geldard began making arrangements to evacuate all of the nurses, along with hundreds of casualties. There was already a hospital ship in harbour, the former riverboat *Wah Sui*, unmistakably painted white with a huge red cross on either side, which it was felt even the Japanese might respect. There would be close to 350 men on board, including 127 ill or wounded servicemen. Geldard chose to send six nurses from the 2/10th AGH along with a number of their patients. Matron Paschke asked for volunteers to leave almost immediately. No one volunteered, so (probably filled with admiration for their humanity) she personally selected the six nurses to go, with just five minutes' notice. Betty later wrote:

Poor Matron! What a decision she had to make! In her usual calm manner she assembled as many of us as she could, then simply divided us into two groups – those on the one hand to go, those on the other to stay. There was no time for anything else – and everyone wanted to stay and carry on. But off they went, under orders, with hardly anyone to see them on their way. We were flat out receiving wounded, and still more wounded, while the bombing and noise went on and on.

According to Sister Veronica Clancy: 'The girls who had to go begged to be allowed to remain, but the orders had to be obeyed. Tearful farewells and last-minute messages and they were gone.' Betty Jeffrey was not one of the six; suspecting that the matron was seeking volunteers, she had slipped away from the meeting and remained in one of the wards, dutifully changing a patient's dressing. It was a typically selfless act on her part, but one that would soon cost her three-and-a-half years of liberty. All of those who left on the Chinese vessel *Wah Sui* that day – the six nurses and around 350 critically wounded patients – eventually made it safely back home to Australia following a long and hellish voyage.

The following day, 11 February, arrangements were in place for a further evacuation of around 30 nurses from the 2/10th and 2/13th – this time on the cargo ship *Empire Star*. Later, another 30 nurses were added to the ship's contingent, eventually making 59 in total. According to Betty Jeffrey, 'The *Empire Star* was to sail . . . so Matron Paschke calmly sent this number off to the wharf while just as calmly she continued supervising her hospital where the rest of her nurses were flat out receiving the never-ending stream of wounded.'

One of those evacuated was Sister Frances Cullen of the 2/13th AGH, who later praised the bravery and defiance of the men they had to leave behind:

> The night we left we had a thousand patients. We had to put them on the floors, in the quartermaster's store, even in the little chapel, where we had boarded off the altar. The boys were marvellous . . . One of our most wonderful helpers was Padre Marsden, a brother of Major Marsden, the registrar of the 10th AGH. The padre worked as a stretcher bearer, gave anaesthetics, made tea, did anything we asked him.
>
> We will never forget the courage and unselfishness of the men of the AIF. In the last days on the island they were begging us to let them leave the hospital. Even the ones with limb injuries said they could be carried to a gun and could lie beside it to fire it.

We all hated leaving the boys. The night we left we were all in tears. Matron Drummond said to us, 'Stop crying, girls, and try to look bright,' ignoring the fact that tears were streaming down her own face.

Each of the 59 nurses was issued with iron rations, a tin of either bully beef or baked beans, a kit bag and a small haversack. Once they reached the wharf, several of them were also given cans of baby rusks.

The *Empire Star* slipped out of the harbour very early on the morning of 12 February with a recorded 2154 people on board, including the nurses. The ship eventually arrived in Australia two weeks later, but only after several instances of being attacked while heading south to Batavia. During one raid by enemy aircraft, with hundreds of servicemen and patients stranded out on the open deck, the ship took three direct hits, killing 17 people and wounding 32 others.

During the raid, extreme courage was displayed by two Victorian nurses from the 2/13th AGH, Sisters Margaret Anderson and Veronica Torney. Disobeying orders to stay below decks during the attack, they made their way up on deck to render assistance to the badly injured, although there were virtually no medical supplies or water to assist them. As the raid continued, they often laid their own bodies over those of their patients in order to protect them from the constant threat of bullets flying everywhere.

Later, back in Australia, the two women were recognised for their courage under fire and for protecting the vulnerable wounded. Anderson deservedly received the George Medal (GM) for gallantry, and Torney an MBE. Sister Torney later said that they were just doing what they had been trained to do. 'There were other wounded and other sisters doing all they could,' she remarked. 'They did as good a job as we did.'

Meanwhile, there had been mass confusion for the remaining nurses of the 2/13th AGH in the hospital that had been set up within St Patrick's Boys' School at Katong. The previous day they had seen 30 of their number ordered to leave straight away – despite their protests and pleas to stay – and driven to Singapore wharf, ready to board the *Empire Star*.

On Thursday, 11 February, even as their depleted numbers desperately tried to tend to an ever-increasing number of wounded soldiers and civilians, there were fresh orders for six nurses, badly needed to assist at the temporary Manor House casualty hospital, perched on a nearby hill, where most of the surgical cases had been admitted. Matron Paschke selected Sisters Jessie Blanch, Mary Cuthbertson, Winnie Davis, Dorothy Freeman, Clarice Halligan and Betty Jeffrey and drove them to the smaller facility.

Betty came close to tears when she walked into the hospital. Wounded men were not only occupying every available bed, but were laid out side by side over stretchers on the floor, on verandas, in garages, tents and even in protective grave-like dugouts. Meanwhile enemy fighter planes constantly roared overhead, blazing away indiscriminately at any target in the area that caught the pilots' attention.

Out in front of the hospital, a huge red cross on a white background had been laid across the front lawn, which hopefully offered the hospital a degree of protection. But once they'd arrived there was no time to dwell on their own safety, so Betty and the five other nurses immediately stepped in and got to work, with nearly a thousand casualties needing their assistance. It was extraordinarily

tough, dirty and dangerous work, made even more so by the continual bombardment and shelling from the sky. As Betty later
recalled:

We went straight into work. I heard Matron Paschke on the phone
saying 'Yes sir. Yes sir. Yes sir.' She turned to me and said, 'Jeff, can
you get 78 patients in by midnight?' I said, 'Yes sir, yes sir' without
thinking. To put the 78 patients in we knocked out the thin walls in
this building and by midnight we were pulling their boots and socks
off while Matron was in the kitchen making soup for them. By
daylight we had been working 48 hours straight and I was walking
along the ward in the first glow of sunlight and I could hear gentle
breathing all around. I thought, 'We've done it.'

We had beds out on an old tennis court under a marquee.
Because it had been raining heavily, 150 beds began to sink into
the soil. Sister [Dot] Freeman and I were out there and they were
actually sinking as you rested your hand on the bed to treat the
men. We were practically nursing on our knees. When the bombs
began to fall, some of the patients put their tin hats on, and for
those who didn't have tin hats, we put bed pans on their heads.

The planes were firing streams of bullets. I had a tray with a
cloth on it marked with a big red cross and I stepped out and lifted
it up. The pilot coming in low must have seen it and he stopped the
stream of bullets just before getting to us and began again after he
passed on. A piece of shrapnel had gone by me, it just missed my
face but seared my skin and hair on one side.

I don't know how many hours we worked . . . Wounded were
arriving all the time. Almost a thousand were there, in the 200-bed
hospital.

It was trauma nursing at its most demanding level. Then, just as they were about to grab a quick lunch break, a car pulled up outside and they were instructed to get in straight away. The bewildered nurses were told they were now among those being evacuated to the wharf, where they would board a ship and flee Singapore. All six stubbornly refused to leave their patients and demanded to stay. As Betty later recorded,

> But our refusal was useless. We were ordered to leave and just had to walk out on those superb fellows lying there – not one complaining and all needed attention – also our young doctors and the senior doctors too, who needed our help so badly – just had to walk out on them – the rottenest thing I've ever done in my life. This was the work we had gone overseas to do. We all hated it – we just sat in that car dazed, it happened so quickly.

On reaching the main hospital, all the remaining nurses and their few essential possessions were thrust into a convoy of ambulances. An orderly managed to grab Betty's kit bag and threw it to her in the ambulance, much to her relief. Leaving the hospital, the convoy cautiously drove down back streets until they reached the magnificent St Andrew's Cathedral near Padang, which was also being used as an emergency hospital. Here they were joined by some sisters from the 2/13th AGH and 2/4th CCS. As explosions and gunfire rent the air around them, their names and numbers were taken by Australian Lieutenant Colonel Glyn White, Deputy Assistant Director of Medical Services (DADMS) for the 8th Division, along with Matron Paschke. Sister Jessie Simons (2/13th AGH) was one of the nurses, and later wrote:

We waited in the dim coolness, invaded here and there by the late afternoon sunshine which streamed through the windows. Within a few minutes an air-raid siren whined and the ack-ack gun mounted at the cathedral door stammered into action . . . News of our going had spread and several men brought in letters for us to deliver when, or if, we reached Australia or some other peaceful point south. In our turn we sent messages to friends to whom we had been unable to say goodbye. These messages were probably never delivered and the letters certainly were not.

Betty also wrote,

It was a queer sensation, sitting in that huge cathedral seeing the rows of Army sisters – some wearing captails, some in tin hats, one or two with outdoor felt hats on (we had all been on duty) – sitting quietly while an air raid raged and ack-ack guns echoed loudly through the church.

All up, 65 nursing sisters including Matron Paschke had been assembled in the church and would be transported to the wharf once it was deemed safe enough to proceed. When the all-clear between air raids was finally given, everyone piled back into the ambulances, which sped off. It was a perilous, nightmare journey through dense palls of smoke, past bombed-out buildings on rubble-filled streets, seeing the unleashed fury of huge, uncontained fires and watching hundreds of frightened people running aimlessly about in sheer terror. The ambulances finally stopped near the waterfront, but with destruction everywhere the nurses had to walk the rest of the way through thick smoke, passing shattered and burning buildings and abandoned or wrecked cars until they reached the wharf. It too was a scene of utter chaos, Betty recalled:

> Singapore was ablaze. There were fires burning everywhere behind and around us and on the wharf hundreds of people trying to get away, long queues of civilian men and women, and a long grey line – us. Masts of sunken ships were sticking up out of the water, but no ships were in sight other than forlorn-looking barges.
>
> As we walked along the wharf we noticed that dozens of beautiful cars had been dumped in the water; some were smashed on top of each other, others were visible only by a wheel or part of the engine sticking out of the water. Cars during that last week in Singapore were literally given away as people evacuated; these obviously were scuttled to prevent the Japanese from using them.

As they waited on the wharf, the British officer overseeing their departure gave the nurses an ominous warning. He said he had seen the atrocities carried out by Japanese soldiers in Hong Kong and cautioned them that, should they somehow find themselves in a position where they were about to be taken by Japanese forces, they should ask the ship's officers to shoot them, rather than allow themselves to fall into their enemy's barbarous hands. Although they were highly unlikely to take such drastic advice, the nurses' blood ran cold.

It took around forty-five minutes to get organised as another air raid took place, with the ominous sounds of shelling and ack-ack fire directed at the aircraft from the ground. The noise around them was frightening. It was with mixed feelings, but mostly relief, and the acrid tang of smoke thick in their nostrils, that the nurses were finally marched in single file onto a waiting tender, that cast off once everyone was on board. It took them down the harbour through choppy waters to where SS *Vyner Brooke* was waiting patiently at anchor, flying the red ensign. The tender pulled alongside a steel door in the side of the ship and, as they were assisted aboard by the crew, each nurse was handed a wood and canvas lifebelt.

Built in Scotland in 1928, the *Vyner Brooke* was a British-registered cargo vessel of 1669 tons gross, named after the third Rajah of Sarawak – Sir Charles Vyner Brooke. Up until the outbreak of war with the Japanese, the *Vyner Brooke* had serenely plied the waters between Singapore and Kuching as a luxury vessel operating under the flag of the Sarawak Steamship Company, and would normally carry around twelve passengers. When war erupted, the ship was requisitioned by the Royal Navy, given a coat of dark grey paint, and became a lightly armed trader with four small deck guns. The ship was under the command of Lieutenant Richard ('Tubby') Borton, RNR, with a crew of around 50, including the gun crew.

As soon as all 65 nurses were on board, joining around 130 civilian refugees crowded onto the ship's deck – mostly women and children – Captain Borton gave the order to prepare to get under way as soon as darkness had begun setting in. Time passed slowly, but once everything was in readiness the engines were fired up and Borton skilfully steered the crowded ship into nearby Keppel Harbour, a little west of Singapore Harbour, where the engines were shut down while he waited for full darkness, giving them the best possible chance of leaving undetected.

Meanwhile, Matron Paschke had been busy organising her nurses in the ship's saloon, and quickly realised there was very little food on board apart from what they had brought with them in their kit bags – mainly tins of bully beef and baked beans, biscuits and water – and decided that it should be rationed throughout the ship. As Betty later recalled,

> The ship's crew were tired out and we were asked to go to the galley and prepare a meal. Some did this and produced a stew of army tinned meat and tinned vegetables. A chain gang of nurses was formed and the plates of food were passed from the galley to everyone on board; civilian men, women and children, ship's crew and finally, us. Army biscuits and cheese were the second wave.

The scratch meal was greatly appreciated, but the nurses were now given additional duties. Each of them was assigned her own particular area of the ship, where they would tend to the wounded in the event of an attack. They were supplied with field dressings, morphine and syringes. Matron Paschke impressed on the nurses that if the ship had to be abandoned at sea due to enemy action, they were to be the last to evacuate, and to wear their Red Cross armbands at all times. The ship had to be thoroughly checked beforehand for anyone still on board, then either she or Matron Irene Drummond would give the order to abandon ship.

'Remember,' she concluded, 'remove your shoes, hold your lifebelt down firmly and jump into the water feet first. If you don't hold your belt down it can come up and hit you under the chin with the possibility of breaking your neck!' The lifebelts were made of thick cork squares sewn into a khaki canvas jacket which was designed to slip over the head and be tied securely at the front.

Sister Jessie Simons from Tasmania would later report on the tumult within Singapore Harbour in her magnificent post-war book, *While History Passed*, saying that they could only watch, fascinated but in helpless dismay, as Japanese dive bombers dropped their bombs over the hundreds of ships still bobbing around in the harbour.

The short tropical twilight sent the Jap planes, serenely ignoring our defences, back across the city to their aerodromes on the mainland. In the dusk, the dark water reflected blazing Singapore, which looked like a huge bonfire, while an island nearby which had been used as an oil store, added its whirling blaze and thick smoke to the lurid picture. Bursting bombs, the distant thunder of artillery, the staccato rattle of machine guns and the drone of planes provided an infernal and very terrifying orchestral background as the curtain of night fell on the doomed city.

While they waited for the ship to depart their Keppel Harbour sanctuary, one of the nurses broke the sombre mood when she began to sing 'Waltzing Matilda'. It was not long before they were all joining in, singing along at the top of their voices, and it certainly lifted the spirits of everyone on board.

'We got under way as darkness fell, leaving behind a scene that we would never forget,' recalled Sister Florence (Flo) Trotter (2/10th AGH). 'Singapore was ablaze; thick black smoke billowed high behind the city. There were 200 aboard – far too many for the size of the ship.' Sister Sylvia Muir of the 2/13th AGH also watched in sadness as Singapore slowly receded behind them:

The sun was sinking behind a pall of black smoke as I watched it at the close of that awful day . . . Beside me a lass murmured: 'There goes all my hopes and plans for the future.' Her fiancé had been killed a few days previously. It was just as well she and I didn't know the future. Four days later she was shot on the beach at Banka Island.

By giving one of the native crew a few of my precious remaining dollars he produced a camp stretcher, some boiling water, two blankets, a pillow and some bananas. We made use of the bedding, put some children on the stretcher and tried to get a night's sleep.

The crew had mentioned that due to overcrowding below decks those who preferred to do so could sleep on the deck. After watching fires burning along the Singapore waterfront, with Collyer Quay well hidden beneath a thick black layer of smoke, the nurses settled down on the deck to try to catch some sleep. Most covered themselves with their coats and used rubber respirators as makeshift pillows. Sleep would prove difficult, however, with the ever-present sound of ships' guns and other hostile sounds of battle echoing across the water, mingled with wistful thoughts of those they had left behind.

One major problem for those on board was a distinct lack of toilet facilities; just two 'heads' and one washroom were available for the nearly 200 people, so there was always a long queue to negotiate. Then there was a frightened scramble after the crew told everyone to don their lifebelts as a precaution, as the ship was about to pass through a British minefield. It was with great relief that they were later informed the captain had successfully negotiated the mines.

The following morning, *Vyner Brooke* was laid up in the lee of the small, jungle-covered Lingga Island, located some 60 miles south of Singapore. Twice that morning, Japanese aircraft were seen flying overhead, but no one seemed interested in taking a closer look at them, so the ship weighed anchor a little before midday and continued its journey.

Despite the circumstances, Sister Vivian Bullwinkel could still admire the splendour and calmness of the day. 'Friday was the most beautiful [morning] I can recall,' she later observed. 'We're just sailing among the islands, and it was difficult to think that there was a war raging not very far from us.' Betty was not quite as taken with their progress that day:

> We spent it keeping our fingers crossed and hiding behind islands, stopping all the time. We all kept wishing we could get on with the journey we were supposed to be making towards Java. And the noise of battle rolled not so far away.

During the afternoon, other Japanese war planes were spotted, but the *Vyner Brooke* continued unmolested. The ship's immediate destination was Batavia (now Jakarta), then the capital of the Dutch East Indies. If this could be reached without incident, a determination would then be made about the possibility of going on to Fremantle in Western Australia. However, to reach Batavia they would have to navigate a path through the danger-filled Banka Strait, while trying to avoid prowling enemy ships and aircraft. The strait had already earned the ominous nickname of 'Bomb Alley'.

On the morning of Saturday, 14 February, the ship was anchored in the lee of Toejou Island, a smaller and less concealed place to anchor than Captain Borton would have preferred, but it was some distance to the next-larger island and they would have been easily visible to patrolling enemy aircraft. After seeing some of those planes operating in the vicinity, Captain Borton decided to make a run for it mid-morning, setting a course for the Banka Strait, and then skirting around the north-western corner of Banka Island.

Major William Tebbutt, who had been attached to the headquarters of the 8th Division AIF in Singapore, was on board the *Vyner Brooke* as the race was on to elude detection and hopefully reach safer waters.

The captain stated to me that he considered it suicidal to remain anchored close to land, that the ship could easily be picked up from the air, and would provide a sitting shot for bombers. From his experience he believed that he might be able to avoid bombs in the open fairway. Accordingly he did not obey his orders to anchor in the daytime.

As the ship headed south, the nurses were busy in the galley preparing a meagre, late breakfast for everyone, while the crew conducted an examination of the six lifeboats carried on board. They determined that, should there be a need to launch them, two would hold 30 passengers each and the remainder 20 each. As a precaution each passenger, including the children, had been handed a lifebelt and instructed in its use. With insufficient room for everyone in the lifeboats, those who were strong swimmers were told that if necessary they should take to the water instead.

Offering a further means of life-saving flotation in the water, several dozen one-metre-square 'life rafts' of various sizes were positioned around the ship. These comprised a number of interwoven wooden slats covered in canvas and containing some cork for flotation. Nurse 'Mickey' Syer later described them as 'gimcrack' – by definition, something cheaply made or shoddy. The smallest raft could hold one person, or two people sitting back-to-back. Each raft was equipped with rope handles for people in the water to hold on to, or they could be used to tie rafts together. All up, there was enough room on the boats and rafts and other life-saving devices for around 650 people, which was somewhat reassuring for those on board.

Meanwhile, as they entered the Banka Strait, leaving Singapore 148 miles astern, the ship and its prominent wake had now become dangerously exposed on the calm flat sea. As Major Tebbutt continued:

After the ship left Toejou [aka Toedjoe] Island there were three or four alerts before about one p.m., when a formation of nine Japanese planes flew over the ship several times and were fired upon by [the ship's] Lewis gun. They then went about two miles ahead of the ship and three dived over the ship, dropping their bombs from 3000 feet. The ship circled at full speed. The bombs all fell harmlessly into the sea, exploding close enough to shake the ship.

At the first sign of trouble, the ship's siren had sounded. Everyone had to don their lifebelts and any other protective gear, including tin hats. They were told to proceed down to the lounge deck and lie on the floor. There was little else they could do. The planes swept over the vulnerable ship in groups of three, but their accuracy was awry, with many bombs missing their mark.

Despite the ferocity of the aerial attack, Betty tried her hardest to remain confident they could see it through.

We had a view – too horribly clear – of it all. First time they missed, but she was a very small ship and the near misses made her rattle. She zigzagged just in the same way as a ship we had seen being attacked off the Malacca Swimming Club two months before. On that occasion the ship was not hit.

I felt certain that the bombs would miss us, too. We were able to relax a little while the planes gathered themselves together to try again, but it was nerve-racking, really, waiting.

Back came the planes . . . and this time we were just about lifted out of the water. The little ship shuddered and rattled. There was a terrific bang, and after that she was still.

Two bombs had finally found their target, with one dropping straight down the ship's funnel and exploding, blowing out the bottom of the ship. As Sister Wilma Oram later recalled,

We were lying flat on our faces, and the side was blown out of the ship. There was broken glass sprayed all over us. I thought my legs had been cut off, but when I had a look they were only just cut by flying glass.

As an immediate result of the explosion, the engines fell silent. One of the ship's officers barged into the lounge and ordered everyone to go upstairs and head for the lifeboats. There was surprisingly little panic as everyone made their way to the upper deck. Once there, however, the news was not good; the Japanese aircraft were now moving in for the kill, viciously hammering the deck and precious lifeboats with bullets. Betty knew they were in deep trouble:

Down the planes came again, and what a crash! It felt as if the bomb had landed right in the room with us. Then shattering glass, tons of it, smoke, and the sounds of crashing walls. We had been given instructions that morning what the drill was to be if we were bombed or torpedoed. Different jobs were allocated to each nurse. Now everyone hurried about the decks doing the task assigned to her.

The damage was catastrophic; ropes holding three lifeboats on one side of the ship were severed and two had plunged into the sea. One sank almost immediately, while the second turned upside-down and drifted away from the ship. Two Malay sailors manned a third lifeboat before it suddenly fell into the water and partially sank beneath them.

Wounded women and children and those nurses who could not swim were allotted to the remaining seaworthy lifeboats. Everyone else, they were told, would have to fend for themselves. There was shattered glass and wood everywhere, and clouds of thick, choking smoke. As people scrambled to get into the remaining boats or jumped into the sea, the *Vyner Brooke* began to slowly list heavily to starboard. The two undamaged lifeboats, now filled to capacity, were successfully lowered and began moving away from the sinking vessel. They were now faced with trying to make it to Banka Island, a largely undeveloped island known only for its reserves of tin. It was some 12 miles distant.

In the midst of the tumult, Matron Olive Paschke stood tall and calm as she organised the safe evacuation of everyone from the doomed ship with the help of the nurses. Once satisfied that all that could be done had been done, and with the ship rapidly sinking, she called out, 'It's time to go, girls!' She then reminded the nurses it would be best if they took off their shoes to aid in swimming, and to go over the side as quickly as possible. As they all followed the matron's instructions, she shouted out one last piece of encouragement: 'We'll all meet on the shore, girls, and get teed up again!'

Matron Drummond, assisted by some of the nurses, managed to load as many medical supplies as they could into the bullet-riddled remains of a lifeboat and launch it into the water. Those who were able to climb aboard desperately tried to keep it afloat by bailing out the seawater using their hands and any type of container they could find.

One of the nurses, Mona Wilton, was killed when she was struck by a heavy life raft falling from the roof of the ship. Despite all that was going on, Sister Sylvia Muir agreed there was surprisingly little panic among the nurses trying to cope with the situation as they deserted the doomed ship:

I remember my friend and I taking off our shoes, placing our steel helmets neatly on top of them and going to the rail. Many of the people were sliding down ropes into the water, but we jumped. We struck out from the side of the ship remembering all that we had heard about being sucked down. When I stopped to rest I started calling to my friend but she did not answer. She was never seen alive again.

Sister Veronica Clancy from Adelaide had leapt off the top deck, swinging out on a rope, but in doing so, and like so many others, she stripped a lot of the skin off her hands. Clancy later recalled seeing the keel of the ship shortly before it vanished beneath the waves.

She then found herself swimming in an ocean of thick oil, surrounded by struggling figures holding on to spars and other debris to keep themselves afloat amid the bodies of thousands of brightly coloured fish that had been killed in the explosion. She managed to cling to an upturned lifeboat, gazing in horror at the oil-covered bodies floating by of those who had lost their lives.

Many years after the event, Sister Vivian Bullwinkel, formerly of the 2/13th AGH, told Perth's *Sunday Times* reporter Robert Wainwright that the years had not dulled her memory. 'We had old-fashioned cork lifebelts in which I had no faith,' she stated, 'so I was surprised to find myself floating with one of those things under my chin. I would have drowned without it.'

Sister Pat Darling was another able to vividly recall that tumultuous time. 'There were dead bodies floating around everywhere, because people had jumped overboard and their lifebelt had gone up and would have broken their necks as they hit the water.'

Despite the *Vyner Brooke* rapidly sinking, the Japanese pilots were not yet content with their carnage. For a few minutes they continued to strafe the ship and anyone they could see in the lifeboats and rafts or swimming in the open water before finally flying away, leaving behind dozens of dead men, women and children bobbing up and down in their life vests. A major concern for those swimming was the terrifying fact that sharks were known to inhabit these waters, and there was certainly a lot of blood to attract them, but there is no recorded case of anyone being attacked – at least no one living.

Another recollection came from Sister Iole Harper, the only Western Australian among the 65 Australian nurses. When told to get into the water as the ship was sinking, she had watched as others leapt overboard:

We had lifebelts on and people were jumping into the water. I didn't like the idea of jumping and so I waited until the ship was rolling slowly over onto its side. Then I walked down its steel plates and flopped into the water. I had been in the water for a few minutes and I remember thinking: 'This is funny. This sort of thing happens in books.' I didn't think it could happen to me. I didn't think I'd be going this way. Then I got on a raft. That made sixteen of us, including two Malays. The raft was overloaded and partially submerged. We realised we couldn't go on as we were. But land was just a distant blur. Most of the girls couldn't swim and as I was a strong swimmer I got off the raft with another sister . . . and, after a lot of persuading, the two Malay sailors got off too.

The sister who selflessly climbed off the raft with Iole was Betty Jeffrey. Before the *Vyner Brooke* sank, she had been busy helping other people over the side and climbing into the lifeboats or rafts or into the water. As the ship began to tip over, she realised it was time to get off herself, kicked off her shoes and looked for the quickest way to leave the doomed ship:

Couldn't find a rope ladder so tried to be Tarzan and slip down a rope. Result, terribly burnt fingers, all skin missing from six fingers, and both palms of my hands; they seemed quite raw. I landed with an awful thud and my tin hat landed on top of me.

What a glorious sensation! The coolness of the water was marvellous after the heat of the ship. We all swam well away from her and grabbed anything that floated and hung on to it in small groups. We hopelessly watched the *Vyner Brooke* take her last roll

60

and disappear under the waves. I looked at my watch – twenty to three . . . Then up came the oil – that awful, horrible oil, ugh!

The thick manila rope had caused lasting, grievous harm to her hands as she slid down its rough length, which she would only realise later, once she was moving away from the immediate danger of being sucked down with the sinking ship. Betty would forever carry rope burn scars on her hands, and particularly one which she said reminded her of the shape of Banka Island, meaning she would carry 'that wretched island' with her for the rest of her life.

She also recalled those on board the raft as the two Malay sailors – 'one a bit burnt' – four or five civilian women and Sisters Iole Harper, Caroline Ennis, Merle Trenerry, Gladys McDonald, Millicent Dorsch and Mary Clarke. She was pleased to see that Matron Paschke had also made it onto the raft and was busy helping those who were ill or injured while trying to organise ways to get the raft to shore. The main problem was that the only means of rowing the raft relied on two small slabs of wood from a packing case. Those who were able to help took turns rowing during the night.

'Iole was wonderful,' Betty later recalled. 'When not rowing she would get off, swim all round, count everybody, and collect those who got tired of hanging on, making them use their feet properly to assist in pushing the thing along.'

Like many others that terrifying afternoon and evening they drifted through thick black patches of oil, retching and vomiting, almost reaching land, only to be swept out again by the currents.

Long after the war, Betty was asked if she ever had any doubts that she would reach the shore. 'No. Never,' she responded immediately. 'I've always been a long-distance swimmer. When I was thirteen or fourteen down at Mornington I would swim Point to Point. I just loved swimming. I knew just give me time and I will get in. I did have a lifebelt.'

Sister Sylvia Muir from Queensland was one of those who was helped aboard a badly damaged lifeboat and she not only helped to bail out seawater using a tin can but sacrificed her uniform dress. Once removed, it was buttoned together with another nurse's dress to make a rudimentary sail, which proved reasonably effective when it caught the wind. The two scantily clad women were in a lifeboat with several soldiers and civilians, but they were in a desperate situation and knew it was not a time for false modesty.

As they slowly made their way towards shore, which they could see through a haze of mist, Sylvia later reported seeing a small life raft in the distance containing Matron Paschke and five other nurses holding babies and toddlers on their laps, but it was dangerously low in the water as a swirling current swung them by. Sylvia was momentarily distracted by a child crying in her own boat and when she turned around again to look for the life raft it had vanished.

By daybreak, those on board Betty's raft, or swimming beside it, were totally exhausted, their muscles moving more by memory than will. The task of reaching shore seemed harder than ever, but their spirits were lifted when they made out some other survivors on a beach on Banka Island, standing beside a small signal fire. They redoubled their efforts, paddling as hard as they could and calling out to those on the beach, but the dull morning light and the pounding sounds of the sea drowned out their voices and no one could hear or see them. Then an adverse current swept them back out to sea and they all cried out in despair and frustration as their raft was carried further down the coast.

They had another lift in spirits when they saw what looked like a number of black rocks protruding from the sea, but as a swift current took them closer, the 'rocks' turned out to be a convoy of small Japanese warships. The current actually took them right up to one of the ships, but as it was still early morning and no one was on deck, it seemed their plight had gone unnoticed.

They managed to use their legs to push away from the ship, but then they heard motorboats heading their way and they were soon surrounded by several smaller boats filled with Japanese soldiers, who called out in their language but offered no assistance. In fact they quickly lost interest in the pleas and obvious distress of the bewildered survivors, turned their backs, and the boats chugged off in formation, heading for the town of Muntok, leaving those on and around the raft in a state of utter disbelief. All the Japanese seemed to care about was landing stores and other goods on the island, which they now occupied.

As they were carried even further away, everyone realised with dismay that they were still a long distance from the shore and were being drawn further out by the strong currents and buffeted by strong winds. They were cold and many of them were weak and seasick. At one stage, unable to row any further, Betty and Iole and the two Malay people climbed overboard once again, joining Sisters Jess Dorsch and Merle Trenerry, who were holding on to the raft's ropes. This left Mary Clarke, Gladys McDonald and Olive Paschke still on the raft, as well as Caroline Ennis, who was sitting precariously on the side of the raft with two toddlers balanced on her lap, back-to-back with Matron Paschke, who had already declared she did not know how to swim. In fact, while boarding the *Vyner Brooke*, she had moved alongside Betty and quietly said, 'If this thing sinks you'll have to help me, Jeff!'

Betty's hands were bruised and swollen and so badly abraded – the flesh on some fingers torn down to the bones – that she wasn't holding on to the raft's ropes, so she and Iole swam alongside the raft, talking and trying to laugh with those still on the raft about what they'd do and drink once they finally reached land.

It was then that they spotted a fish trap bobbing up and down in the water, not too far away. 'We were obviously going to miss it,' Iole Harper later told interviewer Jane Fleming,

So Bett Jeffrey, who was also a very good swimmer . . . said we're going to see if we can get to the fish trap, because if there's a fish trap then there's fishermen [who'll] come down to the fish trap. And even if they weren't we could have a rest and then swim to the island.

They began dog-paddling towards the fish trap, but to their chagrin the strong currents kept pushing them back. Eventually they had to give up the effort, which was sapping their remaining strength, and headed back towards the raft. A strong current then took hold of the raft and rapidly swept it further out to sea before they could reach it and grab the trailing ropes. The Malay crewmen were in a similar predicament, swimming free of the raft, and they could only watch in stunned dismay as their fellow survivors were carried away.

'A current suddenly swept the raft about and took it back out to sea,' Betty recalled. 'We called to them, but they went too fast for us to catch them and we never saw them again.' The four swimmers were now on their own. If they wanted to live, they knew they had to make for the tree-studded outcrop of land in the distance or drown in the attempt. Only two of them would make it.

The two nurses maintained a close watch on each other and occasionally waved to show that they were still okay. After about an hour of swimming with leaden arms and keeping an eye on Iole, who had caught a different current and was desperately swimming hard for shore about 400 yards away, Betty noticed that the two Malay sailors were no longer to be seen. They had simply disappeared.

Around midday, Iole was the first to reach land, which was nothing more than a long stretch of muddy mangrove swamp, but it was sheer relief to no longer be fighting the unforgiving currents. Soon after, Betty's feet also touched some sharp mangrove roots protruding from the slimy mud and she dragged herself ashore. Her lungs felt like they were bursting and she was trembling uncontrollably as she tried to control her breathing. Using the last of her strength and an enormous amount of will, she finally made it across to where Iole was lying on her back, her legs still floating in the silted water. Iole was too physically exhausted to move further inland and Betty joined her.

With all that they had been through, they both shuddered at each other's unearthly appearance – hair matted and slicked down with stinking black oil, faces purple from exertion, and eyes rimmed in scarlet from long and constant exposure to salt water.

Concerned there might be predators such as crocodiles lurking in the mangroves, the two nurses summoned up the last of their strength and wearily climbed into a tree with wide branches. It was a far from comfortable refuge, but wrapping their arms around the trunk they both quickly fell into a deep but disturbed sleep, often hallucinating in their traumatised state about friends and family reaching out to help them.

'People asked us later if we were not worried about crocodiles,' Iole would later comment. 'They told us the coast was infested with them. Well, we tried not to think about them. And when we did see "logs" in the water below us, we told ourselves that they *were* logs.' After a while, they stopped looking for the ominous rising of two dead eyes watching them just above the surface of the water, or the sudden flick of a spiny tail. Danger was everywhere around them and never far from their minds, but they knew they had no option but to press on regardless. Survival was now paramount and fear would only slow them down.

Official war records would later show that, of the 65 nurses who embarked on the *Vyner Brooke*, 12 were killed during the attack on the ship or were lost to the sea. Those who had managed to survive spent anywhere between eight and 65 hours fighting the strong, swirling currents and strong winds.

In her graphic account of survivors desperately trying to make it to shore, Betty Jeffrey described how the raft carrying Matron Paschke, together with other nurses and civilian women and children, was swept back out again on a strong current and none were ever seen again. The presumption is that the occupants all drowned, apart from one curious anomaly – the reported finding on a small beach of an intact identity disc belonging to Sister Millicent Dorsch, who had been one of those on that raft.

As historian Barbara Angell concluded, 'The only way for anyone's identity disc to be found is for it to have been forcibly ripped or cut off.' Did Sister Dorsch or even the raft carrying all survivors manage to finally make it to shore and, if so, what happened to them? Did they fall victim to a Japanese massacre? It remains a mystery that is never likely to be solved.

4

PRISONERS OF THE JAPANESE

WHEN DAYLIGHT CAME, STIFF AND sore all over, Betty and Iole moved back to shore and reluctantly took to the choppy straits water once again, spending the remainder of that day desperately seeking a better place to move inland and hopefully to find some help. They swam up several promising creeks, but each one ended in near-impenetrable jungle, causing them to retreat in frustration and make their way back out again. As Betty would later record in her secret camp diary,

Our progress was slow, for we had to swim breast-stroke. Thank God we had lifebelts, though the canvas had already rubbed our chins raw. The peculiar animals, crabs, and fish we met along the way didn't exactly inspire good cheer. We would be swimming along through these swamps, when suddenly something would go flop into the water beside or behind us. And fish would go flipping along the surface of the water in an upright position on their tails. If only we could get along at that rate!

Many of the creatures inhabiting these waters were sea snakes, eels, sea slugs, anemones and freshwater shrimp – a staple diet of the Malay people on the island, but a constant, nipping nuisance for the two women. Trying to ignore swarms of mosquitoes and whatever sea life they encountered as they made their way inland, they were determined to keep going, although by now the mangrove spikes were continually cutting into their badly wounded hands, feet, legs and stomachs, causing such intense pain they began to feel they could not continue.

At one stage, when Iole was edging along ahead of Betty, she suddenly stopped and turned around. 'By the way,' she called out, 'what's your name?' Betty burst out laughing; after all, by now they had been swimming and sharing all sorts of jungle adventures for 28 hours. Iole joined in the laughter, after which they introduced themselves and shared some background information. Betty learned that Iole was from Western Australia and had joined the 2/13th AGH, whereas she was a Melbourne girl with the 2/10th. They not only served different units, but, despite tending hundreds of patients in Singapore, seemed never to have crossed paths before the perils of escaping from the sinking *Vyner Brooke*.

The heat and relentless humidity during the day and their constant thirst was wearing them down and they kept hoping to find some fresh water; what they were swimming and wading through was far too salty to consume. As the day drew to a close, the tide began seeping out, and it wasn't long before they found themselves sinking up to their knees in slimy, glutinous mud. When they finally found a suitably thick tree trunk, they trudged out of the mud and climbed to wide branches clear of the water, where they could recuperate and hope to catch some sleep.

That night they spent another uncomfortable few hours perched in the mangrove tree, never comfortable enough to do more than nap, occasionally pestered by huge birds flapping their wings and wanting to share their tree. It was still dark when they agreed to give up, climbed down and began striking out once more as the water slowly rose around them. They had to start swimming again, spending another day moving through the murky water, as Betty recalled:

We must have swum many miles that day towards the beach at Muntok. We saw a few crocodiles. Late that night we found a river – a big one this time – so we swam up until we were too tired to swim any farther. Then we found something that looked like grass, so we got out on to it. It was grass, but very squashy. We broke palm leaves with our elbows because our hands were too badly infected and made a bed there.

Sometime later they woke to the sound of a dog barking nearby, which encouraged them to keep moving in that direction, their feet sinking in the mud and plagued by ever-present clouds of mosquitoes and sandflies. Then they heard oars splashing in the water and surged towards the source as fast as they could. Their hearts lifted when they saw two Malay natives paddling a small boat, chatting away to each other. The nurses called out and waved, but to their distress the men stopped talking and simply seemed to ignore them, paddling on towards the sea, not even looking back at them. They realised they must have looked a truly frightening sight by this time, but their disappointment in the fishermen was acute.

That night was filled with further terror for the two nurses when they heard a large animal making its way towards them in

69

the pitch darkness. Whatever it was, it was large enough to break dead twigs beneath its feet as it cautiously approached. 'We were scared stiff,' Betty later recorded in her book. 'Then two large eyes appeared above us; it sniffed us all over, and – thank Heaven – went away again.' They never did find out what the animal was.

As dawn approached, they could hear several dogs barking and knew they had to be close to a village. They slid back into the river and continued swimming until once again they heard the sound of paddles hitting the water behind them. Then they saw the two Malay fishermen returning, this time coming their way, shouting to them with huge smiles on their faces. It seems they had been out clearing their fish trap and while on the way back were ready to help the women. They paddled their boat right up to Betty and Iole and helped them to clamber in.

After three days in the water, it was sheer bliss to see other humans again, and to know that they had finally been rescued and were not going to perish in some filthy swamp. They were hot, extremely thirsty, and had even been suffering bouts of hallucination, so the two men had come along just in time. Between them they knew very little Malay, but used some of this and sign language to ask for water and food. The two men merely nodded, gestured ahead and rowed upstream, eventually coming to their village, where they helped the sodden nurses out onto blessedly solid ground.

As Betty later wrote,

First thing we noticed was a row of thirteen sharks lying on the ground to dry! We were taken to the fisherman's hut, where we sat in the kitchen – after he had put the fowls outside – and dried ourselves by a stove. His wife and a small boy gave us cold tea first, then made us a pot of hot tea and some small hot cakes, which we ate as they came out of the oven. I haven't tasted anything better since!

Once they'd mostly dried out, they were ushered onto a veranda, in front of which the whole village had assembled. There was a lot of talk and pointing at them, their filthy condition and ragged clothing. It seemed they were all concerned about the number of bad cuts, bites and infections on their hands and legs. Then, to add to their surprise, a Chinese man dressed in crisp white shirt and pants approached them and politely said in clear English, 'Good morning.'

After introductions, they all sat down and the man brought them up to date on the events of the past few days. He was shocked to learn about the sinking of the *Vyner Brooke*, the resultant loss of life, and the extraordinary fact that they had been swimming on and off for three days in swampy waters infested by sharks and crocodiles. He was a citizen of Singapore and one of thousands who had been rounded up and held as prisoners by the Japanese, but he had managed to escape and was trying to make his way down to Java. He told them that the island they were on – Banka Island – was now close to falling completely into the hands of the Japanese and the situation was perilous, especially for foreigners. The man said he had just spoken with the people in the village and they were happy to look after the two of them until they had decided what to do.

As Iole later said,

Those Malays were very good to us and offered to keep us in hiding and supplied with food and said that they would help us escape. We thought that a pretty forlorn hope. We could not speak Malay and thought we could never get through Sumatra or down to Java without being caught.

While they pondered their situation, a young girl who introduced herself as Johanna placed a bowl of hot water in front of Betty and Iole, and watched as they tenderly bathed their aching, raw hands and legs. Once that had been attended to, she patted their wounds dry and bandaged them. Already they felt much better. Then Johanna disappeared, returning soon after with a pair of wooden sandals for each of them.

They consulted further with their Chinese helper and he agreed that trying to escape through treacherous, unknown territory was not a wise option, particularly as the Japanese were known to be trigger-happy. He felt their best option would be to surrender to the Japanese in the nearby town of Muntok, and explained that a number of captured foreigners were being held there in a native gaol. They saw the futility of trying to make their ill-equipped way to Java and decided to follow his advice, resigning themselves to waiting for a Japanese patrol which regularly passed through the village.

The two nurses were escorted to a Malay temple and told to stay there. Meanwhile, the Chinese man slipped off on his hopeful journey to safety after they wished him good luck. Soon after, an elderly village man came into the temple and offered them a gift – an opened can of Australian apricots, some rice and cooked fish. 'It was beautifully cooked,' Betty later wrote. 'We ate until we couldn't eat another thing.'

With renewed spirits and physical strength slowly returning, the two women began to get to know each other a little better. They found to their surprise that they both had sisters who not only knew each other, but were neighbours and friends in Somers, Victoria. As well, they each had a sister who had married an officer in the Royal Australian Navy (RAN). As they chatted, they forged a friendship that would endure for many decades to come.

All too soon, they heard the unmistakable sounds of a petrol engine as it entered the village. They stood up and moved to the doorway, watching with interest the arrival of a small truck-like vehicle carrying three Japanese soldiers armed with rifles. Holding hands, the two women moved out towards the vehicle. As soon as they saw them, the Japanese shouted and leapt to the ground, fixing bayonets to their rifles as they approached. It was a traumatic moment, as Betty later recorded: 'We were too dazed to do anything but just stand there while these bayonets rested on our stomachs – actually on the bottom of my belt, which made the shank stick into me. It hurt quite a lot, so I moved the bayonet down a little.'

A few awkward moments followed, with the soldiers shouting in Japanese and the women trying to communicate in English. Once the Japanese realised there were just the two women and no fighting men with them, they began to calm down and lowered their weapons. Betty had a flash of inspiration and pointed to the small map of Australia embossed on their uniform buttons. One of the soldiers peered closely at the button and then began to yell, 'Americano! Americano!' They were finally able to convince the man they were from Australia, not the United States, at which the soldiers visibly relaxed once again.

When it was time to go, the soldiers ushered the nurses into their muddy vehicle before climbing aboard themselves. As they were about to be driven off, a couple of Malay women cautiously approached and handed both of them coconuts, which the soldiers allowed. Once they moved off, Betty and Iole turned and waved their thanks to the gathered villagers, who quickly vanished from sight as the vehicle was driven deeper into the jungle. It was now time to worry about what fate might have in store for them. Their apprehension quickly grew soon after leaving the village when the driver pulled over and turned off his engine. Two unprotected young women and three armed soldiers – they began to fear they might be violated and then killed, but their fears were quickly allayed. Betty recalls,

> As soon as we got around a corner they immediately changed their attitude towards us, removed their bayonets, put their rifles down, and offered us cigarettes and small packets of biscuits. A few miles further on they stopped again, made us get out, changed their minds, made us get in again, then gave us a cup of water each.

Their destination was the town of Muntok, in the western region of Banka Island, once an important harbour town filled with many Dutch heritage buildings. (It would later become the site of the biggest tin smelter in the world.) After negotiating miles of bumpy dirt roads, they finally reached Muntok about an hour after leaving the Malay village. Their driver stopped in front of a large white building, the local Customs House, where they were escorted up onto a wide veranda and sat in two chairs while one of the soldiers went inside, presumably to report the delivery of two female passengers.

As they waited on the veranda they watched as another Japanese soldier carefully disassembled a machine gun, meticulously cleaning each part before reassembling it to his satisfaction, meanwhile keeping a close eye on them. They could not help but wonder if it would prove to be the instrument of their death.

After a while they were motioned inside, but to their relief and surprise discovered that they were being invited to have something to eat. Betty remembers:

> We were given a whole tin of bully beef and some dry biscuits, with a fork, which was an afterthought on their part, but we couldn't eat a thing. They insisted on our drinking hot milk and water. An officer tried his best to be decent to us, but we just couldn't understand each other, so he sat there and smoked and smiled to cheer us up a bit.

Soon after, the officer took them to a room where wounded Japanese soldiers were lying on the floor, clad only in G-strings, and he asked the nurses what they should put on the wounds. 'We could do nothing,' according to Betty, 'since our hands were smothered in bandages.'

Iole recalled having a conversation with an English-speaking Japanese naval officer who somehow knew they had escaped from the *Vyner Brooke*, and was attempting to justify the attack and sinking. 'Why did you not go across Sumatra higher up?' he asked, as if it had been up to her. 'We were not touching ships which had women and children on them provided they kept north of this place. But you came sailing into our fleet.' All Iole could do was nod, knowing the truth was vastly different from what he was trying to say to her.

Once the 'pleasantries' were over, a guard motioned that it was time to go elsewhere, escorting them down a long dirt road that took them out of town until they reached a large, strange-looking building which held what they would come to know as 'coolie lines' – windowless huts built for indentured labourers who worked in the tin mines. The guard indicated that this was their destination and followed them through the wide door.

As they entered and looked around, they walked past two women dressed in sarongs. Suddenly one of the women cried out, 'Jeff!' Shocked at hearing her nickname, Betty wheeled around, and to her astonishment realised that the two women were actually nurses from her unit – Sisters Jennie Greer and Beryl Woodbridge. 'It was wonderful to know that somebody else had come in out of the sea,' she later wrote. As she walked on, looking for other familiar faces, she passed by a Malay woman, and as she did so the woman said in a broad Australian accent, 'A bit haughty today, aren't you, old thing?' It was yet another nurse she knew.

It was not too long before they were surrounded by other nurses who had survived the sinking of the *Vyner Brooke*, many of whom had lost their uniforms and were now in Malay clothing. 'They were all so sunburnt,' Betty recalled, 'and every one of them had the same raw chins as we had, where our lifebelts had rubbed.' Most of the nurses were dressed in sarongs or local *badjus* – a white top made of woven material – while others were wearing navy or army shorts they had found in the camp that seemed to be unwanted, or trousers that had the bottoms of the legs cut off.

Meanwhile Iole had been greeted by friends from her own unit and they would all soon gather in a dormitory where for quite some time they told their incredible stories of survival, some landing on the Muntok pier that jutted out into the water, while others made it to shore all along the coast of Banka Island. Others had even been brought ashore by crews manning Japanese vessels. Betty learned that most of those who had reached shore then headed towards the pier or the town of Muntok, seeking assistance. As she related,

> They were taken prisoner there and herded with hundreds of other people in the Customs House and later on in a cinema, where they spent two awful days before being marched out of town to this place . . . where they were installed when Iole and I arrived on the scene.

Sister Jessie Simons recalls the arrival of Betty and Iole in the camp. 'Physically they were wrecks, but still cheerful.' While there was much jubilation at being reunited with their friends and colleagues, a lot of concerned discussion followed on just how many more nurses were yet to arrive in the gaol, with so many still unaccounted for. A quick count revealed their number now stood at 31, which left 34 nurses still missing, although a few were thought to have been killed during the sinking of the *Vyner Brooke*, or drowned. That still left a large number no one could explain.

What was known for sure was that the lifeboat containing Matron Drummond and several nurses had made it to shore and they had last been seen gathered around a fire they had lit on the beach. That place – Radji Beach – was not too far from Muntok, and they should have been captured soon after. It seemed unlikely they were being held elsewhere, as all the nurses and other foreign and refugee men and women – many of them injured – were sent straight to this place of internment. Grave fears were held for their safety.

Although water was scarce, they had the wounds on their hands and legs washed and strips of cloth bandage applied, after which they were given an injection of morphine by an English woman doctor.

They were shown to a concrete block which they were told held beds for everyone. These were actually raised concrete platforms sloping towards a central passageway, and not surprisingly the cold, so-called 'beds' came to be known as 'fish slabs'. Above each slab was a wooden shelf that could be used to hold their precious possessions.

At the far end of the passageway was a small room containing a *tong*, or open water tank, used for bathing, and a single tap which issued drinking water at little more than a dribble and was in constant demand. The lavatories were basic and horrendous, the primitive squatting kind with no doors for privacy, and were nothing more than open concrete drains that ran through the camp. As a result, mosquitoes were everywhere, especially after sundown.

Sister Jean Ashton (2/13th AGH) described the chaotic scene as her group had moved in: 'Rooms dirty and a lot of rubbish about. Some sailors' clothes under benches which we all made a bee line for. Some native mats and two old mattresses. But! Oh! The smell of those latrines adjoining.'

When the Dutch occupants had been kicked out by the Japanese, local looters had quickly moved in and taken just about everything with them. There were no tables and nothing to sit on. In fact almost no furniture remained in the dormitories. There was no oven, but some enterprising types had made a rough wood-burning stove out of bricks pried from one of the walls, which could be used for cooking and boiling water.

Betty was now feeling the effects of prolonged exhaustion and in spite of being surrounded by friends she felt her eyelids beginning to droop. Despite their discomfort, and with nothing to go under or over their bodies, Betty and Iole stretched out on one of the concrete 'beds' and quickly fell into a deep sleep.

The place they were now occupying was a large, U-shaped barracks block. The women were held in one dormitory of the building and the men in the other, with a central section utilised as a barracks for the Japanese guards. When previously occupied by indentured labourers, the dormitories would sleep around a hundred people; now they held about six times that number. The majority of them were survivors – civilian and servicemen and -women, nuns, and women and children from the dozens of evacuation ships that had been recently sunk by the Japanese in the Banka Strait. The central outdoor area, spanned by a tin roof, was used as an area for exercise and to escape the stifling indoor heat. When it did rain, which was often and generally torrential, there was precious little shelter for everyone. Jessie Simons would later supply a description of life within the barracks:

> Bathing arrangements were very crude, consisting of a *tong* or bath about twelve by five feet with a three-foot wall. To use it, we stood outside the *tong* and threw water over ourselves. The water supply was poor and dirty, and was not improved by the indiscriminate habits of some of the internees who washed their clothes in the communal bath.

Every morning there was a mad rush to have what the nurses called 'dipper baths', in which they would thrust tins into the water and pour it over their naked bodies. Sometimes the Japanese guards wandered in to ogle this spectacle, but after a while they became bored with this activity and walked out again. Whenever there was heavy rain, the women would rush outside and seize the welcome chance to have a natural shower and wash their hair. As Sister Simons also recalled, the stench of the latrines was disgusting:

Sanitary conditions appalled us. Crude and filthy latrines were the only provisions and we had to become used to Japanese guards wandering indifferently through them and around the *tong*. The accommodation inside the barracks consisted of sloping cement benches without any covering. On these we slept, inevitably slipping down to the lower level during the night. The Jap guards, on their periodical rounds, took a delight in rapping our feet with their electric torches but, otherwise, apart from kicking out of the way (literally) anyone who happened to hinder them, they took little notice of us.

The nurses, together with three women doctors – two British and one German – had done their best to set up a temporary hospital after clearing one dormitory for the purpose. Here they were treating the ill and wounded, but with very few medicines, materials or equipment, clean water or decent food, it was always an uphill task. Drinking water was strictly restricted to one cupful per person per day, while the meagre food ration was mainly grey boiled rice twice a day and some watery vegetable soup. Everyone had to queue up in long lines for these meals with whatever bowls or cups they had been able to find. Often there were tiny grubs found in the burnt rice, and sometimes even what looked suspiciously like rat droppings. Bedtime also meant trying to put up with annoying swarms of flies and mosquitoes.

As well as numerous injuries, many were suffering from tonsillitis, dysentery and heavy colds after those hours and even days spent swimming or paddling for survival in the oily sea. Many of the nurses were also suffering from skinned hands, but not to the same degree as Betty. Despite this they continued to work in the hospital but for only two hours a day, as they were weak from the starvation diet. Every day they were subjected to the plaintive cries of hungry children and the ever-present stench of their primitive toilet. There was absolutely no privacy involved in squatting over the concrete drain, especially embarrassing for the growing number now suffering from dysentery.

For two weeks following her arrival in the camp, Betty felt helpless and unable to help out in any way. Her hands, still torn open from sliding down the thick manila rope into the water, seemed to be stuck around her shoulders, 'and for the life of me I couldn't put them down, so I had to be washed and fed by my friends'.

Each day, twice a day, a whistle blew and everyone had to line up for *tenko*, or roll call. The first of these was held at noon, generally the hottest time of the day. Fortunately for Betty, she did not have to attend *tenko* during this time, as the hospital submitted a daily number of patients to the guards. For the rest, however, they had to form straight lines, and when any guard went by they had to bow deeply. In effect, they had learned they were not bowing to the guards, but to the emperor of Japan. Any sign of disobedience, even so much as a smile, was regarded as an insult to the emperor, which could earn the culprit a sharp slap across the face or a savage kick to the shins. Betty would later write in her precious diary about what she recalled of their imposed diet at this time:

We were fed on rice twice a day, the drill being to line up in two queues, men in one, women in the other. We would stand for hours, it seemed, with the tiny Chinese bowls we had found, and then get our ration – a spoonful of the most evil-looking rice I had seen, grey and burnt. The first meal was at midday, the second at 4 pm. At midday we sometimes had a little sugar, which helped considerably, otherwise we were given some salt. With this we were given a cup of lukewarm fluid called tea, but it tasted like nothing on earth. At 4 pm we had 'stew', which consisted of the same awful rice, with perhaps a piece of vegetable, possibly potato, the size of a threepence, or perhaps a tiny pink splinter, one to each bowl, which we were told was pork. Sometimes we had what was called coffee, which to my way of thinking was the best drink of the lot. There was a faint resemblance to the real thing.

TENKO TENKO !

Out of respect for the nurses, who were usually busy treating people, several of the men in the camp would take their place in the food line and carry their meals to them. This simple act of kindness was sadly a cause of resentment for a small number of the civilian women. Instead of everyone working cooperatively to get through their shared discomfort, some petty arguments broke out, especially when it came to the question of who got how much food at mealtimes.

The problem of clothing to replace the nurses' dirty, torn and oil-soaked uniforms was mostly solved when a few kindly civilian women offered them some spare clothing, and they took scissors to pairs of long trousers that had been left behind by Allied sailors who were the previous occupants of the camp, creating pairs of shorts or calf-length pants. At one stage the Japanese guards surprisingly allowed the nurses to enter a deserted house to look for clothing, and to their joy they located a number of blouses and sarongs. At least they were able to be fully and modestly clothed within the camp, even though it would not be a case of high fashion.

Unable to do much more than exist from day to day, boredom soon began to set in for the nurses when not treating patients. As Betty noted, this meant endless wanderings around the compound or playing bridge with a pack of cards that someone had managed to find.

We went to bed about 7 pm, always hungry . . . the rice satisfied us for only a short time. I have never seen such sights as the Australian Army Nursing Service putting itself to bed! A mixture of old pants, sarongs, cast-off pyjamas, old frocks and bits of old material swathed around our persons – anything that would cover and protect us from the swarms of mosquitoes.

It was not only the mosquitoes that tormented everyone as they tried to sleep on the cold concrete slabs; every so often guards would stroll into the dormitory in the middle of the night and flash the beams of their torches on the faces of the women, sometimes smacking them on their feet with the flat of their bayonets. Other times they would simply switch on all the lights, wait till all the women were groaning and complaining and the younger children and babies were crying, and then switch the lights off. It was just another piece of bastardry that gave them some sort of twisted enjoyment.

There was joy one day when someone found a thin mattress, so that night five nurses, Win Davis, Pat Gunther, Jess Doyle, Pat Blake and Betty Jeffrey, all shared the luxury of placing it on the floor and not having to sleep on the untreated concrete shelves, although they would constantly wake up whenever someone wriggled, trying to get more comfortable on the crowded mattress. A few days later, they willingly gave it up when some English nurses arrived at the camp after surviving on rafts for several days. They were sunburnt, injured, covered in black oil and were still in a state of shock, so Betty's little group quickly agreed to offer them some comfort and handed over the mattress. They knew all too well what these poor women had endured.

There were many graphic stories that Betty would not reveal until after the war. In one, she told a truly amazing tale concerning the capture of one of the nurses she only identified at the time as 'Del' from New South Wales, but was obviously Cecilia Delforce (2/10th AGH), who was known by that nickname. She would survive and return home in 1945. Betty remembers being told that after the sinking of the *Vyner Brooke*, Del must have waded ashore well away from the other nurses she had been with in the water, as she walked up and down the beach without encountering anyone.

We had all been told before we left Singapore that the Japanese were not taking prisoners, so we all knew after our ship was bombed and sunk that, for us, the games were over, but not one of us would accept this.

Del could not find a soul on the beach so she walked along a road hoping to reach the town of Muntok. On the way she heard light gunfire and so she walked towards it to see what it was all about. She thought it might have been us and in trouble. Behind a building she saw a terrifying sight. British and Dutch men were lined up facing the wall of the building and one lone Japanese soldier was loading his rifle and shooting the men down, reloading, shooting again and so on down the line. She thought, 'Well, it must be true,' so she walked up to the line of men and stood there waiting beside the last man in the row. The Japanese soldier saw her – was completely non-plussed at the sight of a young woman, stopped firing and waddled over to her, said something to her in Japanese, then took her by the arm and marched her off to the cinema in town and pushed her in the door. Here all the other British and Australian women were temporarily housed as they came out of the sea and were taken prisoner. Del had found her nursing friends again. The Japanese soldier did not return to his work. He went off duty and back to his camp!

And so the lives were saved of the remainder of those British and Dutch men in that firing line. They lived to be prisoners of war.

In late February, the nurses in the Muntok barracks were overjoyed when yet another Australian sister arrived – the much-loved Vivian Bullwinkel from South Australia, who had also surrendered to the Japanese at Muntok after struggling for several days through muddy swamps and dense jungles. She was covered in scratches and septic mosquito bites. As Vivian moved into the compound, a look of sheer relief washed over her face when she saw so many familiar faces rushing over, eager to greet her.

She was the only one to arrive that day, with an army-type water bottle slung over the shoulder of her rumpled uniform. No one knew it at the time, but she was carefully holding the bottle against her side to conceal a prominent round hole in the back of her uniform. Not just a hole through misadventure, but a jagged bullet hole, which she was desperate to conceal from the Japanese guards, as she would later explain.

'We were terribly relieved to see her,' Betty later recounted, 'and she was just as relieved to see us. We hoped this meant that the others might gradually come in, but this hope was dashed when we heard her story.'

Vivian was escorted into the nurses' dormitory, where she soon found herself surrounded by smiling faces, but at the same time everyone was anxious to know why she was by herself. She was asked repeatedly whether there were others coming, at which a look of total despair crossed her face and tears filled her eyes. The nurses were soon to have a graphic account of sheer bastardry and cold-blooded murder and learn the horrifying, brutal truth about the inhumanity of those who now held them captive.

One of the saddest and most despicable practices carried out by Japanese forces during the Second World War was the appalling slaughter of captured or surrendered Allied service personnel. Many of these involved mass executions – often beheading or bayoneting – of totally defenceless, often wounded and helpless prisoners of war. A number of these massacres were carried out during a withdrawal from an area of conflict or in anticipation of an Allied assault. The killings took place so prisoners did not have to be taken along and guarded during an evacuation, or perhaps liberated by Allied forces, meaning they could fight again. A white flag of surrender meant nothing. It is even recorded that members of the Army Medical Corps wearing prominent Red Cross armbands were not spared; these markings were stripped off and personal possessions seized before they were tied up, made to kneel and either bayoneted or shot to death.

These reprehensible killings were in direct contravention of the Hague Convention of 1907, to which Japan was a signatory. It forbade the killing or wounding of an enemy who had laid down their arms and surrendered. Regardless, there were an overwhelming number of instances of butchery, rape and abject cruelty carried out by Japanese soldiers, and even condoned by superior officers. This was the horrifying history behind the ghastly, sickening story Vivian Bullwinkel would reveal to the anxious nurses who had gathered around her, and which would haunt them all for the rest of their lives.

5

MURDER ON BANKA ISLAND

VIVIAN BULLWINKEL WAS THE DAUGHTER of a mining company employee who had migrated to Australia in 1912, at the age of eighteen. George Albert Bullwinkel, from Leytonstone, Essex, had originally found work as a jackeroo/book-keeper on Mutooroo station near Broken Hill, but after marrying Eva Kate Shegog he was employed at de Bavay's zinc mine as a clerk before taking on yet another clerical position with Broken Hill South Pty Ltd. Vivian was born in Kapunda, on the Light River north of Adelaide, on 18 December 1915 and would have one sibling, John William, born in April 1920.

At the age of seventeen, Vivian graduated from the Broken Hill and Districts High School as school captain, knowing she would have to find some sort of employment to help with the family's struggling finances. Her mother tried to convince her to look at nursing as a career option, but initially she wasn't at all keen. When her best friend Zelda Treloar told her that she was applying for nursing training, she was still not convinced, but as her mother had already filled out the necessary papers, she decided to give nursing a chance. In March 1934, along with Zelda and five other local girls, she undertook her probationary training at the Broken Hill and Districts Hospital.

After an awkward, nervous start, Vivian was placed under the watchful eye of the Sister-in-Charge, Irene Drummond. They soon formed a respectful working relationship and friendship that would develop and deepen over time, and was abruptly ended a few years later on a normally peaceful Sumatran beach.

In September 1934, six months after Vivian had begun her nursing career, she lost her father. He had a history of heart problems, and died suddenly in the back of a taxi aged just 55.

By the time she turned 23, Vivian had completed her general nursing qualification at the Broken Hill hospital, and midwifery training the following year, before commencing her nursing career at the Kia Ora Private Hospital in Hamilton, Victoria. It was there on 3 September 1939 that she and the other trainees heard Prime Minister Robert Menzies announce over the hospital radio that Great Britain was at war with Nazi Germany and, as a consequence, Australia was also at war.

In 1940, wanting to assist in the war effort, she began working in the Jessie McPherson Private Wing at the Queen Victoria Hospital in Melbourne. It was here that she met and befriended a fellow nurse, Wilma Oram, and they would remain good friends throughout and after the war.

That same year, Vivian tried to volunteer as a nurse with the Royal Australian Air Force (RAAF), but a medical examination disclosed that she had flat feet, which back then was a disqualifier. Still determined to do something for her country, she and Wilma volunteered instead with the Australian Army Nursing Service (AANS) and were assigned to the 2/13th AGH. They sailed for Malaya with their unit on the Hospital Ship *Wanganella* in September 1941 and subsequently spent several weeks with the 2/10th nurses at Malacca under Matron Olive Paschke, before re-joining the 2/13th at a hospital in Johor Bahru, on the southern end of the Malayan Peninsula.

In January 1942, fearing a possible Japanese invasion of the peninsula through Burma, the hospital staff hurriedly evacuated to Singapore, where a makeshift hospital had been set up under a large marquee erected on a tennis court. The following month, Vivian and Wilma were among the 65 nursing sisters aboard the evacuation craft *Vyner Brooke* when it was attacked and sunk by Japanese aircraft.

Once the nurses had assisted the civilians to evacuate the sinking *Vyner Brooke*, Matron Drummond (who had trained Vivian back in Broken Hill) told her charges that it was time for them to leave as well, and to do so quickly. Vivian and her fellow nurses jumped into the water and swam to a semi-submerged, upturned lifeboat beside the ship. It had sustained a lot of shell damage, the bottom was ripped open, and it would have sunk had it been overturned and filled with even a few people. Best to use it this way, they all agreed. Altogether, Vivian remembers there were about sixteen people clinging desperately to the sides of the overturned lifeboat – twelve nursing sisters, two civilian women, the husband of one of them, and a ship's officer. They drifted for around eight hours, trying to make for the island. They were aided, as she later recalled, by a signal from some survivors who had already reached shore:

Another lifeboat had got away from the ship and it got ashore on Banka Island around five that night; they lit a fire so that when it became dark all of those who were still out at sea could see it and this became the central point for everybody to try and get to. Our boat got ashore about ten o'clock that night. It was still upside-down of course because it had been machine-gunned. We came ashore and walked a couple of miles along the beach and joined up with the group at the fire. All night, small groups – ones, twos and threes who had got ashore at various other places, kept turning up at the fire, and at one stage a raft with about twelve of our girls got within about twenty yards of the shore and we were talking to them and we were saying to get off and come in, 'work harder, get yourselves in', and then a current came and just swept the raft away and that was the last we heard of them.

Soon a third boatload of survivors made it to shore carrying some civilian women and five other Australian nurses – Sisters Peggy Farmaner, Lorna Fairweather, Clare Halligan, Jean Stewart and Nell Keats. Many of those they saw stretched out on the beach were ill or had sustained injuries so, fighting off their own fatigue and injuries, the nurses did what they could for everyone. Some of those who had managed to survive, but were too badly injured or burnt, could not be saved and were buried in the sand. Once they had done all they could, the nurses and other helpers settled down near the fire and most fell into a deep sleep of exhaustion. For many, their sleep was constantly disturbed by huge explosions and gunfire out to sea, accompanied by massive flashes of light, indicating a fierce naval battle.

As the hours passed, more survivors trickled in. Before dawn, two lifeboats drew up on the beach containing twenty British soldiers from another small evacuation ship that had been sunk by Japanese bombers. In the morning, it was decided to try to find some help – particularly for the badly injured – even if it meant surrendering as a group to the Japanese, who they believed had occupied the island. There were two lighthouses in the distance on either side of the beach, so a few men set off for one to seek assistance, while another group made their way along the sand to the second.

Meanwhile, Vivian and ten other volunteers – four civilian women, Lieutenant Bill Sedgeman (a Scottish Merchant Navy officer), and five nurses – moved inland. They were hoping to come across a friendly village where they might be able to obtain some food and blankets for the injured people back on the beach.

They did locate a village (known locally as a *kampong*) about four miles inland, but the inhabitants were fearful of reprisals by the Japanese for anyone caught helping the enemy, and refused to offer anything, despite the group's desperate pleas. They were each given a drink, but no food, blankets or clothing. One of the village elders suggested that instead they should keep going into Muntok, where he thought the Japanese might help them.

Greatly discouraged, and armed with the news that the Japanese were indeed occupying Banka Island, they made their way back to the beach, hoping someone else had been successful. But to their disappointment no contact had been established by anyone, and they would later learn that the second lighthouse group had been seen by a Japanese patrol and taken prisoner.

By Monday morning, things were decidedly desperate, so Lieutenant Sedgeman called everyone together. He said that while they had plenty of fresh water there was still nothing to eat, and as their number had grown to around a hundred, he asked what should be done, knowing there was little to no chance of getting away from the island. The unanimous decision was to send a small party into

Muntok in the morning, let the Japanese know of their dilemma, and state that they were willing to surrender.

That evening, another lifeboat arrived on the beach carrying about twenty men from the English Ordnance Corps. The situation was explained to them and they agreed that surrender was really the only option. Once again, the night air was filled with flashes and the booming of naval guns and explosions out to sea. In the morning, Sedgeman set off for Muntok along with two surviving sailors from HMS *Prince of Wales*.

Meanwhile, Vivian was aware that the situation for the survivors was growing increasingly serious:

Back on the beach we had civilian women and children and the children were pretty testy by this time, having been through a shipwreck and not having had anything to eat for about fifty-two hours. So Matron Drummond decided to get the women and children together and get them started off towards Muntok and we nurses would stay behind as we were trying to make some kind of stretchers and things to help carry the wounded. So that was done and the women took off.

Once the women and children had left, hoping to catch up with the first group of three, the 22 nurses were left to tend to the seriously ill and injured servicemen stretched out on the sand. Altogether there were around fifty servicemen and an elderly English woman, Carrie Betteridge, who had insisted on staying on the beach to look after her seriously injured husband, Thomas.

After an hour's trek, the large group of women and children came across Bill Sedgeman and the two sailors. They were returning from Muntok, heading back towards the beach accompanied by a Japanese patrol, newly arrived on Banka Island. The patrol comprised about twenty soldiers armed with rifles fitted with bayonets, including one man toting a heavy machine gun. The patrol saw the women and children but simply told them to wait where they were, and then continued to march down the jungle track to Radji Beach.

Those on the beach were not to know that the patrol were from the 229th Infantry Battalion of the Japanese Army's 38th Division. On Christmas Eve, two months earlier, they had been responsible for the appalling atrocities, rape and carnage committed on the defenceless staff and nurses of the St Stephen's College hospital in Hong Kong. They were also not to know that the commander of this division in Hong Kong, Colonel Tanaka Ryosaburo, had issued specific instructions on the battalion's arrival on Banka Island that no prisoners were to be taken.

The following is an extract from the transcript of Vivian Bullwinkel's testimony on the Radji Beach massacre, given before Sir William Webb at the Australian Board of Inquiry into War Crimes in October 1945 (AWM54 1010/4/24B). The questions were mostly put by Mr Russell Cuppaidge, President of the Queensland Law Society, with an occasional interjection by Sir William:

RC: About how many people altogether were on the beach?
VB: By this time there would be about 100 men, women and children.
RC: What happened the next morning?
VB: The next morning Mr [William] Sedgeman [a ship's officer] went over to Muntok to get the Japanese to come and collect the party and take us over. While he was away Matron Drummond who

had taken charge of the women suggested that the civilian women and children should commence on the way so that there would not be so many walking off to the jungle path . . . About ten o'clock in the morning Mr Sedgeman arrived back with a Japanese party consisting of about twenty. They [the Japanese] separated the men from the women in two bunches and the ship's officer tried to tell them we were giving ourselves up as prisoners of war. They just ignored him.

WW: How were these Japanese dressed?

VB: They all had khaki shirts and trousers after the style of jodhpurs and little caps with a star in front of them and they all carried rifles with bayonets on them. I did not see any small arms on them. The one in charge was only a small fellow and was dressed very nattily and much tidier than the others. The suit he had on seemed to have been tailored.

RC: Did he have any insignia?

VB: He carried a sword. Afterwards we found out that those who carried swords were supposed to be officers.

RC: You did not know the names of any of them?

VB: No.

RC: You have no idea what Japanese unit it was?

VB: No, only that they belonged to the first lot that ever arrived at Banka. They arrived only the morning before, because the remainder of our girls who came in on rafts actually arrived before the Japanese landed.

RC: The Japanese, you say, ignored Sedgeman?

VB: Yes.

RC: In what way?

VB: They just brushed him aside.

RC: Then what happened?

VB: They took half the men down the beach about a hundred yards behind the headland. There would be about twenty-five of them. Then they came back and took the remainder of the men down the same direction. I suppose they were away about five or ten minutes. Then they came back and sat down in front of us and cleaned their rifles and bayonets. Two men escaped: Mr Eric German, an American, and a naval rating, [Stoker Ernest] Lloyd.

RC: Did you hear any firing while they were away?

VB: We heard some shots from that direction.

RC: Did you notice the condition of their bayonets when they returned?

VB: No; they were wiping them on a piece of rag or a handkerchief.

RC: How far away were the men taken?

VB: A hundred yards.

RC: Did you hear any screaming?

VB: No.

RC: How many shots were there?

VB: Just a quick succession of them; we did not count them. Then they came back and sat in front of us and when they had finished cleaning their rifles and bayonets they stood up and the one in charge suggested that we should go towards the sea and he sent a couple of Japs to push us along. We went towards the sea and kept walking in and when we got up to our waists they started firing up and down the line with a machine gun.

RC: Did the firing come from those two Japanese or from the others?

VB: From others, who were up under the trees a matter of twenty or thirty yards away.

RC: How many of them?

VB: There was only the one machine gun. They just swept up and down the line and the girls fell one after the other. I was towards the end of the line and a bullet got me in the left loin and went straight through and came out towards the front. The force of it knocked me over in the water and there I lay. I did not lose consciousness.

RC: Can you swim?

VB: No.

RC: You say the water was up to your waist?

VB: Yes, but the waves swept me back. It was rather rough.

RC: About how many women were in your party?

VB: There were twenty-three including myself; twenty-two nurses and one civilian.

RC: What did they do with the other women and children?

VB: They passed them on the way and told them to wait until they returned. But the women got tired of waiting and went on and reached Muntok before the Japanese party overtook them.

RC: You did not lose consciousness; then what happened?

VB: The waves brought me back on to the edge of the water. I lay there ten minutes and everything seemed quiet. I sat up and looked around and there was no sign of anybody. Then I got up and went up in the jungle and lay down and either slept or was unconscious for a couple of days. I slept mostly because I remember waking up at odd times.

RC: Was your wound painful?

VB: It was at times, but not so badly that I could not move around.

The questioning did not allow for any personal observations involving the massacre, but these can be found elsewhere in interviews given by Sister Bullwinkel and held at the Australian War Memorial, Canberra. As she recalled of the cold-blooded killing:

> The conduct of all the girls was most courageous. They all knew what was going to happen to them but no one panicked: they just marched ahead. We knew we would certainly be killed. We just mutely waited. There were no cries for mercy. We knew no appeal would touch the Japs' hearts.

Vivian added that her mentor and friend Matron Irene Drummond's last words were a final cry of encouragement to her beloved nurses: '"Chin up, girls," she said. "I'm proud of you and love you all."' As she made it into the water, the machine-gunner shot her in the back and she fell face forward into the shallow water, feebly groping for her glasses before a second burst ended her life. As others began to fall under a deadly hail of bullets, the rest continued marching resolutely into the waves, uttering prayers or the names of loved ones; the last ones were shot as the water reached their waists.

> I saw the girls fall one after the other. Then I was hit. Being young and naïve I always thought that if you were shot by a bullet you'd had it. With the force of the bullet I overturned and lay there. As time went by, to my amazement, I was still alive but having swallowed so much salt water I became sick and then I was terrified that they would see my heaving shoulders, so I tried to stop being sick and just lay there and the water brought me back into shore.
>
> I haven't any idea of time but when I found the courage to sit up and look around, there was nothing – none of the girls anywhere,

none of the stretcher patients and the Japanese had gone. I became suddenly terribly, terribly cold and all I could think of was to get up in the jungle.

In a state of shock, Vivian dragged her way up the beach and collapsed unseen in the sparse fringes of the jungle, trying to make sense of what had happened to her and wondering how badly she might be wounded. She would later discover that the bullet which had hit her high on her left hip had passed straight through her stomach and out, without hitting any major organs. She had been incredibly lucky. Settling down in the undergrowth behind a palm tree, she fell into a deep asleep.

She had no idea how long she slept – hours? all day? – but when she did wake up she had a raging thirst, and was about to get to her feet and head for the jungle track when she heard some clinking sounds that made her crouch down as low as she could. It was then that she saw the same patrol of Japanese soldiers striding along the beach, heading for a nearby promontory. She held her breath, knowing that if anyone looked her way they would probably see her, as she was not well concealed. It was with immense relief that she watched them slowly tramp away, but it gave Vivian enough of a fright that she remained behind the palm tree for the next few hours, trying to decide what to do.

Eventually her thirst grew so bad that she knew she needed to drink some fresh water, and cautiously made her way to a small spring the nurses had found earlier. Just as she was about to take a drink, she was shocked to hear a quiet voice behind her, saying, 'Where have you been, nurse?'

I swung around – it was one of the stretcher cases, an English soldier [Private Cecil Kingsley] . . . and he'd had all the top part of his arm blown off during the sea battle and then he had been bayoneted by the Japs on the beach. He had later crawled into a fishing hut near the beach.

Vivian cleaned up his wounds as best she could while they discussed what they should do. Eventually it was decided to move away from the beach and the ever-present danger of being spotted by a patrol. She would then try again to seek help in the village she had previously visited on Sunday. By this time the beach was completely deserted – not a body to be seen anywhere – and she guessed that the tides and currents had swept her former colleagues and friends out to sea. With Vivian assisting Kingsley, they cautiously made their way down the track, eventually branching off and moving deep into the jungle until they found a small clearing where they both settled down and fell asleep.

Early the next morning Vivian's first concern was to check that Kingsley had survived the night. She made him as comfortable as she could and then went back to the track, walking and stumbling in pain the several miles back to the *kampong* she had visited earlier. On arrival she was bedraggled, thirsty and hungry, and some village men immediately rushed over to help her.

Once again she pleaded her case, saying she needed some food and water for a badly injured soldier, but the elderly village chief, still fearful of possible reprisals on his people, remained as stubborn as before, refusing to give her anything. Instead, he said it would be better if the two of them gave themselves up to the Japanese, who would take care of them. Vivian knew from recent experience exactly how the Japanese might 'look after them' and continued to plead for anything at all, but it seemed to fall on deaf ears.

Dispirited and aching deeply with pain and hunger, she turned around and made her way back to the track. She had only gone a short distance when she heard a rustling sound in the bushes beside her and two smiling Malay women emerged, shyly indicating she stay silent, and placed two packages wrapped in palm leaves on the ground before scurrying back into the bushes. Vivian opened one and found it contained some cooked fish, rice and chopped pineapple. Their kindness made the long trip back a lot easier, and when she returned to Kingsley they divided the food, working out that if they were careful it would last them four days. She knew that this was probably a once-only gift of kindness, and was reluctant to take a repeat advantage of the village women's generosity.

It was time for a decision, and it was one not taken lightly. She told Kingsley that she could not keep relying on the goodness of the Malay women to supply them with food, and they should surrender to the Japanese and just hope for the best. He wasn't keen to do that, and asked for a few more days to consider their options.

Days later, their food now gone, Vivian made the long, lonely trek back to the outskirts of the village in torrential rain and waited patiently on the track where the women had met her, hoping they would see her there. Some minutes passed before she heard a rustling in the bushes, and there they were again, smiling and passing her another two leaf-wrapped packages of food. She thanked them profusely and made her way back to Kingsley.

After they'd eaten some of their food, Vivian worked out that it had been around eleven hard and dangerous days of hiding in the jungle, and said it was time to surrender and take their chances with the Japanese. Kingsley was agreeable but asked if they could surrender the day after next, as tomorrow would be his birthday. He wanted to be able to celebrate it with her, possibly for the last time as a free man.

Two days later, they both made the long, painful trek back to the village, where the head man was relieved to hear of their decision to surrender, gave them some food for their journey, and pointed out the road to Muntok. They thanked the man and set off, although Kingsley had to stop and rest every few steps. Some time after noon they heard a vehicle coming up behind them. As it came alongside, they saw the driver was a Japanese soldier, with a naval officer in the back. After the soldier got out and searched them for weapons, they were ushered into the car and driven along the potholed road into Muntok.

After being questioned by a Japanese officer and his interpreter, and surprisingly being given some biscuits and a cup of tea, which they quickly consumed, Kingsley was driven away after thanking her for saving his life and for all her kindnesses. Vivian feared she would never see him again. A little later, she heard the car returning and this time it was her turn to climb in.

After a short drive, the vehicle squealed to a halt, waking Vivian, who had dozed off. The driver escorted her through an arched doorway into a compound ringed with huts. A young man approached wearing a tattered British army uniform, smiled at her, and said, 'Welcome to the coolie lines, sister, and it is indeed a pleasure to see you.' After jotting down a few of her details, he accompanied her deeper into the compound, where she suddenly heard excited shouts of 'Bully!' Vivian was soon being hugged by her tearful nursing friends.

Once the excitement of reunion had ebbed somewhat, Vivian revealed to everyone's surprise that she had been wounded by a bullet, and anxious faces were soon examining the pus-filled wound in the privacy of a room. She was told that it seemed to be healing well, but that she had been incredibly lucky; had the bullet hit just an inch further away, she would probably not have survived.

She begged them not to say anything about the wound. She did not want the Japanese to find out that she had survived being shot, in case she ever had the chance to testify as to how it happened. If they somehow discovered her secret, her life would almost certainly be forfeited. She had made sure that the burnt-edged hole in the back of her uniform was covered by a water bottle slung over her shoulder. As she told journalist Robert Wainwright in 1993, she tried at first to keep what had happened on the beach to herself:

By the time I gave myself up I was so horrified about what had happened that I decided I wouldn't tell anybody. But the girls kept asking after the others. I tried to deny that I knew anything but finally I broke down and told them. They were horrified. Our senior Sister went to speak to some Englishmen and told them my story. They told her I should forget about it, deny everything and admit to nothing because not only would I be taken out and shot, but everyone else as well. From that day onwards we never spoke about it. We put it right out of our minds and never gave it another thought.

Despite this, there were others at the camp who recognised Vivian from the *Vyner Brooke* and pressured her to know what had become of the others on the beach who had survived the sinking and if she knew where they were.

One of the English women recognised me from the beach but, thank God, she was sensible. She asked me what had happened and I said, 'We're not talking about anything; will you please forget it.' And she did. About two years later a European woman . . . recognised me and asked what had happened. I said she was getting me mixed up with somebody else but she insisted she remembered me on the beach. I said, 'What beach?' I said we all looked alike in our uniforms. I never lied so much in my life. But I had to lie to stay alive.

In 1969, Betty Jeffrey wrote a short account of what happened on Radji Beach, based on what Vivian told the nurses once she'd arrived in the camp at Muntok. Called *The Girls on the Beach*, she said in it that they had kept a tally of the nurses in the 'coolie' gaol, although it was not known how many might have been lost during the sinking of the *Vyner Brooke*, but it still left a lot unaccounted for. Then, about a week after they had been thrust into the gaol, along came Vivian – alone – and she had some shocking news.

I can still see Vivian now, standing by a table in the entrance hall of our gaol, speaking with a guard. She was firmly holding a shoulder-strapped water bottle to her side and waved to us as we gathered in the doorway. She hurried toward us and we took her into our dormitory, sat her down on the bed space and removed her water bottle. This is when we saw the burnt part of her uniform where she had been shot. She then told us her shocking story which remained a deep secret until the end of the war.

It was such a dreadful and dangerous story that we all decided there and then never to mention it again until we arrived home in Australia. As we were prisoners for the next three-and-a-half years it was never mentioned unless we were talking about one or other of the girls and we would say, 'Oh, she was one of the girls on the beach,' which of course meant nothing to anybody but us. We had all been on the beach at some stage of our getting ashore from the sunken ship. Never at any stage did we think of that awful shooting of our girls as a massacre – it was *always* 'the girls on the beach'. It still is to this day.

According to Sister Wilma Oram, she had a pair of blue raw silk pyjamas given to her just that day by a New Zealand colonel named Wynn. She had been looking forward to sleeping in the pyjamas that night, but quickly handed them to Vivian in order to cover up the telling wounds on her back and ribs. She then washed the blood and dirt out of Vivian's uniform as best she could with the limited supply of water. In a talk she gave in 1960, Wilma said:

The bullet that hit Vivian went in just under her ribs and came out just the other side. It didn't apparently hit anything terribly vital. [The wound] didn't really worry her. She's fortunate that she's just that bit taller than the average girl, and . . . it was just a bit lower than it was on the others. Although she was badly shocked, of course, she didn't really look bad.

There would be a sad postscript to the story of Private Kingsley. Despite Vivian's concerns, he had also been delivered to the 'coolie' prison at Muntok, but was desperately ill, weakened beyond endurance, and was straight away placed in the small camp hospital. The day after her delivery to the internment camp, Vivian was abruptly woken from a deep sleep by her friend Wilma Oram, who told her she was urgently needed at the hospital. Once there, a British nurse guided her over to a raised wooden platform where a thin patient was prone beneath a small blanket. 'He's sinking fast,' she said, 'and he's been asking for you.' Vivian was both relieved and shocked to see that the emaciated patient was Private Kingsley, and then the nurse quietly told her he was dying of his injuries and pleuropneumonia.

Kingsley was barely able to talk, but as she sat on the edge of the platform and held his hand he smiled and whispered, 'Thank you, for everything, Sister.' They were able to exchange a few more words before his tear-filled eyes began to flutter and his weak, final words to her were, 'You had better go now.' He could no longer keep his eyes open. But she would not leave and as she continued to hold his hand Vivian said, 'I'll stay with you a little longer, Kingsley.' A few minutes later he sighed and his pain was at an end.

'I never even knew his Christian name,' she later revealed. 'In those days you didn't call people by their Christian name, not even colleagues. He was Kingsley and I was Sister.'

Several days after Betty and Iole had arrived in the gaol at Muntok, a small group of British nurses were ushered into the camp, telling the same grim stories of their survival at sea. Betty recalls them 'looking sunburnt and dreadful . . . blistered, hungry, very thirsty and in a pretty bad way'. One of those half-dozen survivors was Sister (later Dame) Margot Turner, who had arrived on a stretcher, burned almost black from four days' exposure to the fierce tropical sun. They would later become lifelong friends.

Margot had actually survived two sinkings aboard evacuation ships. She had been aboard the *Kuala* when it received a direct hit and sank. Many of the people on board did not survive, and many others died when the Japanese pilots strafed the survivors in the water. Despite strong currents, she finally made it to the shore on Pompong Island, where she spent the next three days with other surviving nurses tending the dozens of injured. Then, on 17 February, a coastal steamer, the *Tanjong Penang*, pulled in, already carrying between 250 and 300 evacuees, women and children. She said once everyone was aboard, the ship was 'loaded to the hilt'. After leaving the island, the nurses on board once again began tending to the wounded. 'All the women and children and the patients were down in the hold.' Margot said they had just settled down to sleep on the deck that evening when the ship was suddenly brightly lit by search-lights, and without any warning the *Tanjong Penang* was attacked by enemy aircraft. 'The Japanese shells struck right in the middle of the survivors packed in the holds,' she later recalled. 'Most were killed instantly, and others had little chance of getting out before the vessel rolled over.'

Margot said she just stepped into the water from the side of the ship as it began rolling over. Fortunately she was wearing a lifejacket and spent the next four days floating aimlessly and near delirious on a small raft before being picked up by a Japanese warship and put off at Banka Island. It was nine days since she had left Singapore on the ship *Kuala*, and she was now a prisoner of the Japanese, having survived two sinkings at sea, and the only known survivor from the *Tanjong Penang*. As Betty later wrote, 'Margot was a very sick girl for a long time.'

*

Meanwhile, the memories of Radji Beach would continue to haunt Vivian Bullwinkel – amazed that she was still alive after feeling a bullet rip through her body, trying her hardest not to cough or vomit, and meanwhile involuntarily swallowing mouthfuls of seawater mingled with her own blood and that of her murdered colleagues. It was a miracle that she managed to survive the massacre; if she had died no one would ever have known what happened to the nurses on Radji Beach, or been able to tell of their collective courage as they met such a violent and merciless end.

As the sole witness as to what happened that tragic day, Vivian was not only able to testify to what had occurred and who was responsible to a war crimes tribunal, but was able to discuss with compassion the circumstances surrounding the loss of the nurses to their families and friends, who would otherwise never have known the fate of their loved ones.

Sadly, post-war politics may have played a part in this and other tribunals by handing out lesser sentences to those respons-ible for most of the heinous crimes carried out by Japanese officers, soldiers and prison guards. After all that had happened over their four years of involvement in the war, it seems America had no wish to antagonise their former enemy, with whom they were trying to re-establish diplomatic, strategic and economic cooperation. Very few known Japanese war criminals faced the hangman's noose or served a lengthy imprisonment. Major-General Tanaka Ryosaburo, who, with the rank at the time of colonel, oversaw the murderous activities of his 229th Infantry Battalion in Hong Kong and Sumatra, would only receive a twenty-year sentence. He died in 1970.

Two years after the end of the war, diplomatic attempts were made to locate and bring to trial Major Orita Masaru, alleged to have been the officer-in-charge at the massacre on Radji Beach. Evidence suggested that he was being held somewhere in the Soviet Union, but despite official representations to the Soviet Ministry of Foreign Affairs asking that he be surrendered to the Australian authorities, it met a stern rebuttal. The ministry's response, when it came, stated that 'the competent Soviet organs have made enquiries but are unable to trace the war criminal Orita Masaru', and the Australian Legation in Moscow was subsequently instructed 'not to press the matter further'.

Nevertheless, Orita was finally 'located' in 1948, repatriated from the Soviet Union to Japan, and detained in Tokyo's Sugamo Prison in Tokyo, where Australia War Crimes officials were anxious to question him about the Banka Island killings. However, he thwarted possible justice for his crimes when he committed suicide in his prison cell just two days later and was never officially implicated in the massacre.

In 2000 – shortly before Vivian died – broadcaster and journalist Tess Lawrence (Independent Australia) stated that Vivian had participated in an interview during one of several meetings at a Melbourne venue. Vivian reportedly mentioned during one of those meetings about that horrendous day in 1942 that she and the other nurses had been 'violated' by the Japanese soldiers before being marched into the water and shot. According to Lawrence, Vivian said that she had wanted to include this in her statement before the War Crimes Tribunal but had been ordered not to by the Australian government.

This has always deeply puzzled Vivian's nephew, John Bullwinkel, son of her brother. He is adamant that his aunt never spoke of such things to any family members, and she was always very open and frank with them in any discussions on what happened on Banka Island. Why, he asks, would she keep such a personal secret close to her chest all her life, and yet reveal it to someone in the magazine media? His comment on the matter is:

It's just not who she was. Vivian was in a really bad way in the last couple of years of her life, bedridden a lot of the time, and yet she is supposed to have made her way to Melbourne and given an open interview to someone at some club or other? Viv never mentioned it to me or anyone else or even hinted that she had revealed the details that were contained in Lawrence's article.

According to Tess Lawrence in a 2017 reflective article on the events on Radji Beach that tragic day, she mentions meeting Vivian 'on several occasions' in Melbourne, but could not recall whether the conversation in question took place in Melbourne's Naval and Military Club or at the nearby Windsor Club. Interestingly, throughout the article, there are no direct quotes attributed to Vivian. The following is also puzzling: 'They were directed to walk forward into the sea only to be mercilessly gunned down from behind by their captors, who paddled into the Bangka Strait to bayonet to death any women still alive.' This is the only account in which the bayoneting of those nurses still living has been raised. And yet Vivian was still alive after being shot and by her own testimony was floating while pretending to be dead. Remarkably, it seems, she not only survived being shot, but also missed being bayoneted.

John Bullwinkel also commented on another sensitive issue concerning his aunt and her medical records:

And as for one writer trying to get access to my aunt's medical records in order to sensationalise an appalling, traumatic incident from eighty years ago that she went through – and lived with for the rest of her life – well, that is simply invasive and outrageous. If they had cared to contact me I would have told them (although probably not) that I have viewed those medical records myself and there is absolutely nothing in them to warrant this speculation – for that's all it is. I know a lot of other family members, and they are just as bewildered and upset as I am with all this recent nonsense.

One prolific and dedicated writer on the subject of the AANS nurses, Barbara Angell, had the bullet-pierced uniform in which Vivian Bullwinkel was shot (donated and on display at the Australian War Memorial) forensically studied by an expert, who determined that there was something possibly awry. As she outlined in her 2003 book, *A Woman's War: The Exceptional Life of Wilma Oram Young, AM*:

I was puzzled as to the position of the exit bullet hole. It is not where it should be. The entrance bullet hole is in the correct position: on the left side of her back, just slightly above the waistline. The exit hole, of what has always been described as a superficial wound, indicates that the bullet came out at the front and centre of her torso . . . Surely Vivian could not have survived such a wound, one that entered her torso from the LH rear, passed through and exited at the centre of her torso?

Additionally, there was some evidence of 'fiercely ripped button-holes' at the front of Vivian's uniform, which Barbara Angell believes indicates that the front of the uniform had been violently torn apart and was still wide open when Vivian was shot from behind. This, she surmised, could explain why the small exit bullet hole was not located in front of her torso.

Despite these questions and other ongoing research being conducted, the truth of the matter may never be known. The only surviving nurse who knew exactly what happened that horrendous day was Vivian Bullwinkel, and she died more than two decades ago. Can the off-centre bullet hole in the front of her uniform have any other logical explanation? One must recall that these nurses had leapt from a sinking ship wearing heavy life vests into murky, oily water. At that time, or as they desperately tried to make it to shore, their torn, oil-drenched uniform dresses may have been lost or damaged or had buttons ripped off. Perhaps some were even ripped into strips and used as bandages on the rafts or on the shore while tending the wounded. We do know that two uniform dresses were buttoned together and used as a rudimentary sail on one raft.

Did Vivian reveal a final, awful truth in Lawrence's report of an interview? One has to ask why she would confide such a deep, long-held secret to a journalist when there is no convincing evidence that she had ever told her fellow nurses and – more to the point – any family members. It is a curious and unconvincing anomaly to the whole unsavoury episode.

Was there any political or other reason behind the Australian government's purported decision to try to prevent Vivian from testifying on this alleged aspect of the massacre at the war crimes tribunal? Surely she would have said something, even if it was kept top secret at the time, knowing there would have been a 70-year embargo on its release? It would be unthinkable not to mention and prosecute the added crime of rape, to seek some sort of atonement for her fellow nurses and punish those responsible. We will probably never know the circumstances surrounding the tribunal with any certainty.

Then again, Vivian may have ultimately and respectfully decided to spare any further and prolonged agony for the families and friends of her fellow nurses by maintaining her silence. Whatever secrets she and the other nurses may have harboured and shared will likely remain that way.

6

THE COURAGE
TO CONTINUE

THE LOUD SHOUTING AND BANGING began throughout the Muntok camp just before 3 am on the morning of 2 March 1942. Japanese guards stormed into the dormitories and their screamed instructions roused everyone from their sleep. Fortunately, word had quickly spread the previous evening that the camp was being evacuated and everyone would be moved to an unknown destination in the morning. It was rumoured to be somewhere on mainland Sumatra, but no one knew where. Given this early notice, the prisoners had quickly gathered up and packed their few belongings the night before, ready to leave in a hurry.

With the camp still swathed in darkness, each person was made to line up with their bowls and received a 'breakfast' of unappetising, stewed burnt rice. They were also handed a further meal of rice wrapped in a banana leaf for the journey that lay ahead. The nurses were able to supplement this with two small biscuits each that had been cooked the day before. This was all handled quickly, accompanied by the constant yelling of the guards, ordering the prisoners to hurry along.

It was still cold and dark as the first group trudged out of the camp with their precious bundles of clothing, utensils and anything else they could carry. Betty's hands were still bandaged and her arms could not be fully lowered, but Sister Win Davis arranged her possessions into a roll of clothing – including her uniform – so she could carry the bundle tucked beneath one arm. The nurses had earlier agreed to keep their AANS uniforms if they could, as they had vowed to wear them again once they'd been liberated. Dawn was still some time away as the long line of evacuees stumbled along in the darkness towards their unknown destination. Betty began the journey walking alongside her friend Iole, whose legs were still stiff and sore beneath a tight wrapping of bandages. She was in pain, but would never complain.

It was very noticeable that many of the civilian women had left the camp with quite an amount of luggage, which they were struggling to carry. As Sister Wilma Oram noted with a touch of resentment, 'Although we'd all been in the compound together, us without any clothes and these people with clothes, they'd never offered us any.' She also mentioned that a British woman had once promised a nurse her dress if she would carry her suitcase for her, which she agreed to do. Later, when they reached their next camp, the woman had the effrontery to seek out the nurse and ask to have her dress back. There would be many such instances over the years when pure selfishness made camp life even harder to endure.

After walking for half an hour, with the sky just beginning to lighten before dawn, they saw their destination ahead of them – the long Muntok pier. Betty realised it meant a boat trip across the Banka Strait.

We are all sure Muntok has the longest pier in the world – how we missed it that night on the raft I don't know. To our surprise there was nothing resembling a ship at the end to take us across to Sumatra, so we sat there until dawn, then we noticed a few awful old ships about half a mile away. We waited about an hour or so, then two small launches appeared, manned by two Australian men and one [Japanese] guard, and we were taken, about twenty at a time, to the dirtiest old tramp thing, where we sat on the deck or on a pile of wood and watched the most perfect sunrise we had ever seen, complete with a double rainbow. Women and children only in our ship, the men travelled in a larger one that followed us.

Their journey aboard the two rusty, twin-decked, foul-smelling freighters would take them roughly south across the Banka Strait and then 60 miles south-west down the muddy, mangrove-lined Musi River to the port city of Palembang. It would prove to be a nightmare journey – overcrowded, hot and sticky, with no protection at all from a merciless sun. For whatever reason, a machine gun mounted on the upper deck was uncovered and a volley of shots fired over the heads of the passengers as the ship left Banka Island behind, perhaps as some sort of warning. It was a rather pointless exercise; there was simply nowhere to go if anyone decided to slip over the side.

There were no toilet facilities on the women's ship apart from two separated planks projecting over the stern of the ship and perilously positioned right above the propellers. Many of the approximately 200 women and children on board were forced through dysentery and tropical illnesses to use this toilet, stepping down over the stern under the watchful eye of a guard armed with a rifle and bayonet and trying to balance between the two planks while holding on grimly to the ship's flagpole and having to endure water spraying upwards from the propellers churning below.

Then the sun vanished behind thick, rolling clouds and the rain began hammering down. For a time it was ferocious and some managed to find shelter under a heavy tarpaulin. For the rest, there was no shelter until the tropical storm had played itself out. Everyone was drenched and then the sun came back with a vengeance. The Sumatran mainland came into view and the ships entered the estuary leading into the Musi River. As they proceeded up the highly polluted river they saw several small native villages and watched fishing boats being rowed upriver or drawn up at the water's edge.

'We were interested to see the river was thick with oil and the banks were singed,' Betty later wrote. 'There was a huge oilfield nearby. Two ships were sunk, one rather large one, which was sideways on, blocking a large portion of the river.'

Exhausted in the stifling humidity, they finally reached the Palembang ferry station around 4.30 pm. Before they were allowed to disembark, teams of native workers came on board under Japanese supervision to unload the ship. Once this had been completed, the prisoners were ordered off, making their way down a narrow plank gangway, and made to line up. Most took the chance to sit down on their wet bundles, and for nearly two more hours sweltered in the sun before a roll call was held, following which their photographs were taken. By this time, the second ship had docked and the cargo unloading process began as before. The men then disembarked, but unlike the women and children they were marched off straight away.

Meanwhile, a fleet of run-down, open-sided lorries had pulled up. Once the guards had opened up the backs and sides, all the women and children were ordered to climb aboard. It was standing room only on the crowded trucks. The Japanese drivers then took off, travelling at a near reckless speed, jostling the passengers around as they tried to hang on to the sides of the trucks.

A curious thing happened as the drivers slowed while passing through the streets of Palembang. Japanese soldiers had ordered the town's citizens out onto the footpaths, and as the trucks passed they were forced to jeer and laugh at the jammed-in occupants in order to humiliate them, and to wave small Japanese flags. Sister Veronica Clancy later likened it to crowds during the French Revolution jeering at prisoners on their way to the guillotine. Rather than meekly accept this, the nurses began booing back and yelling at the townspeople, poking their tongues out at them and making rude gestures. The locals were startled at the women's reaction; they fell silent, despite the urging of the soldiers, and everyone on the trucks began to laugh at the lunacy of the situation.

The lorries soon pulled up at their destination, the abandoned former Mullah School, where some British and Dutch men from Muntok had not only arrived a day or two earlier, but to the women's joy had already prepared a large pot of hot vegetable stew with traces of meat and gravy and brewed some tea, which was a thoughtful and welcome meal after such a gruelling day.

Then it was time to inspect their new quarters. If they had been prepared for more comfortable arrangements, they were disappointed, as Betty later recorded:

We were divided into groups of forty to each room, and put ourselves to bed as quickly as we could, lying in rows on the cement floor. An electric light glared in our faces all night long. We never looked like going to sleep with that light and the mosquitoes and children and babies crying . . . In the morning we were a very odd-looking crowd, our faces had swollen and our eyes were almost invisible.

It had been an agonising few months for the nurses. Not only had they managed to escape the Japanese occupation of Singapore at the very last minute, they had somehow survived the sinking of the *Vyner Brooke*, during which they lost at least twelve of their number. Then they had been captured by a brutal enemy on Banka Island and thrown into the most disgusting of places of internment, starved, humiliated and treated like animals. Then they learned the sad fate of another 21 of their fellow nurses on Radji Beach.

Throughout all these tragic circumstances they had not only managed to hold their heads high, but the women had formed a bond of friendship and mutual support that would enable them to carry on despite the hunger, deprivation, lack of medicines and clothing, and a total loss of privacy to a belligerent and uncaring enemy. Emotions could often run high, but they would stick together under adversity, look after each other and even find some elements of humour in their circumstances. Betty would often remark on these noble qualities after the war, but for now they were facing the challenge of a new, remote camp in the primitive wilds of Sumatra.

Among those who greeted the new arrivals was Air Commodore Charles Modin of the RAF, whom they had known in the Muntok camp. He fell into talks with the nurses, still aggrieved at the treatment they had been receiving. At one stage he held a private talk with Vivian Bullwinkel, who told him in confidence about the nurses who had been murdered on Radji Beach, and he wrote down all 21 of their names. As Wilma Oram's biographer Barbara Angell would record in her book *A Woman's War*, 'This was as a safeguard in case she did not make it through captivity and, in any case, it was rumoured that some of the men had access to radios that might relay the information to Australia.'

The air commodore also tried to convince the Japanese officers that the 32 nurses were part of the AIF, and as such deserved to be not only treated as military personnel, but be attached to wherever the servicemen were being transferred, rather than as part of the larger civilian group. The servicemen would later be sent to a nearby camp. His entreaties fell on deaf ears, and that afternoon the civilian men, women and children were ordered to prepare to leave the school for what they were told was 'a ten-minute walk'. No food was provided for their journey and many had no footwear. Fortunately a villager had earlier come to the fence selling bananas, and was quickly sold out. Jean Ashton said they had a banana each 'and thought we had never tasted anything so good'.

The Japanese ordered them to begin walking, accompanying the straggling crowd in cars. Their route was down a main road leading to the aerodrome and as they trudged along the dusty road they quickly picked up anything along the way that they might find useful, including 'coolie' bowls and discarded pieces of clothing. Anything and everything could prove precious. A few nurses were able to barter with local spectators along the way, exchanging some small personal items for bananas, eggs and pineapples.

As they trudged on, they were the object of curiosity for the local population, many of whom would have offered them food and other

Above: Australia's first active nursing casualty Frances (Fanny) Hines, who died serving in the Boer War (Photo: https://trove.nla.gov.au/newspaper/article/198175352#)

Left: World War I Australian Army Nursing Service (AANS) Sister Edith May Toan in full uniform

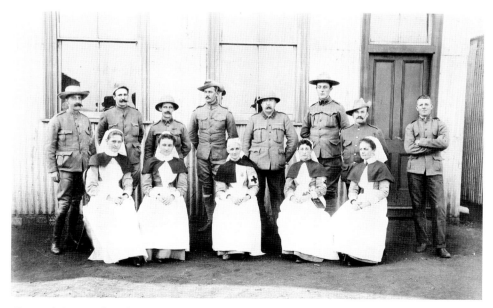

General Sir Frederick Carrington (fourth from left, back row) and some of his medical staff in Rhodesia. Sister Fanny Hines is the nurse at left, front row (Photo: Australian War Memorial PO4544.003)

Left: William (Will) and Amelia (Mill) Jeffrey passing by Melbourne's Flinders Street Station (Photo courtesy of the Jeffrey family)

Below: Betty Jeffrey at Warwick Girls School (Form VB) in 1923. Betty is fourth from the right, front row, with neatly knotted tie (Photo courtesy of the Jeffrey family)

The Jeffrey siblings. From left: Mary, Rex, Jo, Mickey, Alan and Betty (Photo courtesy of the Jeffrey family)

The newly married Aimée Jeffrey (right) with bridesmaid Betty Jeffrey in 1935 (Photo courtesy of the Jeffrey family)

Above: The good ship TSMV (Twin Screw Motor Vessel) *Manunda*, which would play two significant roles in Betty's life
(Photo by Mr Allan C. Green, courtesy of the State Library of Victoria H91.108/827)

Right: Sister Betty Jeffrey in full AANS uniform
(Photo: Australian Nurses Memorial Centre)

Waiting to disembark in Singapore, October 1941 (© Imperial War Museum FE49)

The hospital in Malacca, Malaya, to which Betty Jeffrey (2/10th AGH) was assigned (Photo: Australian War Memorial PO5289.003)

2/10th Australian General Hospitals (AGH) nurses holding air raid equipment, with steel helmets and respirators. From left, back row: Sisters Joy Bell, Dorothy Elmes and Pat Gunther. Front row: Sisters Beryl Woodbridge, Betty Pyman and Nell Keats (Photo: Australian War Memorial PO1180.004)

Sisters of the 2/4th Casualty Clearing Station. *Back row, from left:* Millie Dorsch, Bessie Wilmott, 'Ray' Raymont, Elaine Balfour-Ogilvy, Peggy Farmaner. *Front row:* Dora Gardam, Matron Irene Drummond and Ellen Hannah. Sister Hannah would be the only one in this photo to return home (Photo: Australian War Memorial 120518)

Ward G of the 2/13th AGH near Johor Bahru (Photo: Australia War Memorial PO9909.024)

Enjoying a cup of tea at the Johor Bahru hospital are four nurses of the 2/13th AGH. *From left:* Vivian Bullwinkel, Matron Irene Drummond, Margaret Anderson and Margaret Sellwood (Photo: Australian War Memorial PO1344.008)

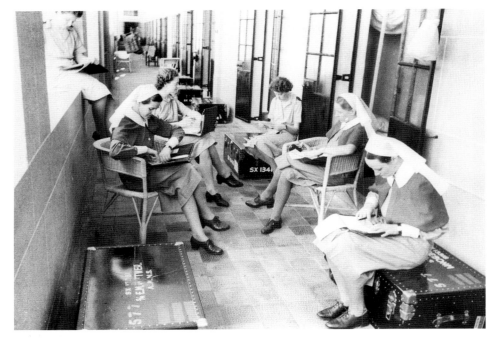

A group of AANS nurses relax by writing letters home in one of the AGH units
(Photo: Australian War Memorial 009921)

St Patrick's Boys School was used as a hospital by the 2/13th AGH to treat the ill
and wounded prior to the fall of Singapore (Photo: Australian War Memorial 116471)

A group of nurses and patients in the St Patrick's school/military hospital following a bombing raid (Photo: Australian War Memorial 012451)

HMS *Prince of Wales* arriving in Singapore on 4 December 1941. It was sunk by Japanese torpedoes just six days later (©Imperial War Museum, A 6784)

Fire engulfs the Singapore naval yards following a bombing raid (Photo: Australian War Memorial PO 1182.010)

The view looking back from the city's Rochor Canal (Photo: Australian War Memorial PO 1182.012)

Civilian women and children desperate to evacuate from the besieged city
(Photo: Argus Newspaper Collection of Photographs, State Library of Victoria, H99.200/548)

General Percival signs the document of surrender, witnessed by Lt General Yamashita

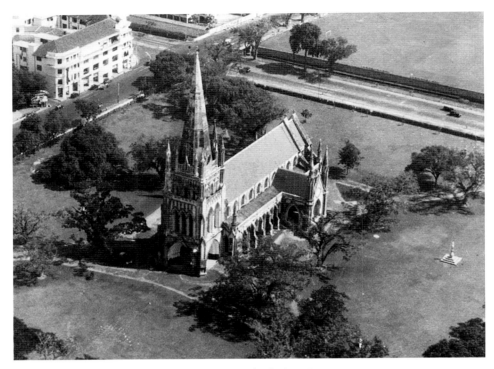

An aerial wartime view of St Andrew's Cathedral in Singapore (Photo: St Andrew's Cathedral, courtesy of Richard Gilham)

SS *Empire Star* (Photo: State Library of Victoria, courtesy of Allan C. Green, H91.325/196)

Informal photo of AANS nurses aboard the *Empire Star* which evacuated 2154 people from Singapore in February 1942. *From left:* Sisters Kath McMillan, Mary Marsden, Dorothy Ralston (with hand on her shoulder), Betty Pump, Joy Bell, Margaret Sellwood, Bonnie Howgate (physiotherapist), unknown, Mavis Clough, Ida Morse, Thelma Gibson (physiotherapist), Betty Pyman, Merrily Higgs (physiotherapist), Margaret Oliffe, unknown (Australian War Memorial PO 99090.005)

AANS nurses on deck as the ship approaches Fremantle, Western Australia (Australian War Memorial PO9909.030)

Together on leave in Melbourne in September 1942: Sisters Margaret Anderson (2/10th AGH) and Vera Torney (2/13th AGH). For their courageous actions when the *Empire Star* was attacked by Japanese aircraft, Sister Anderson was awarded the George Medal and Sister Torney an MBE (Photo: Australian War Memorial 136836)

SS *Vyner Brooke* (Photo: Muntok Peace Museum)

Matron Olive Paschke, in charge of the 2/10th AGH nurses, lost her life following the sinking of the *Vyner Brooke*. She was awarded the Royal Red Cross (RRC) in 1942 and (posthumously) the Florence Nightingale Medal (Photo: Australian War Memorial PO2426.001)

THE SINKING OF THE *VYNER BROOKE*, FEBRUARY 14, 1942

A drawing by ex-POW Geoff Tyson (2/40th AIF Battalion) of the sinking of the *Vyner Brooke* (Photo: Geoff Tyson)

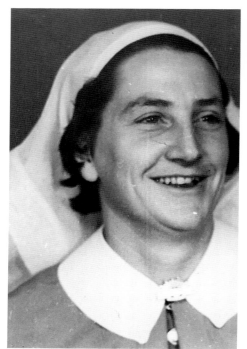 

AANS Sisters Betty Jeffrey (left) and Iole Harper who managed to survive the sinking and made it to shore on Banka Island (Photo of Jeffrey courtesy of the Australian Nurses Memorial Centre; Harper photo courtesy of Army Museum of Western Australia)

Pre-war photo of Muntok, the long pier, and the cinema where those captured were assembled (Photo: Muntok Peace Museum)

aid but were fearful of the Japanese guards. Despite their hunger and discomfort, the nurses were constantly amused at the obsessional antics of Japanese photographers accompanying them, as Sister Jessie Simons later recalled:

> Some took their pictures openly, but others hid in hedges and behind buildings, hoping to catch us off guard. Presumably the photos were for propaganda purposes, though we could not imagine what a polyglot crowd of incongruously clad prisoners, decorated with looted rubbish, would illustrate.

Nearly an hour later, their 'ten-minute' walk brought them into the Palembang district town of Bukit Besar (Big Hill), where they were halted and grouped together in a narrow street filled with empty, double-fronted Dutch bungalows. They would be billeted in groups, and the 32 nurses were able to secure two of the bungalows to themselves: those in the 2/10th AGH were allocated one house (No. 24), while the 2/13th nurses and those of the 2/4th CCS moved into another next door (No. 26).

'There was very little furniture,' Betty later wrote, 'one double bedstead, quite bare, a few chairs and a small couch, but what thrilled us was an electric stove! This was much more than we expected. So we settled in.'

The former Dutch occupants had been ordered to vacate the houses with very little notice and once they had left the looters rushed in, grabbing whatever they could take away, including most furniture items, which meant that the nurses would have to sleep on the floor, stepping over each other in the darkness at bedtime.

Despite the many discomforts, the first few weeks were at least tolerable. Food supplies had improved somewhat and they were now given some green vegetables resembling spinach, and a daily ration of their own army biscuits. There was also an occasional issue of a lump or two of pork – sometimes water buffalo – which was carefully diced and used to supplement the otherwise bland soup they were able to boil up on the shared stove.

Betty recalled that on a few occasions they received visits from some good-hearted Malay and Dutch people, soon to be interned, who brought the nurses a little bread and hot soup, toothbrushes, packs of cards, chess sets and small cushions, as well as a few other essentials that they would normally take for granted. They did this despite the risk of Japanese reprisals. 'It was a great help,' she stated, 'to know we had friends outside the barrier who were not afraid of the Japanese.' Sadly, this welcome arrangement would not last much longer; it came to an end when the male occupants of the two Dutch houses separating the nurses' houses from the rest of the camp were forced to leave.

We were sorry when these Dutchmen went; they had been very good to us, and had managed to get a little bread and sometimes cheese over the fence to us on odd occasions. We sisters then had to move into these two houses so that the Japanese could run a club in the two houses we left. A Japanese officers' club right next door to us – we didn't like that.

The move from houses 24 and 26 to 20 and 22 took place on a Sunday and it rained all day. Despite being soaked to the skin, the nurses busied themselves by forming a line and transferring furniture items over the low concrete fence, along with everything they could find that might be useful, including flyscreens and light fittings. The prized possession that was handed from hand to hand and finally passed over the fence was their little electric stove. Then, as Betty noted, 'the fun started again'.

Saturday, 14 March, was a day on which all 32 nurses would find themselves in a terrible situation, and it was all to do with the so-called 'club' that the Japanese had announced would operate in three empty houses. The Japanese officer in command of the camp was the well-groomed and conceited Captain Miachi, who spoke a reasonable amount of English. It was Miachi who announced the establishment of an officers' club (even though there were only six officers in the camp). The nurses were told they would be needed not only to scrub out the houses in the street opposite the club and make up the beds, but were to make themselves available to 'entertain' the Japanese officers. The nurses were fully aware of what 'entertain' meant and felt increasingly helpless.

A nurse boldly asked one of Miachi's officers why they were picking on them, when there were so many other women in the camps. 'Because you are medically clean,' he replied. 'Free from disease and tall.'

After a restless night, those orders were repeated the following day, with an announcement that the club would open on Wednesday. 'We felt sick; we couldn't eat,' Betty wrote. 'We were told that if we refused the whole camp would have to go without rations for four days.' At this point, they rebelled and firmly declared they would not 'entertain' the officers. As a consequence, and as threatened, there were no rations supplied.

To their joy, however, a Dutch doctor managed to sneak a small bag of Australian flour into both houses and the nurses enjoyed themselves making small plain scones and dampers, as well as fried scones and pastry with pork fat. It was a wonderful change from the eternal diet of mildewed rice, which had to be picked over, grain by grain, and rinsed in water before it was cooked.

The grim spectre of the Japanese club still hung heavily on the nurses, but they were resolute in their determination not to become mere playthings for any Japanese officers. On the Wednesday morning, the dreaded day had arrived. Six nurses, including Betty, were ordered to scrub out the three empty houses. To their relief, this was all they were required to do and they even had a little fun as they cleaned the floors and walls, naming the road the houses were on as 'Lavender Street', after a particularly notorious red light thoroughfare in Singapore. The fun faded when they were told that the club would open that night, and five of the nurses had to attend a meeting that day with four Japanese officers and an interpreter, read some written questions and supply answers.

Eventually the first five names were read out: Jessie Blanch, Winnie Davis, Jess Doyle, Nesta James and Pearl Mittelheuser. Betty's heart was in her mouth as she watched the girls being marched away. Just ten minutes later, to everyone's relief, the first of the nurses came back, and Win Davis was in a furious mood. She had been first to front the officers and they checked her name against their list. The interpreter then handed her a sheet of paper containing questions in English and she was asked to sign the document, which said, 'I am

124

willing to entertain the Japanese officers'. She glanced through it, looked up and uttered an emphatic 'No!'

The interpreter was taken aback, then suggested she did not know what she was saying. Win knew all right, and said, 'No, no! N – O spells NO!'

'But why not, sister?' stammered the interpreter as the officers looked at him, noting his discomfort.

'No!' Win repeated.

'But you will die, then,' he said.

'I would rather be dead at your feet than do this!' Win responded, before storming out of the room. The die had been cast, and as each of the nurses fronted the increasingly confused group and had their names marked off, they all gave the same answer to the questions – a resounding *no*.

They knew this collective insolence would have repercussions, and they spent some time discussing their options. It therefore came as a surprise when a tall English lady – the mother of two children – visited the houses on behalf of the Japanese, promising money to those who agreed to attend that night. It was a deeply disturbing act on the part of the woman, who had somehow managed to survive the sinking of the *Vyner Brooke* along with her two children. She was well aware of what was expected of the nurses, but was desperate enough to have already used her own sex to gain money or food from the camp's officers and had been tasked with trying to recruit others to do the same. Despite their concern, and not a little outrage as this turn of events, a couple of nurses asked what the payment might be. They were told it would be one dollar for each attendee, and her commission would be 30 cents.

As it turned out, no one was seduced by the money on offer and the woman had to report this failure back to the Japanese officers. They in turn issued new orders: twelve women were to report to the club on opening night. As Betty later recorded in her diary,

Even the gallows humour that had sustained the Aussies through most of their trials could not hold the misery and dread at bay. They held a council of war and decided that safety, if anywhere, would lie in numbers. Rather than select martyrs they would all go.

Some nurses were still hospitalised and others too ill to take part, but the number of participants would be around double what the Japanese were expecting. And if they were looking forward to a group of good-looking, well-dressed women turning up, Betty said they were in for a rude surprise, as the nurses deliberately set out to make themselves as unappealing as possible. Those who still had their AANS uniform, no matter how tattered and torn, put them on, while others donned any sort of ill-fitting, overly modest clothing they could find. Footwear consisted of filthy sand-shoes, football and hobnail boots without socks, while some just decided to go barefoot, ensuring they placed some mud between their toes. One sister even wore a pair of scuffed Wellingtons. No make-up of any kind; in fact they looked like a collection of female street beggars.

Sister Pat Darling and some other nurses rubbed ashes and small twigs into their hair, washed most of it out and rubbed the residual grey ash into their skin. When Pat walked into the main room, she heard somebody say, 'Who's that?' So she knew she'd done a good job. Others had a little odorous fat rubbed into their hair, which was then combed flat against their heads, and another nurse poured some of her own urine over the front of her dress.

Further reassurance came in the form of two English male prisoners named Tunn and Stevenson, who were deeply concerned for the safety of the nurses and wanted to do something. They decided to accompany the motley group to the club, act as waiters, and keep a close eye on them.

The two Englishmen lived up to their promise to the nurses when they took up a position as barmen in each of the two club-houses. It can only be imagined how shocked the four Japanese officers in the first house were that night. Not only did a far larger number of nurses turn up than they were expecting, but each of them was in a bedraggled condition, looking as if they'd been caught in the middle of a hurricane. Trying to overcome their dismay, one of the officers told the nurses that six of them had to report immediately to the second clubhouse. After a quick discussion, they split forces and fourteen of them descended on the other house, once again to the surprise of the two officers in attendance, who did not quite know how to react. When they were offered alcoholic drinks by a young boy acting as a waiter, they settled instead for soft drinks. The English 'barman' Stevenson winked at the nurses and Betty heard him whisper, 'Keep it up, girls, you're doing well!'

Some basic snacks had been laid out, and the nurses quickly began munching on the biscuits, cakes and salted peanuts on offer, meanwhile stuffing some of the goodies and cubes of sugar into their pockets. Betty later reported that the hosts' conversation, albeit limited, was almost comical:

They wanted to know why we didn't have powder and lipstick, and would we like to go into town and buy some? No, thank you very much. They also wanted to know what girls in Australia drank on Saturday nights. We told them milk. But it didn't do any good, we didn't get any.

Blanche Hempsted, who could often be heard swearing like a trooper, put on an angelic face and said sweetly, 'Australian girls are nice girls and do not drink alcohol.'

Dealing with these crazy, unkempt Australian women proved beyond the disappointed officers' power to comprehend, tried their patience and limited English (which the nurses pretended not to understand), and so around 11 pm they instructed the women to leave and return to their quarters. However, they warned the women that next time they had to dress properly, or there would be consequences.

It was not the end of the dramas that evening; when they returned they found out that all but four of the women from the first club-house had also been sent back, and there was immediate concern, even though the gallant English minder Tunn was meant to be looking after their welfare. They would later find out that the four women, Sisters Mavis Hannah, Blanche Hempsted, Eileen Short and Val Smith, were escorted out of the house by four of the officers. As Betty recalled,

They had to go out of the club, each one led by a Japanese officer, who tried to get them across to the houses in Lavender Street. The girls refused to go and kept them walking up and down for some time until the whole eight of them were exhausted wrecks. At last one girl [Val Smith] had a bright idea and began coughing. She was dropped like a red-hot coal – the [Japanese] are scared of TB. After an awfully anxious hour they came home.

The four women returned to their house around 1 am, and Mavis Hannah was worried sick. Trembling violently, she told them that one of the officers had led her away from the others and tried to kiss her. She was so angry that she slapped him and he fell to the ground, following which she ran back to the others. She expected that at any moment someone would come banging on the door and drag her away – probably to her death. That knock did not come. They never knew if the officer was embarrassed by being assaulted by a woman and was too ashamed to do anything about it. Mavis lived in fear for some time, but gradually realised that, for whatever reason, the incident had been forgotten.

The next few weeks would prove hellish and miserable; the Japanese were growing increasingly angry at the incalcitrant attitude of the women and their stubborn refusal to cooperate with orders. Food rations were further slashed for the entire camp population as a result, leading to outrage directed at them by many of the civilian prisoners. The nurses were growing increasingly fearful that something bad was about to descend upon them; the tension and mental anguish were almost unbearable. They were starving and existing on a diet almost entirely made up of tapioca roots they managed to dig up. Meanwhile, any sound outside at night ('the steps of the loathsome creatures on the gravel path' as Sister Veronica Clancy described it) would have many of them sitting up, their hearts pounding.

Suddenly, it was all over. The camp's Scottish doctor Jean McDowell also ran a clinic in town and while she was there she was able to talk to some higher-up Japanese military authorities and tell them what was taking place within the camp, and what the nursing sisters were being ordered to do. As well, the two senior nurses, Carrie (Jean) Ashton and Nesta James, made a formal complaint through the Dutch Red Cross representative in the camp, which soon reached the office of the Japanese commander-in-chief for all Japanese forces in Sumatra.

The following month, a representative of the Japanese Imperial Army arrived at the camp and had a long and obviously heated conversation with Captain Miachi, following which there would be no more talk of clubs and 'entertaining' the officers. After a punishment time ordered by Miachi, the rations gradually returned to normal. The nurses were finally able to breathe easy once again; a huge burden had lifted from their shoulders. They had stuck together and proved that non-cooperation with the enemy could have a good outcome.

They later learned that following the nurses' defiance, the British woman who had conspired with the Japanese to bring them to the clubhouses decided on an alternative plan that didn't involve the nurses. She approached the officers and said that she had spoken to some of the Eurasian women and found them willing to 'entertain' the men in exchange for payment for their services. It was a truly murky deal, but after that the nurses were mostly left alone.

Iole Harper would later state that,

there were plenty there that were quite happy to have it on, so why bother about haggish looking nurses? You've got five hundred or something women, and at least fifty of those who are only too anxious. They'd be given food and money, and if that was their scene, why not?

According to Sister Jessie Simons, 'I think all the girls would agree that this club experience was the most repulsive and unpleasant in our whole imprisonment, I know it stands out grimly in our memories.'

By way of celebration after all the club drama, the nurses decided to break into a locked Dutch store room to see what was inside. Once they'd gained entry they were disappointed not to find any food stores, although they did take possession of an Australian airman's greatcoat. But the greatest treasure of all was when someone discovered a few issues of *Women's Weekly* magazines within a stack of similar Dutch publications. As they read through these back in their house, one sister cried out in delight, and they all crowded around. It was an article on their nursing unit at work a few months earlier in Malacca, complete with photographs. They all enjoyed a good laugh. 'We did look well-dressed then,' Betty later commented. 'Shoes! Stockings! Capes! Captails! Starch!' It was just the sort of tonic they needed after such an agonising experience.

There was more good news to come, when a friendly young native met some of the nurses at the barbed-wire fence when there were no guards in sight and told them he had been listening to a secret radio and heard news that a large group of Australian nurses had escaped from Singapore aboard the ship *Empire Star* and had safely arrived back home in Australia. It was the best possible news at such a dark time.

Just as they had adjusted to life and a daily routine in the camp, the nurses were rudely awakened on the morning of the first day in April by guards bursting in, yelling *'Lekas! Lekas!'* to get them moving. They were told that they had to assemble in a nearby *padang* (open park) on top of a hill in half an hour, ready to travel to a new camp. As two guards sat watching on the lounge in Betty's house, telling the nurses to hurry, there was a frantic scramble to grab as much equipment and rice as they could carry for the unexpected move. 'It broke our heart to leave the precious stove,' Betty later wrote.

Once all the prisoners, military and civilian, including the Dutch, had gathered in the park, the guards went through everyone's possessions to make sure they weren't hiding knives or scissors and other utensils that could possibly be used as weapons. Then they were made to sit down in the sun, with no shade available (except for the guards, who sat beneath the shelter of some trees), to await further instructions. At around 2 pm fresh orders were barked out and the men were forced to form up in columns of about twenty and marched off to Palembang gaol to the cries and wailing of their family members. Half an hour later, the distraught civilian woman and children were made to stand and form up and they too were sent off, but in a different direction, with the nurses following behind them.

The prisoners were made to walk about a mile along the main road in the blazing afternoon sun until they reached a street containing a group of eighteen Dutch houses and a garage or two. Betty wrote that the group was told they would be living there for a short time, and the guards indicated it was necessary to 'nanti nanti' (wait) before they were moved on. They found out this area of Palembang was called Irenelaan, and the expectation was that it was only temporary accommodation and 'very soon' they would be placed elsewhere. For the nurses, that promise of relocating 'very soon' would eventually string out to seventeen long and difficult months.

There were a lot of people to accommodate, somewhere around 300, and it took quite a while to sort out, but eventually the confusion settled down as numbers dwindled. Soon it was the nurses' turn, and they were allocated two of the Dutch houses. Fifteen sisters from the 2/13th AGH and 2/4th CCS were placed in house 7, along with eight other people, including four children.

There was immediate tension when the mother of these two boys and two girls, an Irishwoman named Close, married to a British soldier who'd been serving in Malaya, selfishly insisted on taking over an entire room in the house for herself and her family, which led to severe crowding elsewhere. As Betty noted: 'To start with, fifteen sisters lived in the living room and dressed in the tiny dingy room at the back of the house while the Closes lived in one large bedroom and managed to keep it filthy, stinking and noisy all day long.'

Meanwhile, Betty and the other sixteen sisters from the 2/10th AGH were allocated house 8, sharing with seven other women. 'This was good, apparently,' she noted, 'for a slightly larger house farther along had 36 people in it.' One of the garages would serve as a nursing and dressing clinic under the administration of a Scottish doctor, Jean McDowell. She would try in vain to get any medical supplies. Each morning there would be a long line of women and children desperately hoping to get something to heal their sores.

An inspection quickly revealed there were taps but no water; electric lights were installed but there was no power. Later on, a trickle of water came through, and the electricity was switched on. Not surprisingly, there were no beds or mattresses and they were resigned to sleeping on the floor once again. For a while at least, one nurse was fortunate; there was a cot in a bedroom and, as Sister Nesta James was only 5 feet tall, it was agreed that she could sleep there.

The kitchen was small and lacked a stove and cooking pots. There was a small fireplace but there was no wood to be found. To cook meals and boil rice, the women began stripping wood from their windows and doors and ripping off fascia boards to use in the fire. The search for wood meant that Nesta James' cot slowly surrendered all but one side, which she asked to keep so she could lie on that instead of the floor.

Despite assurances this was only temporary accommodation, the day after they arrived at Irenelaan some workers began erecting a barbed-wire fence around the entire area. Sister Jessie Simons would later recall that,

> There was a good deal of friction at times because of the different customs and traditions represented (for example in hygienic standards and cooking methods), but we soon learned to tolerate each other's ways and gradually shook down into a well-organised camp.

To maintain some sort of order in each house, the nurses appointed a 'captain' who would liaise with the Japanese to improve their conditions and food supply and be the focal person if there were any problems within the house. Sister Jean Ashton was appointed to this task in house 7, while Pearl Mittelheuser took on the task for the 2/10th nurses and the seven civilian occupants in house 8. With those two sisters supervising proceedings, a list of duties and a daily roster were drawn up.

One unfortunate consequence of stripping all the wood from windows soon became apparent after local Malay looters noticed this and began slipping in through the open windows to steal whatever they could find. This was just one of many major irritations that would plague the nurses as they tried to cope with the appalling conditions and constant hunger.

Sanitary provisions were disgusting. Effluent from the small shared septic toilet in each house – designed for around three people – flowed into an open concrete drain running down beside the dwellings and then out into the street, resulting in blockages and a foul, constant stench throughout the camp. It was a disgusting job to clean the drains and carry the effluent away, but it had to be done. Those civilian women who were unfortunate enough to be allocated to live in the filthy garages were even worse off; their toilet was just a hole in the ground outside, open to the elements and the eyes of those who passed by.

As there were no pots and pans available, the nurses were forced to use old half-gallon Mobil Oil tins for cooking. Even though they continually scrubbed the inside of the tins clean, the food and tea always had a lingering aftertaste of engine oil. They also learned to be a little creative when it came to food; one of Betty's 'housemates' was Sister Florence (Flo) Trotter, who discovered that privet hedge and hibiscus leaves were actually quite tasty when made into a soup with a small amount of rice.

There should have been running water available, but the supply had been controlled by the Dutch, and they had either been moved on or interned. The local people simply didn't understand how the water supply worked, and all the nurses had for domestic and sanitary purposes was a mere and occasional trickle through their taps. As a result, they would have to get permission from the guards to leave the camp and trudge two miles downhill to a communal hydrant. As they waited patiently in a long queue to fill their containers, they would often have to endure hours spent under the hot sun and it was not unusual to find the water supply had been exhausted just as their turn arrived. Fortunately it rained often, and heavily, and they filled every available container while it lasted. According to Sister Veronica Clancy of the 2/13th AGH, 'When it rained, we had a glorious bath, and washed our few clothes.'

They also had to endure the occasional surprise visit by lowly Japanese guards hoping to catch a glimpse of the women washing themselves in the bathrooms, but once they had amused themselves in this perverted way they generally wandered out of the houses again. The occasional sight of a naked breast or two seemed to be enough to keep them amused and satisfied.

At least the search for wood, which had become acute, was finally resolved after numerous appeals to the Japanese guard house by Dr McDowell. At first, there was just a small amount wheeled into the camp in a baby's pushchair, but that was snapped up in seconds. Later that day a truck came and a large number of burnt poles of wood about 15 feet long were rolled off the back. It needed chopping, so, following deputations made to the Japanese, they finally provided two axes, which were in constant use, particularly when there were two deliveries of wood every day for a week. Everyone now had so much wood they didn't know where to store it all.

Wood may have been plentiful, but food was not and what was supplied was close to inedible. The vegetables, mostly decayed, came into the camp in the back of a truck and were literally shovelled out onto the ground. This was a rotten mixture of cabbages and scrawny carrots, or a type of wild spinach called *kangkong*, which grew in profusion in the gutters and sewers, and did at least provide some vitamin A to the prisoners' diet. Each house had to send a representative who would bring along a card showing the number of people in their house and would be given the appropriate amount of food, now covered in dirt. In her diary, Betty wrote that they could smell the rotting vegetables and Chinese cabbage before the truck even arrived. Every so often, however, a piece of wild pig would be tossed from the truck, and was immediately surrounded by hungry dogs. Betty recalled:

We were not allowed to call the dogs away. The drill then was for a Japanese guard to cut it with his penknife into so many pieces – one piece to each house. He would put his dirty boot on the meat to steady it, since it was so tough, then he would throw each piece on a heap nearby for us to take away when he said so. Our ration for 24 people would not cover the palm of a hand. Consequently there was great excitement if you found a small piece of pork in your stew.

In April, the camp numbers swelled even more when two trucks arrived carrying some British nurses, women and children from the gaol in Muntok. Any hopes that some more Australian nurses would be among them were quickly dashed. Three of the British nurses were allocated to Betty's house 8: Sisters Edith Castle, Mary McCallum and Alice Rossie. Betty recognised Mary McCallum, having met her in Malaya before the outbreak of war.

It is at this point of the nurses' saga in her book *White Coolies* that Betty first mentions her secret diary, written whenever a chance presented itself. Beginning on Banka Island and throughout her years of captivity, Betty would secretly keep diary notes, first on blank pages torn from the front leaves of unwanted Dutch books and later in three children's exercise books. This was done at huge risk, as keeping notes about life under the Japanese was probably punishable by death if caught. At the time she wrote:

We are not allowed to have papers or do any writing. Our belongings are searched periodically, without warning, and marriage certificates, birth certificates, or any personal papers at all are smartly removed and burnt by the guards. This diary lives in a small pillow at the moment.

Betty had managed to steal the exercise book (the first of three she would complete) from a Japanese guard hut and later admitted that keeping a diary was a tricky and dangerous business. The diary notes were carefully set down in tiny writing, as paper was precious, sometimes written using a borrowed pen, but mostly with a small pencil she had found in a heap of rubbish. 'Of course we were not permitted to do this,' she reflected after the war.

Whenever I moved I had to find a way of transporting my diary. I had a little cushion for my head and sometimes I would put it in that. Once I had a bag around my waist and pulled my pants over that but that didn't go too well. They transported us in this boat thing and because I was sick I couldn't climb out so [they] had to heave me out and I felt the bag go. Next day a Japanese came down asking us who owned the bag and I called out, 'Me! Me!' It hadn't been opened.

One day that month she also recorded the occasion when strident guards ordered everybody out of their huts and told them to line up in two rows. After a count had been conducted, they were told that some important Japanese officials were visiting the camp and when they walked past everyone was to bow down low and not make a sound. Although the women felt like rebelling, they thought better of it and the inspection went off without a hitch. Obeying the order brought about some good news for several of the Dutch Eurasians and Indo-Dutch in the camp when they were released from imprisonment and were free to leave the camp.

Some opportunist locals used to hide in bushes behind the camp's bungalows and sell or exchange clothing, eggs, bananas, brown sugar and cakes to anyone who could afford to buy or trade their goods, although most people had nothing to offer. It seems that somebody alerted a guard to this practice and one day the guard caught an elderly local hiding behind some trees trying to sell a few eggs. The guard ran at the man, hit him with the butt of his rifle and kicked him several times. He then grabbed a length of barbed wire from the fence which he looped around the battered man's neck and marched him down to the guard house. Once there, he drove a heavy stake into the ground, made the man kneel, tied his hands behind his back and wound the barbed wire around his neck to the stake. He then told the internees that anyone caught trying to help the man would suffer the same fate. Each time guards walked past the kneeling man they would strike him. The next day the man was gone, and no one knew what had happened to him. They could only hope that if he was dead the end had been quick.

Medical care arrangements sorted out in the camp dictated that the very sick were transported by ambulance to the old Charitas

Hospital in Palembang, where they would be tended by the Dutch Sisters of Charity. There were actually two hospitals in town; the old Charitas and the new Charitas, but the Japanese had taken over the new hospital, giving the nuns just a few hours to return to the old hospital, which had been turned into a school. The nuns were told they could not transfer any equipment apart from beds, although they did manage to get an operating table past the guards. Meanwhile the Australian nurses looked after those in the Irenelaan camp. There was a lot of illness to cope with, a direct result in most cases of an inadequate diet, unavoidable malnutrition, a lack of vitamin C, and the inevitable effects of filthy drains and open sewer lines.

While living under these miserable, taxing conditions, several people went out of their way to make things not only a lot easier, but a good deal happier. Some of this fun occurred around a battered old piano the nurses had acquired from a deserted Dutch house, which they managed to wrestle with great effort into house 7. One of the main contributors to the entertainment was the redoubtable Margaret Dryburgh, who was quite masterful on the discoloured ivory keys, even though it badly needed tuning after a lengthy exposure to tropical humidity. Every Saturday night, people would gather in the house, filled with anticipation for the entertainment that evening. It was normally a happy singalong, mostly organised by Mina ('Ray') Raymont, with Shirley Gardam on piano, in which the Dutch women also participated.

Everyone was delighted when Sister Raymont penned a ditty that everyone loved, sung (and sung often) to the tune of an old favourite, 'The Quartermaster's Store':

THE COURAGE TO CONTINUE

We are POWs, pouring out our woes
On a dreadful diet, this is how it goes.
There is rice, rice, mouldy rotten rice
Nothing more, nothing more.
There are eggs, eggs, growing little legs
Let's heave them at their shaven heads.
They are so blind they cannot see
This is not enough for you and me
And we are all so damned hungry.

There is spinach, spinach; how the grubs thrive in it
Nothing more, nothing more.
There are spuds, spuds, most of them are duds
Let's heave them at those yellow mugs
They are so blind they cannot see
This is not enough for you and me
And we are all so damned hungry.

There is pork, pork, a skinny bit of pork
Nothing more, nothing more.
There is yak, yak, yak we cannot hack
Let's heave this tough yak back.
They are so blind they cannot see
This is not enough for you and me
And we are all so damned hungry.

There are leeks, leeks, oh my how they reek
Nothing more, nothing more
There is cabbage, cabbage, rescued from the garbage

141

Only good enough for yellow baggage.

They are so dense, they do not know

How tired of this we all do grow

And we want to go right home.

What followed was a weekly skit based on life within the camp, often quite hilarious. For these, the nurses dressed up as Hollywood stars: Vivian Bullwinkel played Greta Garbo, Wilma Oram was Mae West, Beryl Woodbridge was Shirley Temple and Sylvia Muir played a sarong-clad Dorothy Lamour. Those who attended would go to sleep that night hoarse from singing and laughing. 'Mrs [Mary] Brown, who must be in her sixties, gave an admirable performance one night as Dame Pêche Melba,' Betty wrote in her diary. 'We nearly died laughing at her.'

Betty was quite in awe of the remarkable Margaret Dryburgh. An English and music teacher, missionary and qualified nursing sister, she had been born in Sunderland, England, in 1890. On 12 February 1942, she was aboard the evacuation ship *Mata Hari* trying to flee Singapore, sailing soon after the *Vyner Brooke*. Those on board were mostly women, children and nurses, as well as a few servicemen. Fortunately they did not suffer the same fate as those on board the *Vyner Brooke*. Their ship was located and seized by the Japanese navy in the Banka Strait off Sumatra.

Following her capture and within days of arriving at the Palembang camp, Margaret had already begun organising church services and hymn singing for anyone interested, as well as putting together a Glee Club, a writing class and poetry sessions. She would later create one of the most remarkable things ever seen or heard in a prisoner-of-war camp, which, many years later, would even be the subject of an award-winning film. As Betty wrote in her diary,

> Miss Margaret Dryburgh must have been in her late fifties when she was taken prisoner. She is English and had been in the East for many years as a missionary schoolteacher. She is very, very quiet and greatly admired by us all. She works hard for our entertainment, organising church services every Sunday, running the glee club, and taking a hand in producing a camp magazine [the *Camp Chronicle*] every month. This magazine has interesting articles written by people with us and includes a cookery section, a children's section, and even a crossword puzzle! In her own quiet way Miss Dryburgh is a very valuable member of the camp.
>
> At the present time she is busy writing music in three parts for the 'Camp Choral Society' or glee club. She writes from memory the music of well-known songs, so that each singer may sing from the music. Miss Dryburgh or Mrs [Margery] Jennings conducts the singers and their efforts are really marvellous. How everybody enjoys it!

As mentioned by Betty, a non-denominational church service was held in one of the camp garages each Sunday, so well attended that most attendees had to sit in the driveway, right back to the barbed-wire fence. The service would be given by one of the missionaries who lived in the garage, and a choir of five would lead the prisoners in the singing of hymns, with the words written on pieces of paper. Remarkably enough, the Japanese would not interfere in these weekly religious gatherings.

One momentous event took place on Sunday, 5 July 1942, when Margaret Dryburgh, Shelagh Brown and Dorothy McLeod sang for the very first time an original hymn, which had been written by Margaret. It was so moving that it would be sung every Sunday service thereafter, with everyone joining in. It was called 'The Captives Hymn', and it perfectly expressed not only the captives' faith and humility, but their indomitable, unbreakable spirit. That unchanged hymn is still performed by women's choirs to this very day.

THE CAPTIVES HYMN
Music and Lyrics by Margaret Dryburgh
Father in captivity,
We would lift our prayers to Thee,
Keep us ever in Thy Love,
Grant that daily we may prove
Those who place their trust in Thee
More than conquerors may be.

Give us patience to endure.
Keep our hearts serene and pure,
Grant us courage, charity,
Greater faith, humility,
Readiness to own Thy will,
Be we free or captives still.

For our country we would pray,
In this hour be Thou her stay,
Pride and sinfulness forgive,
Teach her by Thy laws to live,
By Thy grace may all men see
That true greatness comes from Thee.

For our loved ones we would pray,

Be their guardian night and day,

From all danger keep them free,

Banish all anxiety,

May they trust us to Thy care,

Know that Thou our pains dost share.

May the day of freedom dawn,

Peace and justice be reborn,

Grant that nations loving Thee

O'er the world may brothers be,

Cleansed by suffering, know rebirth,

See Thy kingdom come on earth.

As Betty recorded in her diary: 'To hear people of all colours and creeds singing this each Sunday, is one of the things I shall never forget.'

The Japanese continued to infuriate everyone with their daily penchant for the roll call known as *tenko*, which meant that they had to dump anything they were doing and line up in columns day after day to be counted in the heat of the sun or the belting rain. The house 8 'team leader' Pearl ('Mitz') Mittelheuser would stand before her hut of nurses, bow at the waist and recite '*Dua puluh empat*', which was 'twenty-four' in Malay. Regardless of this, the Japanese soldier doing the count would check several times before he was finally content that it was correct.

Someone in Japanese authority finally decided that the women did not present any threat to the camp guards. They ordered that some Javanese policemen be brought in to keep an eye on the women, arming them with a single revolver. They turned out to be relatively friendly guardians, turning a blind eye to many activities the Japanese would not tolerate, and even playing with the children in the camp. At first the only casualty of this new order was a stray dog that had wandered into the camp. It was shot and wounded. But then, as noted by Betty in her diary, the nurses finally found something to secretly cheer them up, recording that a few nights earlier a Japanese guard had fired a hasty shot from his rifle at a shadow in the camp, very close to the nurses' quarters, but the bullet struck and killed another guard. 'That's the spirit, boys!' Betty wrote. 'Makes one less for our chaps to polish off somewhere else.' For some days after there was a lot of confusion among their captors, although it was some time before any of the nurses were brave enough to venture out at night.

By this time the number of internees had swelled to four hundred women and children, crammed into the same fourteen small three-bedroomed houses and garages. This could have been greatly eased if the Japanese had opened up the three empty houses, but they remained that way. At least some of the British nurses had finally been permitted to travel into town to look after local people in a small clinic run by two doctors.

Day followed weary day. On 11 November, a short service was held to commemorate Armistice Day in World War I and Christmas was approaching. Much to her pleasure, Betty had been given an enjoyable task with the so-called 'canteen committee'. Every Sunday since August, a local black marketeer named Gho Leng was allowed into the camp in his bullock cart to sell some precious items to those who still had money or goods to barter. His 'shop' was filled with over-ripe pineapples, bananas, coconuts, limes and sugar, as well as small amounts of tea, coffee, peas and weevil-infested brown beans. Many of the nurses had earned some money by doing a number of different tasks for other civilian prisoners, so they were eager to buy some of Gho's goods, even at highly inflated prices, and his regular visits were a much-anticipated event.

GHO LENG.

Things were getting a little out of hand when Gho visited the camp, with a lot of elbowing, pushing and shoving, so a special committee of four British women and two Dutch internees was set up to administer things every week. Betty was selected as one of the 'British' women, and Jessie Simons wrote that she did a fine job of it:

Betty Jeffrey was appointed a sort of shop labourer, and spent hours on Sunday counting limes, bananas and pineapples. She had two Dutch assistants or observers, one of whom, Josh by name, had the special job of looking after the interests of the Dutch. What a job it was. Jeff handled delicate situations very capably, and I decided she had missed her vocation – she should have been a greengrocer.

147

The men's camp was not too far from where the women were held and occasional bits of war news were passed on, carefully hidden in some of the food supplies, but so much of it was unreliable and was dismissed awaiting confirmation. There was one occasion when the Japanese openly divulged some news from earlier that year to the Australian nurses. This concerned a suicide attack on the city of Sydney on 29 May 1942 by three two-man Japanese midget submarines, which was certainly alarming news.

The lurid description of the raid told of the *Queen Mary* and *Queen Elizabeth* being sunk, and the centre pylon of the Sydney Harbour Bridge being badly damaged. At this the women relaxed, knowing that the bridge did not have a centre pylon, so for the most part this news lacked credibility. The raid had actually ended quickly, with two of the submarines lost, but only after one of them had torpedoed the military-converted ferry HMAS *Kuttabul*, resulting in the loss of 21 Allied naval ratings when it sank almost immediately. The third submarine had vanished (the wreckage was only located in 2006 off Sydney's northern beaches).

The reason the Japanese wanted to pass on this news was that they were genuinely impressed by the fact that the bodies of four of the Japanese submariners were recovered from the sunken vessels and their bones graciously and respectfully returned to Japan for burial. The officer who gave the nurses this news then said, 'Some good news is coming for you.' If it gave the nurses some sort of hope, this was eventually dashed when nothing came of it. Sister Wilma Oram did cause much laughter when she later said, 'We were hoping they would send our bones home, but with us outside them!'

*

There was real excitement in the camp one day close to Christmas 1942 when someone at the end of the nurses' road happened to spot the male prisoners marching to work, two abreast, in the distance. There was an open space between a low retaining wall and the barbed-wire fence where the women used to gather, and now they had the chance to wave to the men, who were building a new camp about a mile away. As their guards at this time were Javanese police, the men were able to wave back to those in the camp. On Christmas Eve, a mixed group of prisoners including a Dutch nun stood silently – for the first time – at the end of the road.

Sumatran internee (and later priest) William McDougall was one of those men walking by, and he wrote the following about that unforgettable day:

The day before Christmas I marched out with the working party. As usual we began to wave and shout when in sight of the Women's Camp. But the women were silent, standing motionless in the open space . . . Their stillness silenced us. We slowed to a halt and asked each other, in whispers, what was wrong? The answer came in song. Across the no-man's-land which separated us sounded the melody of 'Come All Ye Faithful'. Our guards were as astonished as we and let us stand there listening. The music softened on the second song, 'Silent Night, Holy Night', and grew stronger on the third, a Dutch carol. Leading the singers was a woman in the habit of a nun. Her arm rose and fell, as though waving a baton. The guards finally asked us to move on. 'Please walk,' they said in Malay. 'Japanese may come.' We walked, moving quietly and slowly in order to hear those voices as long as possible.

When the women had begun singing, they watched with smiles on their faces as they saw the men stop to listen. Once their songs had ended the men were moved along amid faint cries of 'Thank you!' Two days later the women and children assembled once again and this time it was the turn of the men; they stopped along with their guards and they sang the same Christmas carols before being moved on to their work site. There was many a tear shed that day. As McDougall later wrote:

> Different as was that Christmas to all of us, there was about it something which brought us closer to the real significance of the day than many of us had ever been. We had Christmas in our hearts, instead of on an electrically lighted tree or in gaudily wrapped packages from a department store.

On Christmas Day, a Japanese officer handed over a typed paper of Christmas greetings from Australia. It was signed by the Prime Minister, John Curtin, and read: 'Australia sends greetings. Keep smiling. Curtin.' It could only be imagined the comments that provoked from the underfed, undernourished, under-dressed, weak, ill and tormented nurses, and not all would have been of a complimentary nature.

Two days after Christmas, just to make conditions even worse, the nurses were ordered to take some more Malay prisoners into house 8. Three were women – one heavily pregnant – and four children, and Betty wrote that, 'All of them are lousy with scabies and lice. We are now 31 in a three-roomed house. Heaven help us!' Room had to be found in the tiny house, so the nurses ended up clearing floor space in the kitchen and the new inhabitants settled in there.

On New Year's Eve, the men in the nearby camp managed to smuggle in a veritable feast for the nurses of meat, onions and potatoes, which went down very well indeed. As for celebrating the coming of the New Year, that simply did not happen, especially if the past year was any indication of things yet to come. The nurses still recognised the occasion, however, by forming a circle and holding hands, followed by the singing of 'Auld Lang Syne' as near as they could estimate to midnight.

As if the unresolved situation with Mrs Close in house 7 wasn't bad enough, another two civilian women named Murray and McKechlie were moved in and they immediately allied themselves to Mrs Close, which created further ongoing arguments and even fights. When another woman and her five children were also allocated to house 7, Dr Jean McDowell, who had recently been elected British Commandant, called on Mrs Close and ordered her to move her family to a much smaller room at the back of the house. The furious woman, supported by Miss Murray and Mrs McKechlie, argued loudly, but eventually had to vacate the bedroom. To make matters worse, the Dutch family was eventually housed elsewhere in the camp and Mrs Close demanded a return to the large room. When this was denied, she broke into the room occupied by the nurses on New Year's Eve and began throwing their belongings out the door, at which Wilma Oram interceded and tried to reason quietly with the woman. Things turned violent when the irate Irishwoman pulled Wilma's hair and clawed her across the face.

The Close family was made to stay in the smaller room, but from then on they and the other two women made life intolerable for the nurses, constantly reporting them to the guards for any trivial matter that upset them. Things escalated on 2 February, when Jean

Ashton wrote in her own secret diary that she was cooking some jam on the house's veranda when Murray and McKechlie stormed out of the door, screaming that the smoke was blowing through their window, and tried to knock the jam pot off the little fire. Elizabeth Simons heard the commotion and rushed over, at which both women were attacked and had their sun tops violently ripped off. Then, as Jean later recorded, 'Miss Murray hit me with [a] tin over left eye and blood flows down. What a life!'

Things became even worse five days later. Early that morning, Sisters Val Smith and 'Ray' Raymont were suddenly attacked in the bathroom by Mrs Close. Jean wrote in her diary,

We others are still in bed. We rush out to help. Miss Murray, from the back room, joins in the fray by standing behind Mrs Close and hitting Sr Gladys Hughes on the head with a piece of wood. Mrs Close goes down to [the guard house] and reports us. Nothing eventuates.

It would take some time and many heated meetings to try and resolve this unprovoked hostility towards the nurses. Eventually it was decided that rather than cause any further problems, it would be best if the nurses found lodgings elsewhere. Betty wrote:

So the sisters moved out. Ten of them are here, the other 5 sleep elsewhere and mess here, and the whole thing is miles better and now old Mrs Close has 32 good Australians to contend with if she dares cross the border.

7

SURVIVING THE ENDLESS YEARS

As PREDICTED, 1943 PRESENTED the same difficulties as before; every day was a continual struggle for survival while constantly battling illness, starvation and tropical diseases.

In January, the nurses were ordered to tidy up the grounds around their houses, including the wood-heaps and fireplaces, and cut the long grass, as some prominent Japanese dignitary – a general – was visiting the camp from Singapore. They had no means of cutting the grass, apart from a knife without a handle they had to borrow from the kitchen. When it was done, the guard in charge, a foul-tempered fellow they nicknamed 'Lipstick Larry' (he hated the sight of women wearing lipstick) told the nurses to sweep the camp roads. Once that task was finished, he would order it done again, just because he could.

On the big day, the nurses were told to sweep the streets again and clear all the drains. Other women were given handfuls of branches broken from bushes outside the camp and told to stick them into the ground at regular intervals, creating an artificial 'garden' to show that the prisoners were being well fed. They soon began to wilt in the heat of the sun. By the end of this clean-up everyone was exhausted.

According to Betty's diary,

> Then the rations arrived. The natives on the truck in their usual style threw the vegetables, bad *brinjals* [a type of eggplant] and *towgay* [bean sprouts], on the beautifully cleaned roadway just inside the camp entrance, then drove off smartly, leaving this untidy mess smelling to high heaven.

Before anything could be done, they heard the sound of car horns approaching the camp. The dignitaries' vehicles halted near the pile of rotting vegetables, the occupants got out and everyone had a look at the rations before glancing around what they could see of the camp before climbing back in their cars and driving off. The so-called 'gardens' of broken branches were pulled up. Had the general revisited later that day, he might have thought a swarm of locusts had passed through.

There was some joy in the camp mid-March when those who were prisoners of war were each presented with a yellow services card so they could send a message home, but limited to just 25 words. It would be two weeks before the cards were finally collected and it would take several months for the cards to reach home, but at least it gave some overdue comfort to their loved ones.

When not engaged in taxing manual labour, the nurses would often get to work with their single sewing needle – they only had one, and it was in constant demand – making blouses, pillows, towels and work bags from any scraps of material they could find. They also found that bicycle wheel spokes made passable knitting needles, fashioning garments out of thick string bought from an Indian merchant. Others unravelled long woollen underwear – 'long johns' – that had previously been knitted for sailors by the Australian Red Cross. 'The weather was never really very cold,' according to Sister Jessie Blanch, 'but when it is wet and windy, and you are hungry, you feel cold.'

For a while they also had only one toothbrush, which they all shared. It had to be washed after every use and placed out in the sun to dry before the next person could brush their teeth. It was soon worn down and Betty later said the problems with their teeth began. 'Fillings have fallen out,' she reported, 'and we cannot get any dental treatment any more at the hospital. We shall all go home toothless and white-haired.' Fortunately a Dutch woman heard of their plight and gave them a few toothbrushes.

Betty decided to try her hand at becoming the camp barber in order to earn some money to purchase a little extra food to share. At first she practised on the other nurses, and then spread the word that she would trim people's hair for 10 cents, although they had to supply their own scissors, which were usually small, curved nail scissors. It worked well and later she even dared to raise the price to 20 cents.

HAR KANIPEN!

On 25 April, the Australian nurses held an Anzac Day service in house 8. There was a brief service and some choir singing, but Betty later said the whole service was very hard to take, given their circumstances. The singing was carried out by a camp choral society – mostly British – that had a slow beginning, but was soon singing some fine English, Scottish and Irish songs. After one concert they began singing 'Jerusalem' and the whole audience joined in. It was the beginning of something special that would evolve as the months went by.

In June, Betty resumed writing her diary after an enforced break of several weeks, following word that the guards were searching the nurses' few belongings, although no one knew exactly what they were looking for. Out of caution, she sewed her diary inside a small pillow and did not touch it for a while.

Over the next few months, Betty's diary reflected little more than the growing incidence of illness and death throughout the camp. There was very little to colour their days and they could only wait for the day when they could leave that dreadful place. On 8 June, an earthquake tremor woke most people in the camp, and the nurses agreed that it would be good if it was centred in Japan. There was a second tremor the next morning, but no more after that.

By now the incidence of illness was so prevalent in the camp that only the very worst cases would be admitted to the already over-crowded hospital. As Jessie Simons later wrote,

... even for them only the barest minimum of treatment was possible. Chronic bronchitis, dysentery and dengue fever were common complaints, and tinea, a skin disease, was widespread. Viv Bullwinkel had a spell in hospital with tinea, and when discharged was gravely advised that butter or margarine rubbed into the affected parts would be beneficial. This struck us all as a good joke since we had not seen either since we slipped out of Singapore; if by any remote chance some did turn up we would have been too diet-conscious to use it as an ointment.

In August the nurses were given injections to help prevent the spread of typhoid, and the following month they began hearing increasing rumours that they would soon be on the move. Then, on 19 September, a note was found hidden in a piece of wood that had arrived as a shipment from the men's camp. Such secret notes were often found in the wood piles brought into the camp and care was taken to check each log carefully before use. It said, 'Leaving today – destination unknown.' Someone keeping watch reported seeing a number of trucks leaving the men's camp.

The imminent move and the possible searches it entailed meant that Betty's precious diary had to be sewn back into her small pillow, where it would remain for several months until things settled down. Although the move began on 10 October, Betty's next entry wasn't until 25 January 1944 and briefly told of the transfer to the men's camp soon after it had been vacated by them.

If they had been expecting better conditions, they were in for a rude shock. It began when six officers marched into the houses and told the nurses to be ready to move that day. They had antic-ipated this and had already stripped the camp of anything useful, packed their meagre possessions and were ready just ten minutes later.

Shortly after, a truck pulled up outside Betty's house and they brought everything outside. Along with two other nurses, Betty climbed into the back of the truck and they began packing things in as they were handed to them. There was so much loaded that the three sisters were also packed in, meaning that they went with the truck as it left the camp. The rest of the occupants would leave a little later in another truck.

The trip across to the new camp did not take long and the women nearly cried when they looked around. It was built on a low-lying swamp below sea level. 'Oh, this place is so ghastly,' Betty later wrote. 'This new camp is like a pigsty.'

A barbed-wire fence encircled the camp, and there were high sentry boxes positioned at each corner, commanding views of the outer barricade and inner yard. The camp was basically rectangular, a little over an acre in area, containing a number of large, airless *attap* huts, three near-empty wells and a single, barely working water tap, which would always have a long queue in front. There were only two bathrooms on either side of the compound, each containing a large cement trough, or *tong*, but with non-working taps, and a single lavatory, which was essentially a long cement drain. All this was meant to house and service the 500 internees.

The male prisoners who had constructed the camp before moving on did not know who it was being built for, and left it in a truly sorry state. Had they known the Japanese were planning to move all the women across, they would have taken much more care, so they were not really to blame for the atrocious conditions now encountered by the new occupants. Betty was certainly unimpressed:

Down the centre of each hut is a long mud or clay passage with a wooden shelf each side, 2 feet from the ground and about 5 feet 6 inches wide, on which we sleep. We are 60 to one hut, and lie alongside each other like sardines. Our belongings sit on a narrower shelf above our heads . . . The Dutch live in the huts on one side of the camp and the British on the other; all seem happy that way.

The place is thick with bugs, rats, fleas, mosquitoes, and mud. For days we worked hard trying to clean it all up.

Whenever it rained the water penetrated straight through the palm-leafed roof, leaving the clay walkway in each hut boggy and treacherous. The rain also meant that toads and huge rats would shelter beneath the sleeping platforms. The Japanese did something worthwhile when they built a large shelter shed (or *pendopo*) right in the centre of the camp where the children could play and church services could be held each Sunday, as well as the occasional concert.

Holding back their disgust with the new surroundings, the nurses began to organise their activities and duties, many of which were imposed on them by the Japanese. With no men to help them, many of the nurses later said they had come to realise their own strengths while existing every day for years in the camps.

Along with three other nurses, Betty set up a small camp 'bakery'. She and Iole were one team and, along with a second team, Dot Freeman and Rene Singleton, they would hunt out every bit of rice they could, which was usually a difficult task. They would turn this into little rice savouries that they would either sell to the civilians or trade for different food items.

According to Sister Jessie Blanch, some nurses were able to visit a nearby Chinese cemetery where, with apologies for the act, they managed to collect some food that had been left on graves for the spirits of the dead.

Despite all their hard work trying to prevent the spread of disease, with virtually no medicines to aid them, conditions at the camp quickly grew worse. Beriberi, typhoid, tuberculosis and dysentery were setting in at an alarming rate. If the Japanese had displayed even the most fundamental grasp of sanitation and prevention of illness, the incidence of these diseases would have been far less, but they remained callous and indifferent to the suffering going on around them.

Soon after their arrival in the camp, a black cat strolled into the area occupied by the nurses and had soon attached himself to them. They called him 'Hitam' (Malay for 'black') and he proved a real hero by killing many of the rats populating their area. Unfortunately, he came to the notice of one of the nastier guards, who kicked the poor animal to death.

Gradually, many of the Japanese guards found themselves being needed for the war effort elsewhere and were replaced by volunteer auxiliary soldiers chosen from local Javanese who were members of the Japanese-recruited 'People's Army'. These guards were referred to as 'Heihos', and that's how they were known to the internees.

The months passed by in the mud swamp they called 'The Men's Camp', but then something quite extraordinary began brewing within the camp, and it would prove to be one of the most remarkable and inspiring things ever conceived and carried out in a place of mass internment and sorrow.

As Betty Jeffrey recorded in her secret diary, Christmas 1943 was not as elaborate as the one the previous year, and was celebrated Malay style, consisting of precious scraps of food saved for days.

Despite the poor Christmas, more 'spiritual' events were developing. There were now 600 women of all nationalities in the camp – predominantly Dutch, with the British making up about a quarter of the camp population. During what would ordinarily be the festive season back home, they tried singing traditional songs and carols, but hunger and exhaustion meant these melodies soon died out.

Then Norah Chambers, a one-time graduate of England's Royal College of Music, had an inspiration which she took to Margaret Dryburgh in October 1943. At the time, Margaret was ill with dengue fever and her morale was faltering badly, but she quickly rallied when she heard the plan. She had a musical background, which included learning the piano at the age of twelve. In the camp she was never known as Margaret; it was always the respectful 'Miss Dryburgh'.

The idea was not to form a choir as such, but what they would call a vocal orchestra, uniting voices instead of musical instruments, and putting together a program of familiar orchestral pieces. As Norah Chambers would later remember of her musical collaborator, 'You could go to her, hum a tune and straight away she could write it down and harmonise it.' Chambers' own skill was in copying the sheet music at great speed. The pair would quickly become a close and highly collaborative team. Together they worked from memory to transcribe and arrange over thirty short classic pieces for the four-part vocal harmonies, the different voices representing the violin, viola, cello and bass.

'Norah Chambers conducts her "orchestra" in the Dutch kitchen at night,' Betty duly recorded in her diary. 'About twenty women of all nationalities hum or "ooh" very softly music that has been written down from memory by Miss Dryburgh and Norah – glorious music.'

"ORCHESTRA" PRACTICE –
IN THE DUTCH KITCHEN.

Betty wrote that the Japanese could never understand why the women went about their work singing and smiling. 'They said we should be serious, for there was a war on.' The women hardly needed reminding about that.

Of necessity, practice sessions had to be carried out in small groups, as the guards forbade the internees congregating in large numbers. As well, the singers had to frequently sit on stools (generally just tree stumps), because they were simply too weak to stand. Betty, an admirer of the classics, was enthralled by the way in which the vocal orchestra developed and grew. She wrote that she 'loved listening to them doing the Largo from the *New World Symphony* and *Raindrop Prelude*, but they are doing more and more each week.' Post-war, she recalled:

I used to go and sit there and watch them practise. I used to sit on a log in the kitchen and listen and I would just sort of hum it to myself. I knew it as well as they did really. And then Norah asked me if I could read music. And I said, 'Well I did learn music when

I was a kid at school. I'll try.' And she found that I could and she helped me and I soon picked it up again. They made me a first alto.

I was just watching and carrying on with everybody. We were singing along beautifully and I was watching our conductor and there was this little bit of a hesitation before we went on to the next bar and I came in a little bit too soon and did a solo! Norah's hands just dropped and she just collapsed. Everybody collapsed with laughter. It was terribly, terribly funny. It really was! They said, 'Who did that?' And I sort of looked around with the others and said, 'Who did that?' I knew exactly who did it, but I always denied it just for fun – just to get them excited, you know! The way I finished the *Unfinished*! It was always a bit tricky after that when we did the *Unfinished*. I just watched Norah like a hawk. I never did come in too soon again. Perhaps I didn't even sing that note – I left it to the others in my row! I didn't make the same mistake again! It really was funny!

Betty loved being a part of the orchestra. 'It is absolutely marvellous, the most fascinating thing I have ever done,' she wrote in her diary. 'We are doing the *Moonlight Sonata*, *Morning* from the *Peer Gynt Suite*, *Country Gardens*, *Sea Song*, *Bolero*, and quite a few others.' Then another two Australian nurses joined in the fun: Flo Trotter and Ada ('Mickey') Syer.

Sister Florence (Flo) Trotter from Eastwood, New South Wales, had arrived in Singapore in February 1941 aboard the converted *Queen Mary* as a nursing officer with the 2/10th AGH in Malacca. Post-war, for the Returned Sisters Sub-Branch of the Queensland RSL, she had participated in writing essays on life as a female prisoner of war, along with some other former POWs. Titled *We Too Were*

There, these stories were later published in the book *Medicos and Memories*, compiled by ex-POWs Jim Dixon and Bob Goodwin. One of her stories was about her favourite recollection during the years of captivity – the vocal orchestra:

> One very good thing that happened in this camp was the birth of the camp choir, later to be known as the vocal orchestra. There were thirty of us who joined – Dutch, British and Australians. The talented missionary, Margaret Dryburgh, who, from seemingly hopeless conditions, gave the world *The Captives' Hymn* and Norah Chambers, a graduate of the Royal Academy of Music, London, were the driving forces behind this endeavour. Margaret, who had a most retentive memory, wrote down page upon page of classical music. Together she and Norah rearranged the scores for choral singing, condensing a fifteen-minute symphony to a five-minute work without losing the sense of balance and flow. The orchestra was divided into four parts. We each copied our part on to any paper we could find and, on practice nights, we would meet in a little room behind the Dutch kitchen. The music was absolutely wonderful. It was so good for the soul and lifted our spirits immeasurably.

As recalled by former Dutch prisoner Helen Colijn, who was captured along with her two sisters in 1942, 'It seemed a miracle that among the bedbugs, the cockroaches and the rats, among the smells of the latrines, among the fever, the boils and the hunger pangs, women's voices could recreate the surging glorious music of Debussy, Beethoven and Chopin.'

To mark their second year of captivity, a vocal orchestra Christmas concert was planned for 27 December. Among the singers was

Norah Chambers' best friend in the camps, Audrey Owen, as well as Norah's sister, Ena Murray. Others included Shelagh Brown and Dorothy MacLeod, British nurse Olga Neubronner, Dutch sisters Antoinette and Alette Colijn, Dutch nun Sister Catharinia, three Australian nurses, 'Mickey' Syer, Flo Trotter and Betty Jeffrey, and Sigrid Stronck, a Dutch mother of two. At 4.30 that afternoon, the 30 women filed out of the central kitchen behind Norah Chambers and headed towards the *pendopo*. Each woman carried pieces of paper in one hand and a little stool in the other.

Word had quickly spread around the camp that something special was about to happen, and everyone made their way to the *pendopo*, curious to see what was in store. Not everyone could be seated in the small area, so they took any vantage point around the perimeter.

All the singers sat on their stools apart from Norah Chambers, who would face and conduct the 'orchestra', and Miss Dryburgh, who stayed on her feet and welcomed everybody. She explained the background behind the concert and what they were about to hear, using the words 'vocal orchestra' for the first time before an audience. After describing the music and melodies, she then asked for a little tolerance from the audience:

We do not profess to reproduce the effects or quality of stringed or reed instruments, but as the lovely melodies and harmonies of the great masters greet your ears, you may imagine you hear them. The choir will remain sitting, as does an orchestra, to conserve their energies. Mrs MacLeod is contributing two solos to the program, 'The Lord Is My Light' and 'Here In The Quiet Hills', thus enabling the performers to rest for a short while. And to give them a further chance of recuperating, there will be an interval of 20 minutes when refreshments will be provided for all, thanks to the generosity of the Dutch ladies. The Australian sisters are kindly serving the coffee.

So close your eyes, and try to imagine you are in a concert hall hearing Toscanini or Sir Thomas Beecham conduct his world-famous orchestra.

With that, Norah Chambers raised her hands before the choir, signalling the start of the concert. As Flo Trotter later wrote:

We put on our first concert on 27 December 1943 and performed the [Dvorak] Largo, [Tchaikovsky's] *Andante Cantabile*, and Mendelssohn's *Song Without Words*, a Brahms Waltz, *Londonderry Air*, Debussy's *Reverie*, Beethoven's *Minuet* and *To A Wild Rose*. It was a glorious concert. All the women put on their best dresses, curled their children's hair and dressed them as best they could for the occasion. That concert did wonders for the camp. The women said it helped to renew their sense of human dignity and feeling of being stronger than the enemy. That night, everyone forgot about the rats and the filth of the camp.

As described by one camp survivor, Helen Colijn, in her 1995 book *Song of Survival*, there was an incident which threatened to end the performance prematurely when an enraged Japanese guard burst onto the scene:

'Huu, huu,' I heard behind me. It was the ugly, raw voice of an angry guard. No doubt he had his bayonet ready. No one in the back row looked behind her, and neither did I. Norah must have heard the guard, too. Would she stop conducting? Norah went on waving her hands.

'Huu, huu,' I heard again. The guard was now close behind me. He must have reached almost the back row. I stepped aside, as did others, to let him pass. Yes, he did have the bayonet on his rifle. And he was clearly furious.

The guard was quite short in stature, and as he pushed his way forward he seemed to disappear from view, swallowed up by those taller than him in the closely packed audience. He finally reached the railing of the *pendopo*, and everyone was waiting for the angry shouting to begin again. They held their collective breath, but the only voices to be heard were those of the vocal orchestra harmonising on Dvorak's Largo. There were no more cries of 'huu, huu' and to Helen Colijn it even seemed that he had lowered his rifle and bayonet.

Could he be listening to the music? As the Largo moved toward a great, glorious crescendo, the guard remained as still as we. He remained still during the rest of the program . . . We had been asked to hold applause until the intermission. When the applause began, it was hesitant at first. The guard, after all, was still in our midst. But he, too, seemed to be savouring memories behind his stony face, and the applause slowly took on volume until it surged into a loud outpouring of enthusiasm, with cries of 'Jolly good!' (from the English) and 'Bravo!' (from the Dutch).

The program concluded with a glorious rendition of 'Auld Lang Syne', which was sung again to another eager audience when the entire concert was repeated four days later, on New Year's Day. There would be a third concert, held on 17 June 1944, but it lacked the vitality and spirit of the previous two performances, most likely attributable to the further weakened state, illness and even death of some of its members. The vocal orchestra would not be heard in the camp again. As Norah Chambers later reflected, 'Our vocal orchestra was silenced forever when more than half had died and the others were too weak to continue . . . it was wonderful while it lasted.'

Curiously enough, in her diary for that period, Betty Jeffrey makes no further mention of the original concert or those that followed – or even her part in them – though without question they would have provided her with one of the better and more moving highlights of her lengthy captivity.

Sadly, the incredibly gifted and inspirational Margaret Dryburgh would not live to see out the war. A near-starvation diet, dengue fever and dysentery eventually took their toll on the 55-year-old Englishwoman and she passed away on 21 April 1945, just days after the women were transferred from Palembang to Belalau camp at Loebok Linggau. She was buried there two days later. In 1951, her remains were respectfully reburied in the Dutch War Grave Cemetery in Java.

In their 1982 book *Women Beyond the Wire*, Lavinia Warner and John Sandilands stated:

[T]he loss of Miss Dryburgh was sorely felt . . . She was the vigorous and inventive spirit who made a large and disparate body of women coalesce to find strength against a common peril . . . The church services she initiated, amid the doubts and impatience and even embarrassment of those around her at the start of the imprisonment, endured as a vital rallying point to the very end. But in fact she did more, fostering the tribal strength that became the foundation of survival when the desperate fight at Belalau forced each person there to call upon their last individual resources.

Norah Chambers managed to survive the war, along with many members of the vocal orchestra, and would not only live to see the music she had worked on in the camps with Margaret Dryburgh published, but heard with pride of it being performed in the 1980s in the United States and the Netherlands, and later across Australia.

Along with nine of the twelve remaining members of the wartime choir, Betty attended a special performance of the songs by the Peninsula Women's Choir, held at the Grace Lutheran Church in Palo Alto, California, in 1983, which brought back many memories. 'Saturday night's concert here was unforgettable,' she said in a post-concert interview.

It was one of the most marvellous things that has ever happened to me. To meet women from the prison camp after all these years. To be with them – it was terribly emotional – the whole thing. We were all churned up inside. The choir knew our music. They could sing our music. When they started with [the] Largo from the *New World Symphony* I thought how am I going to cope with this? It was just so beautiful to listen to and so full of emotion.

Another special performance was held in St Paul's Church in Chichester, England, on 26 October 2013 to celebrate the 70th anniversary of the first vocal orchestra concert, held in the Palembang internment camp. On that day, the Chichester Women's Vocal

Orchestra performed selected pieces from the original repertoire. The choir was made up of 24 women from all walks of life and was formed especially for the occasion under conductor Christopher Larley.

The person most responsible for bringing the concert together was Margie Caldicott, who had a very personal connection to the story; both her mother and grandmother, Shelagh and Mary Brown, had performed briefly in camp choirs and later in the original vocal orchestra. Sadly, Mary Brown did not survive and died in Sumatra. However, Margie recalled her mother, Shelagh, talking about the music. 'She said that rehearsing helped them forget about the squalor of the barracks camp in Palembang and when they sang the music went out, it was free, giving them spiritual release.'

In 1997 the film *Paradise Road*, directed by renowned Australian film-maker Bruce Beresford, was released. It told the story of the camp and the vocal orchestra. In the film, a slew of Oscar winners played the main roles. Pauline Collins took on the lead role of Margaret Dryburgh (with a name change to Margaret Drummond – curiously the same as the matron killed on Radji Beach). Others in the cast were Glenn Close as Adrienne Pargiter (based on Norah Chambers), Frances McDormand as the German-accented Dr Verstak, and Australian actor Cate Blanchett as a lovelorn nurse, Susan McCarthy, who was hoping to be reunited with her boyfriend.

One of the actual participants assisting Beresford as an adviser/ consultant in telling the story of the vocal orchestra on film was Betty Jeffrey. It remains unknown whether one of the film's minor characters, played by Anita Hegh, was named Bett in acknowledgement of her helpful insights into camp life. Once Bruce Beresford had completed filming on *Paradise Road*, Betty was invited to a private screening, as some aspects of the film were drawn from her book.

She later told a friend that, after the nurses (in the film) slipped over the side of the sinking *Vyner Brooke*, she had simply tuned out. Later, asked by an interviewer how the film might have affected her, she replied that she could not remember much of it at all.

> Yes, I was numb after it. I was in the theatre awake, aware. All I know is that it was pretty good. But there was one bit which was very violent and it just didn't happen. I think that was going over-board a bit. I must speak to Bruce about taking it out. Apart from that, I thought it was very good and very well done.

Betty's great-niece, Emily Malone, was quite disappointed the first time she saw the film, expecting the nurses to feature more prominently in the story:

> None of the nurses were individually represented in *Paradise Road* and Aunty Bett never told me if the character Bett was a nod to her or not. I remember being quite shocked when I saw the film, that the nurses were not part of the story.

On the first day of April 1944, there was a dramatic change in the administration of the camp, from being under civilian control to that of the military. It also brought with it a change in commandant, and a quickly despised Japanese Army captain, Siki Kazue, was now in command, along with a few new offsiders.

On that day, a table was set up in the *pendopo* and the prisoners were sorted into groups of different nationalities, waiting in the blazing heat of the sun. Then every single prisoner – even young children – had to be 'presented' to Captain Siki by his bulky second-in-command, named Mizumoto, who would soon earn the secret title of 'Ah Fat'. Everyone had to bow to Siki, give their name and age, and when this was finally over they would have to remain standing while Siki gave a speech relayed by his interpreter.

As expected, he regaled them with stories of the many victories of the Japanese empire, but also warned the prisoners that the flourishing black market for food within the camp must cease. He spoke on the dangers and safety concerns of Allied air raids in the area (raids which actually lifted the morale of the prisoners), and that if these continued they might have to be moved again to a 'nearby' rubber plantation. One consequence of this warning was that any concerts by the voice orchestra were temporarily postponed. He would also leave the daily running of the camp to his Japanese and Javanese guards.

There was some good news when injections became available against typhoid, dysentery and cholera, which undoubtedly saved a lot of lives, but Siki also ordered a punishing edict which basically said, 'No work, no food.' He said that due to food shortages in Sumatra, the prisoners would be required to establish gardens both within and outside the camp and grow their own vegetables. This announcement resulted in the already pathetic rations being cut even more. As British nurse Margot Turner later commented:

The area we had to dig was the space in the centre of the camp, consisting of hard clay, and also some ground outside the camp. All the digging had to be done with heavy hoes called chunkels [known locally as *cangkuls*] which made little impression on the iron-hard ground and jarred the diggers horribly at every stroke. In addition we had to tidy up the roads outside the camp, including the gardens of the houses in which the Japs were living, and clean their drains daily.

As they learned to adapt to their new camp, the nurses continued to tend to their patients, chop wood with a blunt axe and do the cooking, as well as the revolting task of attending to sanitary arrangements. They were also made to carry water for different Japanese requirements, which included cultivating their potato and tapioca fields and even private baths. The water pump was located 400 yards away, and squads of women had to trudge there and back with tins and buckets of clean water, which went onto the sweet potatoes or into Japanese baths. This was infuriating for the nurses, as that water was clean, but they had to use muddy water from the camp wells for cooking and bathing.

Some nurses were also assigned with other women in the camp to what they called 'potato squads'. For the first working shift, this meant reporting to the guard house at 5 am to be counted (and then re-counted) before being marched out in pairs to the potato fields. There they would be given a cup of weak coffee without sugar as their breakfast, before commencing work, mostly preferring to do this barefoot rather than ruin whatever footwear they possessed.

While working in the fields, the women were dressed in their usual sun tops and shorts, and would soon suffer from sunburn. It was tough work and some fainted from hunger, thirst and sheer exhaustion. Fortunately each shift was only required to work for four hours a day before returning stiff and sore to the camp, when another group would be marched out to continue the work. As Sister Flo Trotter remarked after the war,

We certainly were white coolies. We would stand in the midday sun and then move out of the camp carrying whatever utensils we could find, walk about half a mile down the hill to a pump beside the road, fill up with water and carry it back to water the vegetable gardens. Goodness knows how many trips we made each day. We were not allowed to keep any for ourselves, so when it rained we all stood under the leaking roof to have a bath and wash our hair.

As well as working in the potato squads, the women were forced to cut grass in the nearby town, much to the amazement of the local people and the amusement of the guards.

There were some small acts of defiance. Sister Veronica Clancy remembered carrying clean water intended for Japanese baths. 'We used to all spit in the bath water,' she once recalled with a chuckle.

When the first crop of sweet potatoes was ready, they were pulled out of the ground. To no one's surprise, the Japanese took all the tubers and very generously told the women they could keep and cook the vines!

On the afternoon of 17 August 1944, there was a very welcome surprise for the Australian nurses when Gertrude Hinch, a representative of the British Young Women's Christian Association (YWCA), and Dutch woman Tine Muller, the camp's unofficial Japanese interpreter, emerged from the guardhouse with a guard nicknamed 'Rasputin'. They were carrying a large wad of letters and letter cards, which had all been forwarded months before by the Japanese Red Cross. Betty was sitting in the sun along with Sylvia Muir when Mrs Hinch called out to everyone with a smile on her face, 'Letters for you, girls!'

An excited group quickly gathered around the two women, but it wasn't as easy as just handing them out – every letter had to be signed for. The nurses queued up, but it was still an hour before 'Rasputin' was ready to begin the process. Iole Harper was several places ahead of Betty, but when she emerged her disappointment was evident – there was no mail for her. However, she told Betty there was a letter waiting for her, and was keen to hear everyone's news from home. It seemed to take an eternity for Betty to reach the head of the line:

First letter for three years! I looked over Mrs Hinch's shoulder and suddenly saw my mother's handwriting. I went cold and goosey all over. It was so familiar, and to see it in all this awful mess and slum conditions amongst people from all the ends of the earth – it didn't seem real.

Betty signed for the letter and walked away with it, but found herself unable to open it. She just stared at the so-familiar handwriting on the front. Iole noticed her standing there with the letter clutched in her hand and asked if she could help. At that, Betty opened the letter.

I quickly read the 25 words in the message from home. Everything was forgotten temporarily; the whole camp life was wiped out while I read those few words. Everyone at home was well and I had two nieces! I was thrilled, for I had always wanted a niece.

Betty was the recipient of wonderful news from her family, even though the letter was two years old. Once again the Japanese had demonstrated their cruel nature by withholding the mail. At least it was something that brought some sunshine into that day, and there was extra excitement when they were told they could send replies of no more than 50 words, but they were not to mention anything about the shortage of food, that they were forced to work, or the condition of the camp. Not everyone had received good news; some learned of the death of loved ones, and there was an emotional mixture of tears and smiles as everyone retired that night.

In October, a large batch of American Red Cross parcels, intended strictly for the prisoners, were delivered to the camp. Completely ignoring international law, the camp's Japanese helped themselves to the contents of the parcels, including hundreds of packets of cigarettes. This meant that when they were handed over to their rightful owners the Red Cross parcels were almost empty, apart from a few cigarettes and a bar or two of chocolate, some powdered milk, loaf sugar, soup powders, jam, meat, salmon, cheese, coffee essence and butter. However, these were in such small quantities, and spread over so many people, that they barely made any difference to the hunger and well-being of the prisoners.

Around this time rumours began to swirl around the camp that a move back to the more familiar surrounds of Muntok might be about to happen, and everyone was hopeful that it would turn out to be more than just idle gossip. Back in late August, Captain Siki had let it be known that 'sometime soon' everyone should prepare themselves for a move to Muntok, but weeks passed by and nothing more was heard.

Five weeks later, rumours of the promised evacuation turned out to be correct; around lunchtime on Wednesday, 5 October, the nurses were told to be ready to leave in two hours. Eight of them were to go with an advance party of 40 British women, and Betty was one of those selected to go with this first group. They were told they could only take small bundles of personal possessions. They were also warned that the new camp only had oil lamp lighting – no electricity – and no running water. Many of them were furious that the vegetable gardens they had endlessly slaved over would now fall into the hands of the remaining Japanese.

Just after 2 pm, the lorries arrived and the women climbed aboard. As they left the camp, sitting on their bundles of clothing and with their other possessions tied to their backs, the rest of the camp turned out to cheer them on their way. Following the usual manic drive, they arrived at the wharf, where a three-decker river boat was waiting for them. They would occupy the middle deck and as there were only 40 of them they took great pleasure in being able to move around and lie on a clean surface.

That evening the boat moved across the Musi River to where around 120 internees, mostly Dutch and including about a dozen Dutch nuns, were waiting at the nearby Kertapati railway station, ready to board the boat for the trip up the river and across the stormy Banka Strait to Muntok. They had arrived there from another camp in Bencoolen, and many were weak and suffering from malaria, beriberi and malnutrition. The immediate problem was that they had been allowed to bring along *all* their possessions: books, china, silver, chairs and loads of bulk food items, including heavy sacks of corn. To expedite the boarding, the Japanese guards ordered ten of the women, including Betty, to get all this luggage on board:

> It took us until midnight to get it on, and it nearly killed us. We have never lifted anything so heavy, some of it we couldn't raise from the ground, so we had to drag it on board. It felt like lead.

To think of what we had left behind, and now we had to burst our boilers carrying heavy stuff for Indonesians who had been travelling all day. When we stopped for a rest, or when it got too heavy to even drag it, [the] officers would make us do it by flashing their swords very close to our arms and legs, far too close to disregard, in fact we had to skip aside smartly to miss the sword.

They finally managed to load everything on the river boat, and there was one small incident, when Sister Catharinia, a Dutch Charitas nurse, was so exhausted that she wobbled off the gangplank and fell into the river and had to be retrieved.

Just as they began to flop back down on the deck, along came the Japanese officers once again, who ordered the women to go back to the station, where they had to unload a truck full of rice and carry that on board. 'Then on went dozens of coffins, a gruesome sight at that hour of the morning. Two of the girls found a sack of sugar and poked a hole in it, and we all filled our pockets.'

They were finally finished around three o'clock in the morning, but Betty was in agony for some time afterward, suddenly developing a sharp pain under her ribs while dragging a heavy trunk, and was still suffering badly from diarrhoea. Meanwhile, the women back at the camp had been allowed to make some fried rice cakes for those camp women on the boat, which even contained small pieces of pork, as well as some tea. They enjoyed these for breakfast, although wisely keeping some aside, knowing it would probably be the only food and drink they would get before reaching Muntok – and that's how it turned out.

Eventually the river boat captain and the guards were satisfied, and the crowded vessel pulled away from the wharf, heading north up the Musi River. Sixty miles later, at around 2 pm, the boat entered the Banka Strait, and everyone on board revelled in the smell and fresh air of the sea after the sticky heat of the river. There was time for quiet reflection when they passed close to the area where *Vyner Brooke* had gone down two-and-a-half years earlier with the loss of twelve fellow Australian nurses.

It was later that afternoon when the river boat pulled up and anchored about a mile from the long pier at Muntok. By this time some ugly, stormy weather had rolled in and the sea was so choppy that it would have been incredibly difficult to transfer anyone onto the smaller craft that would carry them to the pier. Nevertheless, a few hours later, 40 of the women on board, including all the nurses, were made to board the filthy coal lighter that would transport them. None of the new internees they had picked up at Kertapati were in that number; they had elected to stay on board rather than risk the treacherous seas in a small, unsafe junk:

We entered a tiny hole in the roof, then came down a few steps and had to jump the rest of the way to the bottom into two inches of kerosene. What a smell! We had to sit and soak in this. Our luggage was thrown at us by half a dozen [Japanese] who were constantly screaming at the top of their voices. Nearly all of us were sick, and just as we left the bigger vessel an air-raid siren screamed. The [guards] screamed more, put out their torches and closed the trap over that tiny hole, leaving us in pitch blackness.

Then came the nightmare of being constantly flung around like corks in complete darkness for what seemed ages, until they felt the junk bump up against something solid. They knew they couldn't have reached the pier, and when the trapdoor was finally flung open they found they were still alongside the river boat. Once the Japanese decided it was time to try again, the trapdoor was closed and they set off.

This time they reached the pier, after being tossed around, with evil-smelling water sloshing all over them. By now they were so weak that they could not get up onto the pier unaided and had to be assisted by the Japanese soldiers. They were feeling faint, cold, ill, hungry and no longer cared what happened to them or their meagre possessions. Fortunately the fresh air helped them to revive somewhat before they staggered along the long, seemingly endless pier, at the far end of which they were loaded into four lorries that would take them to the camp.

As there were only 40 being transported, there was plenty of room in the back of the truck and, just when they had begun to feel they would never see them again, their possessions were thrown in to them. As a precaution before leaving Palembang, Betty had secured her precious diary and drawings in a bundle around her waist. The last thing she needed was for guards to go through their possessions at some stage of the journey and locate them.

The ride to the camp that night along deserted roads was quite pleasant under the circumstances, passing along a road bordered by elegant coconut palm trees. When they reached their destination and clambered down from the trucks, they were surprised to find it was nothing like they had expected; the camp was quite large and practically brand new, with lots of room in each of the *attap* huts and plenty of bed space, which meant they could spread out rather than sleeping jammed together. The only water supply came from nine wells that were almost empty, and water would have to be hauled up from about 50 feet down using frail ropes that would often break. One sour note was that the wells were both unhygienic and situated just a few feet from the latrine pits.

They later discovered that the male prisoners had been moved into their old 'coolie' gaol not too far from the camp and were expecting them. When they sent over some food, the new arrivals found it difficult to cope with such luxury. When she next had a chance, Betty wrote in her diary:

> Rice porridge cooked in coconut milk, buckets of rice, vegetables, and fried salt fish, with gallons of tea arrived for us. After eating all we could we filled everything we owned with cooked rice so we could dry it in the sun next day and store it away for our next rainy day. We all slept soundly that night.

A tour of inspection the next morning showed that the camp was built on a gravel base and situated on a rise, high enough that cooling sea breezes kept conditions pleasant enough. There were three kitchens; one was quite large and centrally located, while two smaller adjacent ones contained about fifty small concrete fireplaces. The unfortunate feature of the camp was that the latrines had been constructed beside the kitchens, and once the camp was full and hundreds were using them daily, the putrid stench drifted through the cooking areas. As in previous camps, anyone using the latrines would have to squat down, one foot on either side of bamboo slats, with a filth-filled tank below. There were community bathrooms with cement floors located right next to the latrines.

A day later all nine wells were empty, so guards had to escort the women down to a small fresh-water creek a ten-minute walk from the camp. Betty's diary notes indicate that it all seemed very promising:

> We have to do heavy work sinking posts and putting a barbed-wire fence round the hospital, and carrying sacks of rice, wood, and so on, but we are allowed to go to the creek and bathe and do our washing if we have been on a working squad. The first day I went in a small water-carrying squad at 6 am and it was perfect. We all remarked that it was good to be alive.

The day after Betty's group arrived at the camp, the others from the river steamer turned up and settled in. They were followed by the second group – all Dutch – coming from the camp at Palembang, and they were met by a nice hot meal prepared in the new kitchens, which they really appreciated.

There was plenty of firewood available and enough food until the numbers began to increase, but there were still some welcome surprises in store, such as when they were given supplies of so-called 'fresh' fish. They believed the small fish were caught in nets in the morning and left in the sun until mid-afternoon, thus attracting hordes of flies, but were then retrieved and brought to the camp. The women would wash the fish and then deep-fry them whole until they were nice and crispy, at which time they would be eaten. One afternoon a large stingray was also brought to the camp, cut into small pieces and deep-fried in some palm oil supplied by the new Japanese rations officer. A few days later, a shark was brought in with the tiny fish and it too provided everyone with a delicious meal.

It would be two weeks after the first group arrived that the remaining Palembang prisoners turned up in that camp, including the rest of the Australian nurses, the hospital staff and their patients. There were some joyous reunions, although the new arrivals were in a terrible state, having endured an even worse rough voyage, with no food, no room to lie down, and worst of all no means of going to the toilet. When the trucks arrived, the women in the camp assisted them to get down, at which some fainted from sheer exhaustion. 'They were cold, hungry, and utterly worn out,' Betty observed, 'a nightmare of a trip for the older women amongst them.'

As with the second group, a meal had been prepared for them, consisting of rice, vegetables, fried shark, and gallons of tea and coffee. Just as they were able to hand this out, Captain Siki arrived on the scene, much to everyone's dismay. He took one look at the food and shouted, 'No food tonight!' No one who took in the plight and condition of the new arrivals could comprehend this latest act of cruelty on his part. All he would allow until the morning was the tea and coffee. He then posted guards on the kitchen and would not allow anyone in. The next morning the food was distributed and consumed and, even though it must have been quite awful by then, they ate every scrap. It was after this that the new arrivals discovered to their consternation that somewhere on their journey their luggage had been rifled and precious items, along with any small amounts of food, had been stolen.

Betty was quite appalled by Siki's unrelenting sadism, but reasoned that if the Japanese hated the British so much, then the Allies must be giving them merry hell somewhere.

8

CONQUERING DESPAIR

IN HER DIARY NOTES FOR 10 November 1944, Betty revealed that she had been placed into the camp hospital with a mixed infection of what they called 'Banka fever' and her first dose of malaria. 'Suddenly felt very ill one morning and was carried over here to the hospital, hoping somebody could remove my head; it felt as if it were about to burst.' At least this hospital was much bigger and better organised than the previous one at Palembang.

Within a week, she was joined in the hospital by 'Mitz' Mittelheuser, Shirley Gardham, Mickey Syer and Jennie Greer. All had a raging fever and uncomfortably high temperature, often lapsing into unconsciousness. Sister Wilhelmina ('Ray') Raymont, who had earlier fallen seriously ill, was eventually discharged from hospital, but warned not to do anything too strenuous. There were four doctors attached to the hospital, and they were run off their feet, now having more than 700 internees to look after. One of them would work in the hospital along with the Charitas nuns and the Australian nurses, once they had been released from their camp chores. Another doctor was in charge of the daily clinic, while the other two looked after everyone in the six internee blocks. With so much fever and other diseases rampant throughout the camp, they were always busy.

The Australian and British nurses held a meeting and were quickly organised, now divided into two groups: hospital staff and district nurses. As Betty stated: 'This was the only way to cope with this dreadful fever that has hit the camp. It recurs every few weeks and nothing seems to stop it.' She added that the Japanese could have helped enormously if they had allowed medicines and quinine to be brought into the camp, but all they did was 'bring in a small bottle of 100 quinine tablets for 700 people once every five or six weeks – practically useless'. As she wrote these and other remarks, nine of the AGH nurses were in hospital, 'and two very ill in the blocks. All have Banka fever. There are at least 30 people sick in each block and things are grim.'

Another problem facing everyone was the presence of parasites, which would get into their hair. For this reason, the nurses made sure they had close haircuts and tried to keep their hair as clean as possible.

After the camp had been occupied for a few weeks, the latrine situation reached a critical state. It was nothing more than a large concrete pit about 5 feet deep, filled with excrement, surrounded by flies and crawling with maggots. There was no drainage from the tank and it soon began to overflow. Volunteers had to be recruited for the awful task of emptying it every so often, with the aid of a coconut shell hammered onto a stick. They would use this to scoop out the faeces, swimming with maggots, and empty it into a bucket. Two women would then place the bucket on a pole and empty the disgusting mess outside the camp. Sometimes at night a fearful cry would be heard when someone slipped and tumbled through the wooden slats where they had to squat above the latrine pit. The poor person would have to be hauled out and washed down – a terrible humiliation for anyone.

A week after moving into the camp, three young Englishwomen had died, two more were unconscious, and 210 were down with the mysterious but virulent Banka fever.

Whenever someone died, the women had to carry the body out of the camp in the afternoon to a small Chinese cemetery located on a hillside in the middle of the jungle. It was otherwise a very pretty spot, with colourful wild jungle flowers in profusion, which they often picked to take back to their hut. A corner of the cemetery had been set aside for those who had died in the camp. Young boys from the camp would help the Japanese making the rough bamboo coffins. Sister Pat Darling (then Gunther) recalled:

> It took 20 of us to carry out a coffin. Three poles were placed under the coffin. Eighteen people lifted the poles. One person led out, holding her hands behind to steady the coffin, and kept her eye on the track, as we all had a dread of walking on graves. The end of the coffin was supported by the twentieth person to avoid any risk of it slipping.

The squad of women would have to dig graves using the unwieldly chunkels, although a couple of spades would have greatly assisted them in this laborious work. Once the body had been lowered into the grave and covered up, either nuns or missionaries would take the service. In one small concession, the Japanese officers allowed small wooden crosses to be placed at the head of each grave. The names and inscriptions were patiently burnt on these by Norah Chambers and New Zealander Audrey Owen, both of whom did a wonderful job. After the service, the women would quickly gather up firewood on the way back to the camp despite the screaming and shouting of the guards.

Many grim memories of their captivity, especially at Muntok, would haunt the surviving women for the rest of their lives. Life to the Japanese had been considered cheap and expendable and any death just meant one less person to feed.

Englishwoman Shelagh Brown had been evacuating Singapore aboard the *Vyner Brooke* with her mother Mary when it was sunk. Miraculously both survived and became prisoners of the Japanese. Shelagh was a devoted member of the vocal orchestra set up by Norah Chambers and Margaret Dryburgh. Her mother did not survive through to liberation, dying in captivity in Muntok on 17 January 1945, aged 67. After the war, Shelagh (who died in 2005) set down many recollections of her mother and their shared time in the Sumatran camps – essays later donated to the Imperial War Museum, London. One particularly poignant memory concerned the sad, unnecessary death and crude burial of an unnamed woman from the camp, which typified the respect the camp women had for each other, both in life and death:

'Volunteers to dig a grave.' So the word went round. XX has died, her body no longer able to withstand the great demands made upon it, her Spirit ready for her Master. Her last words were, 'I will pray for you all in Heaven'. She had had typhus, and then there was no food to build up her strength. In the so-called hospital, there was only enough water to allow one cupful per person per day for washing purposes. This is in the tropics in sweltering fever heat and those nursing the sick, themselves in need of rest and care. And now the call for 'Volunteers to dig a grave'. When will the rough coffin be sent or will the body have to lie in the open for 24 hours and quiet vigil be kept, as on a previous occasion? Out of the barbed wire they go, those able at the time and with the strength for the digging. Peace? Quietness at any rate. No longer the noisy, dusty, dirty squalor behind the barbed wire. Human bodies, skin and bones, struggling for existence, struggling to help each other – orphaned children in a bewildered small world – and sights – only happier memories of a past existence. The task is finished, back they come, weary, silent – no water to wash off the dirt, the sweat, but triumph only that a need has been met, a task accomplished. A rough box is brought; will the boards hold? The small procession forms, how heavy the load, how slow the pace. The camp is silenced, another body laid to rest. The way was steep, the clay heavy, the service simple, the prayers sincere. The hymn 'Oh God Our Help In Ages Past' never more appropriate, and favourite scripture more inspiring. One broken body now triumphant – for her Faith was sure and her life of service and witness supreme in her death. Women honoured woman.

There is no one now to care for her grave; no one is responsible for her last resting place. The end came soon for her, but there were many more like her, both men and women. Is she Chinese, is she English, Eurasian or Scotch? Is she Roman Catholic, Presbyterian, Church of England or a Plymouth Brethren? She had loved Malaya, in her work or in her home. It was only the sad fate of war that caused her to die so soon and in such hardship in an Allied territory, now Indonesia. She was proud to be British in 1943.

No tombstone or cross now marks her last resting place – no neat mown grass covers the site. No, for all she did, all she was – only the tropical growth of twenty-three years covers the grave. The birds will be singing, the sunrises and the sunsets will lighten the spot, and the sun give warmth. Will there be buildings erected here in years to come or more battles fought?

She was just one of God's children, but let us not forget . . .

Throughout their years as prisoners, the Australian nurses remained a cohesive group, taking strength from each other and even using humour at times to get them through every wretched day. They were admired for these qualities by others in the camp. As Sister Jessie Simons later explained, if decisions had to be made, they were made as a committed group. 'We were like sisters of a family. Of course we did not always see eye to eye, but what sisters do?' It was difficult to remain optimistic under the dire circumstances, but they all knew that strength lay in unity and this was always of paramount consideration in planning and carrying out every action.

On 8 December 1944, Betty – who had been in and out of hospital with her fever and other ailments – noted:

It is three years today since this war started, and I notice we are sitting behind a [Japanese] flag flying gaily over the entrance. How we hate that infernal red blob! They are so proud of what they did at Pearl Harbour. We all hope we don't celebrate their fourth anniversary with them. Surely not?

The following day she finally felt well enough to leave the hospital, only to see two of her AGH colleagues admitted.

The nurses' third Christmas in captivity was not cause for much joy, but they set about making the most of it. There were no presents to exchange, although a few hand-drawn cards changed hands. As Betty later recorded in her diary (which only came out when it was safe to do so), Christmas dinner was Chinese-style – mostly fried rice with a few 'oddments' through it:

> These oddments were a little piece of pork, half a garfish, and a few prawns, so we really had a feast. The [Japanese] gave us two tiny pigs and a small sack of rice for 'being good'. When the pigs were prepared and ready to be cooked a guard walked into the kitchen, cut off the hind legs, and walked off with them. So that was that. We had the rest.

Towards the end of January 1945, Betty revealed the sad fact that 31 of the 32 Australian nurses now had bad cases of malaria and they knew things could not go on as they were. 'You can't treat tropical fevers, ulcers, etc., on this diet and lack of water; it just won't work.'

On 26 January, she wrote in her diary of a nasty accident involving her friend Iole Harper:

> Vivian and Iole have had an accident carrying. Something slipped, they both juggled with the long pole they carry on their shoulders, one behind the other. Iole missed it and it poked her in the

chest heavily. As the pain didn't die down at all she reported to the doctor, who has bandaged a fractured rib. This is the first fracture we have had in camp. Just as well, we could do little with fractured arms and legs, and as for surgery, if anybody needed immediate surgery she would have to go without; there is no equipment here at all.

The year 1945 would prove to be a tragic and disheartening one for the nurses, in a camp filled with desperately ill women and children. On 8 February, Sister Raymont of the 2/4th CCS became the first of the AANS nurses to die, and in the following eight weeks another three were lost – Sister Rene Singleton of the 2/10th AGH on 20 February, Sister Pauline ('Blanche') Hempsted of the 2/13th AGH on 19 March, and Sister Shirley Gardam of the 2/4th CCS on 4 April. Banka fever (a mystery virus seemingly only evident on Banka Island), beriberi, malaria and other tropical diseases would continue to decimate the ranks of the nurses, who no longer had the strength, the will or medications to continue their unwinnable fight against these insidious killers.

South Australian-born Wilhelmina ('Ray') Raymont had suffered a sudden attack of malaria, fell into a coma, and died just 36 hours later. Betty would record that her fellow nurse had never fully recovered after an incident several months earlier, when a small knot in the wood behind Ray's bed-space had been either pushed out or fallen out. Along with Sister Val Smith, she was accused of peeping through this during an Allied bombing of the nearby Pladjoe oil refinery, watching Japanese soldiers running around the camp in a state of confusion.

This trivial occurrence somehow enraged the guards, especially the one known as 'Rasputin', who accused them of damaging Japanese military property and made the two women stand outside in the heat of the sun without hats or water. After an hour, Val was allowed back indoors, but Ray, being seen as the main offender, was ordered to stay where she was. Eventually someone noticed that she was near collapse in the ferocious heat of the sun and brought out a hat.

When he saw this, 'Rasputin' rushed out of the guard house, knocked the hat off and smacked Ray across the face so hard that she fell backwards. Elected camp commandant Mrs Hinch and a German woman doctor, Dr Goldberg, were summoned by the nurses and tried to have the punishment terminated, but despite their pleas 'Rasputin' ordered her to stand up again for another hour. The nurses could only watch on feeling utterly helpless. After a while, Ray tottered and collapsed. Everyone rushed out, ignoring the hated Japanese soldier, and carried the unconscious Ray to the camp hospital, where it was believed she had suffered from a heart attack. From that time on, she was in and out of the hospital, but never fully recovered from her ordeal.

'We are all absolutely rocked,' Betty wrote at the time of the sad loss. 'Our girls gave Ray a military funeral, all wearing their uniforms. It made the Japs sit up; they even stood to attention and removed their caps as it went past their quarters, a thing they had never done before.'

Just twelve days later a second nurse, Rene Singleton, died of beriberi after a lengthy and agony-filled period in hospital. She died without ever knowing that Kenneth, one of her two elder twin brothers, had died of his wounds in Alexandria, Egypt, on 25 July 1942, while serving with the 2/24th Australian Infantry Battalion.

Betty was herself in and out of hospital during this time and said she found it difficult to write any new entries in her diary, mostly as she felt there was nothing pleasant to write about, declaring, 'Camp life is just an existence now. No more concerts or charades or sing-songs; when the day's work is done people go off to their beds and lie there until morning.'

The following month, a strong rumour began to sweep through the camp that the internees were going to be moving back to Sumatra, to a different camp in Palembang. Despite that area's mud, heat and mosquitoes, the nurses were somewhat optimistic; they knew they had to get away from this indescribably disgusting camp before they all perished. When the move was announced by Captain Siki, it was not a return to Palembang at all; instead they were going to embark on a three-day journey by boat and train to another unknown camp on the southern side of Sumatra, in a place called Loebok Linggau.

Confirmation of the move came too late for Sisters Blanche Hempsted and Shirley Gardam. Vivian Bullwinkel was feeding Shirley Gardam in hospital and they were happily discussing Shirley's training days at Launceston General Hospital, when Shirley's eyes went wide, she arched upwards, cried out, and fell back, lifeless. She died just four days before the first of three groups of women, children and nurses were packed into trucks on 8 April and taken away. She was so ill and frail she would never have survived the transfer.

When the first group had assembled, the Australian nurses were given the exhausting task of loading the stretcher patients – many of them dying – onto the waiting lorries and accompanying them to Muntok pier, then assisting them onto the waiting ship. On arrival at the long pier, the nurses unloaded the stretcher cases, but in what Betty called 'a typical case of callous mismanagement' they were left on the pier for hours, fully exposed to the heat of the sun. Inevitably, the Japanese then ordered *tenko*, and everyone had to be counted – the usual slow and laborious task that took forever. One of the women died, and her body was conveyed back to the camp, where the nurses' final task at Muntok was to gently place her in a rough coffin which they lowered into a shallow grave they had just dug.

Once the count had finally been completed, the prisoners all had to be loaded onto tenders that would carry them out to the waiting ship. There was a steep staircase down to each tender, which meant that all the stretcher cases – seventeen in all – had to be carried down the stairs while the Japanese guards simply looked on. The 400 prisoners were eventually crammed on board the larger, ancient vessel, many of them herded below decks where they had to endure the stinking, stifling heat in darkness, sharing the hold with sacks of verminous rice. The rest, including all the stretcher cases, had to remain on the overcrowded open deck again, with no shelter from the elements and very little room to move around. A Japanese doctor was on board, but he was neither helpful nor sympathetic.

In all, eight people died during the sea voyage across from Banka Island and down the Musi River. The bodies could not remain on board; they had to be wrapped in sack material and lowered into the water as the ship sailed on. With nothing available to weigh the bodies down, they floated alongside in the drag of the ship – a horrid, undignified sight. Veronica Clancy reflected after the war:

All our journeys with the Japs were bad, but this was appalling. All the transports lacked sanitary arrangements or any civilised comforts, and on this trip we spent three days and nights crowded into the hold of the ship without any sanitation. The only ventilation was a small hole in the deck, and at night we froze, dressed as we were in our shorts and sun tops, and during the day the sun was sweltering. Our bodies became swollen and distorted and eight women died. The boats had to circle to get away from the floating bodies. There were heartrending scenes when children refused to leave their dead mothers.

After negotiating the Musi River, they finally reached Palembang wharf in the middle of a torrential downpour, but once again the Japanese showed their indifference to the plight of their ill prisoners by insisting on yet another *tenko*. After another lengthy count, they determined that the count was wrong; people were missing. It took someone telling them to add the eight people who had died on the voyage to their count before it finally tallied, after which they were marched to the railway station for the next leg of their torturous journey.

Betty was in the second group to leave the camp in pouring rain on 12 April, with the evacuation ship now back and berthed off the Muntok pier. This time there would be around 100 other people and more hospital patients to face the journey. The Japanese once again showed a complete lack of humanity. Those listed had to depart in the second group, whatever condition they might be in. Those remaining would vacate the camp in a third group four days later. As Betty later recorded in her diary:

What a business! About six people were desperately ill, some of them unconscious, and in spite of the doctors' begging . . . to allow them to remain until the last party left they had to travel that day. They obviously had only a few hours to live, and it seemed criminal to move them.

Setting-off time was announced as six o'clock that morning. After assembling, they ate some cold rice that had been cooked the previous evening. The rain was relentless, and as usual they were kept waiting in the open for hour after hour until they were finally loaded into the lorries for the trip to Muntok pier. The drivers were obviously under orders to get to the pier as soon as possible, so they drove as fast as they could, without a thought for those banging around helplessly in the back.

On reaching the pier, the nurses unloaded the stretcher patients, this time onto the grass beneath some trees, and out of the sun. As they waited for the next phase of their journey, one Dutch woman died. When they were permitted, those able to walk to the far end of the interminably long pier set off, carrying or dragging their baggage with a frequent number of stops.

A few nurses who were not as ill as the others carried the stretcher cases to where a small tender was waiting at the end of the pier. Once there, they turned around and went back to where the other seriously ill patients were positioned and carried them along the pier. They did this several times. 'How they kept it up nobody knows,' Betty observed. There were several Japanese soldiers lining the way, but as before they did not lift a finger to help; instead they just looked on as ragged, pathetically thin women staggered past.

Once loaded, the tenders relayed the prisoners out to the waiting wooden cargo ship until everyone was on board. It was the same filthy ship that had brought them to Banka Island the year before.

Once again the deck was completely filled with those unable to walk, while the rest were consigned to the stinking hold. Betty recorded:

As Pat Blake and I were walking patients, we were made to go down into the hatch and squat on crawling rice sacks with so many other women and children and babies that it was impossible for anyone to stretch her legs. And hot! It was like a furnace. The thought of 24 hours of that didn't help matters, especially as we both had dysentery, and we knew it was not fair to these people to stay there with them, since they were not, as yet, suffering from this complaint. So just before we started I scrambled out and back to the crowded deck where the stretcher patients were lying, packed like sardines, and facing the glaring sun. Fortunately the rain had stopped. I saw a tiny ledge just below the tiny ship's bridge and out of everybody's way, so climbed up there and sent a message to Pat down below to join me. It was very hot there in the sun. The ledge was about four feet square, and Val Smith and Iole joined us.

On this decrepit ship, apart from the single, rickety plank toilet jutting out from the stern, the only form of lavatory readily available to all the women and children was a small number of bedpans with handles that the Dutch nuns had managed to procure, and with dysentery rife these were in constant use. The nurses looking after those unable to care for themselves had the onerous task of standing on a narrow ledge on the outer side of the boat while two people held onto them, then lowering the excrement-filled bedpans on ropes down the side of the ship and letting them drag in the water for a while (which nearly dragged them over the side as well) and then raising them.

Iole Harper was constantly on this appalling duty, leading Betty to later comment of her friend, 'As long as I live I will never forget Iole emptying and dragging bedpans in the sea . . . I can't remember how often the girl did that, but she must have done it 50 times. If ever anyone deserved a Victoria Cross she did.'

On that first day at sea, they were given a meagre ration of boiled rice and some water, which they were told would have to last for all three days of their journey. Despite this warning, on subsequent days they would each be given some more boiled rice along with some salted fish, which only served to make their thirst even worse, but they received no additional water.

It was not long into the journey that the first patient, an English woman, died. Once the nuns working on the deck noticed, they had the terrible job of lifting the thin, soiled mattress with the woman's filth-covered body still on top and dropping it over the side of the ship. It was all they could do for the poor woman under the circumstances, and there was a mixed sense of sadness and contempt for their unfeeling captors as the mattress and body drifted away behind them.

The death toll continued to rise on the ship, but the decision was made to keep these bodies on board and bury them with some form of dignity once they reached Palembang. As Vivian Bullwinkel later stated,

We lost about twelve women through death on that ship. Cause of death: exposure to the sun. They were all sick women, and being exposed on the deck and without medical supplies or water, and the tropical sun was just too much for them. They died from sunstroke, because of their emaciated condition.

To everyone's relief, they finally arrived at Palembang's Kertapati wharf just after midday. 'Twenty-six hours in that awful tub for those sick people,' Betty later reflected in her diary, 'and everyone was sunburnt to glory.' Following a wait for the tide to rise and allow them to disembark, the desperately ill people were finally allowed onto the wharf.

Despite their own illnesses, the nurses and nuns were now fully engaged in carrying the stretcher cases off, crossing some railway lines and placing them in some shade. As expected, they were not given anything to eat, and yet again they had to put up with another *tenko* on the wharf, prior to which they had to bow to the Japanese preparing to conduct the head count. Once again there was confusion with the numbers, and yet again this was caused by not counting the stretcher cases and those who had died. Cruelly, they ordered the stretcher cases to be brought back to them by the nurses so they could be included in their count.

As it was only a short walk to the railway station, most were able to walk there, but others on the point of collapse had to be assisted or carried across the steel tracks and onto a grassed area alongside the station platform. Despite earlier plans to transport the dead to the camp for burial, they had to be left behind and nobody would ever know what became of their bodies. It was with a great sense of relief that the weary prisoners were finally able to sit on the grass and some lowly Japanese soldiers brought around buckets of liquid they called 'tea' for them to drink. Although tasting of vegetables and filled with unidentified lumps of foreign matter, 'It was hot and wet and we all enjoyed it,' according to Betty.

Those suffering from dysentery were permitted to use purpose-dug ditches along the path to the station. As before, those using this 'sanitary arrangement' had to do so in front of everyone who passed by, although years of living under the Japanese had almost inured them to this complete lack of privacy.

If they thought the worst was behind them, there was more sadness and tragedy to come on their onward journey to the new camp, and the continuing but easily preventable loss of life would forever haunt those who managed to survive the ordeal. Betty continues:

> At last a train came in, and we were told to get in. The stretcher patients were put into cattle trucks, the walking patients and others into carriages, filthy with black grit, but with padded seats, which rather surprised us. This was better than that blazing sun.
>
> We had to sit there on a siding all night, with windows and doors closed, blinds down and no light. It was airless and pitch dark. We sat there and stifled and put in another hellish night sitting up. Six of the patients in the cattle trucks died that night before we ever left the siding.

There was some good news during the evening when a person came through the train handing out 'bread'. What everyone received could hardly be described as bread; it was in the shape of a small, heavy loaf about the size of a fist. It was tough to bite into and chew, but it was a first cousin to bread and the first they had seen or tasted since becoming prisoners back in early 1942. Betty would regard the bread as something of a miracle, as it seemed to clear up their diarrhoea.

Promptly at seven o'clock the next morning, amid much clamour and movement, a locomotive hooked up to the carriages and they

A local boy stands in front of a group of Irenelaan houses, photographed prior to their occupation by the Japanese (Photo: Australian War Memorial 11462.002)

Before the Japanese moved into the area, and observed by Dutch residents, local villagers stand outside houses 6 and 7 at Irenelaan. The 2/10th AGH nurses would occupy house 6, while the 2/13th AGH and 2/4th Casualty Clearing Station (CCS) nurses were allocated house 7. They would spend a total of seventeen months living here (Photo: Australian War Memorial P11462.001)

Palembang Ferry Station (Photo: Muntok Peace Museum)

Illustrating how female internees were made to bow to any Japanese guards and dignitaries at each *tenko*, or roll call (Photo: Singapore National Archives)

Margaret Dryburgh

Norah Chambers

A drawing of the Palembang Barracks Camp by Margaret Dryburgh

The freshwater spring at the Belalau camp (Photo: Muntok Peace Museum)

The freed nurses arrive at Singapore airfield from Sumatra wearing their original, ragged and oil-stained uniforms. Betty Jeffrey is between the nurse at front with a bedroll and the nurse with the white cap (Photo: Australia War Memorial 044480)

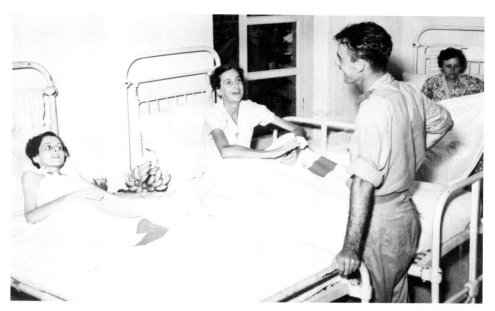

Sisters Jean Greer (left) and Betty Jeffrey chat with an Australian soldier while recuperating in one of the wards at the 2/14th hospital, Singapore, where they were being slowly nursed back to health (Photo: Australian War Memorial 305369)

Four nurses recuperating on the verandah at the AGH. From left: Jessie Simons, Mavis Hannah, Wilma Oram and Vivian Bullwinkel (Photo: Argus Newspaper Collection of photographs, State Library of Victoria, H98.103/3669)

Above: A group of AANS nurses on board the converted hospital ship *Manunda* on its arrival at Fremantle. Among them are Vivian Bullwinkel (third from right, holding flowers), Matron-in-Chief Annie Sage (centre, in full uniform) and left of the Matron is Betty Jeffrey (Photo: Argus Newspaper Collection of photographs, State Library of Victoria, H98.103/4102)

Left: Hospital ship *Manunda* arrives in Sydney Harbour on 27 October 1945, the final port of call after delivering repatriated 2/8th Division soldiers and AANS nurses (Photo: Argus Newspaper Collection of photographs, State Library of Victoria, H99.201/847)

At a homecoming celebration in Adelaide, Sister Jean Ashton (2/13th AGH) stands between her parents Caroline and Walter, with her brother Leslie standing behind (Photo courtesy of the Ashton family)

Betty is reunited with her family on 24 October 1945. From left: Frances (Mick), Dr Charles Gale (Breeze), Amelia (Millie), Betty, Marjorie (Jo), William (Will) and Gwenyth (Mary) (Photo courtesy of the Jeffrey family)

Vivian Bullwinkel looks on as Betty Jeffrey opens a first edition of her book *White Coolies* (Photo: Australian Nurses Memorial Centre)

The magnificent Madowla, which would be transformed into the Nurses Memorial Centre (Photo: Australian Nurses Memorial Centre)

Betty assisting at the opening of the Nurses Memorial Centre in 1949 to the delight of Sisters Holden (Epworth Hospital) and Crameri (Royal Women's Hospital) (Photo: Argus newspaper, courtesy of the Jeffrey family)

Anzac Day, 1955: Vivian Bullwinkel, Betty Jeffrey and Beryl Woodbridge march through the streets of Melbourne (Photo: Australian Nurses Memorial Centre)

Matron Annie Sage and Betty Jeffrey flank Sister Ida O'Dwyer, a World War I nurse, while visiting the Edith Cavell memorial on St Kilda Road (Photo: Australian War Memorial PO4585.001)

Betty Jeffrey addresses the audience at the official opening of the Woodhouse-Nareeb Soldiers Memorial Hall in 1955 (Photo: Australian Nurses Memorial Centre)

Betty outside Madowla with her beloved dog Robbie (Credit: Australian Nurses Memorial Centre)

A proud Betty Jeffrey after receiving her OAM at Government House in 1987 (Photo courtesy of the Jeffrey family)

A reunion photo taken at Melbourne's Fairfield Hospital, circa 1978. *Clockwise from bottom:* Ken Brown (pilot who helped rescue the nurses from Belalau), Beryl Woodbridge, Wilma (Oram) Young, Vivian (Bullwinkel) Statham, Betty Jeffrey and Nesta James (Photo: Australian Nurses Memorial Centre)

Doll of the Japanese guard nicknamed 'Bully' – a birthday present to Betty in camp that she managed to hide and bring to Australia, where it is now on display at the Australian War Memorial, Canberra (Photo: Emily Malone)

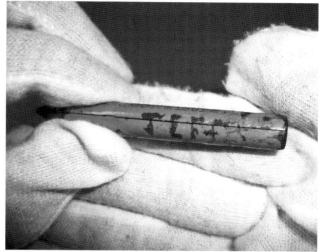

The pencil Betty used to write her secret diary is also in the AWM collection, carefully held here by Betty's great-niece, Emily (Photo: Emily Malone)

The family of Sister Jean Ashton in front of the Radji Beach Memorial in February 2012. *From left:* Brian, Rose, Sue (Ackroyd) and Maxie Ashton (Photo courtesy of the Ashton family)

Fellow Sumatra survivors and lifelong friends Jean Ashton and Wilma (Oram) Young, taken at a POW reunion in November 1990 (Photo courtesy of the Ashton family)

Betty with one of her handwritten diaries in her East Malvern apartment. The brown suitcase which always held her precious memorabilia is behind her left arm (Photo: Emily Malone)

Taken on the balcony of her apartment in October 1986 were, at back *(left to right):* Patty Blake, Vivian Bullwinkel, Wilma Oram, Betty and Flo Trotter. At front: Jessie Blanch and Joyce Tweddell (Photo courtesy of the Jeffrey family)

Golf played an important role in Betty's post-war life. Betty Jeffrey (left), Burtta Cheney and Dora O'Sullevan at the Huntingdale Golf Club in the late 1990s (Photo courtesy of Huntingdale Golf Club)

The Jeffrey girls: Mary, Betty and Jo, photographed in 1994 (Photo courtesy of the Jeffrey family)

Sister Agnes Betty Jeffrey OAM, RN: 14 May 1908 – 13 September 2000 (Photo: Australian Nurses Memorial Centre)

were finally on their way. Once they were well clear of the station, the guards allowed everyone to raise their blinds and windows, which had been closed in the event of an air raid, letting some refreshing air gush through the stuffy carriages. There were no toilets on the train, so any excreta had to be tipped through a sliding hatch located high on the carriage walls. Despite the fresh air now flowing, the smell of this and dozens of sweaty bodies was quite overpowering.

As the train moved steadily south-west across Sumatra, the lush, mountainous scenery was ever-changing, and under normal circumstances would have been regarded as picturesque, but this small enjoyment was tempered every time they passed a tree heavy with bananas or other tropical fruit, which they would have given anything to feast on.

Throughout the next long night, Sisters Iole Harper and Val Smith walked back and forth, tending to the ill and trying their best to make them more comfortable. Betty was simply too ill to help them, later writing,

we were nearly dead with weariness, thirst and hunger, yet those two sisters of ours had to put up with these conditions and help the sick, who were getting worse, and others becoming ill all the time. Iole and Val didn't sit down for more than ten minutes at a time during the whole of the journey in that train.

At least there was some relief at midday when the train pulled into a station and they each received some rice and fish with a sweet sauce.

They finally pulled into the station at Loebok Linggau at around 8 pm that evening. Loebok Linggau was a tiny town perched in the jungle-clad foothills of Sumatra's west coast, home to many rubber estates. Most people took the opportunity to climb off the train under the watchful eyes of the guards in order to breathe in some fresh air. Several more patients had been lost along the way, but their bodies were not allowed to be removed from the cattle cars. Those few minutes of open-air relaxation did not last long, as they were soon ordered back into the train carriages, in which the atmosphere was still stiflingly warm and stuffy. Once again the blinds and windows had to be closed. The next morning, as dawn was breaking, there was renewed shouting as the guards ordered everyone off the train.

A convoy of trucks was waiting to transport everyone the 7 miles to the camp, situated in the middle of the Belalau Plantation, then the largest rubber plantation in Sumatra. It was surrounded by jungle and had earlier been subjected to the widely implemented 'scorched earth' policy, when the Dutch citizens of Sumatra destroyed anything that might be of use to the invading Japanese, burning rice paddies, cutting down banana plantations, and doing as much as possible to prevent food and other supplies falling into enemy hands. Unfortunately for the new arrivals, it was also situated in an area known to have a high incidence of malaria. Of some small comfort was the fact that the men's camp was nearby, but for Betty it was the very welcome sight of the Australian nurses and others who had arrived four days earlier:

We arrived at the camp soon after 8 am and were met by Woodie [Beryl Woodbridge], Jennie Greer, Win Davis, Jess Doyle, and a few English nurses. It was good to see them. They thought we all looked awful and were very concerned about us, but what a relief to have that hell journey behind us.

The first thing I saw was a huge heap of sweet potatoes. What a change from sour, dry, cold rice! Win said they had been given sweet potato stew that had carrot in it, and she had kept a spoonful each for us. That is Win, always doing something for others. It was luscious.

The latest arrivals were soon given information on their new camp, and not much of it was good to hear. A barbed-wire fence encircled the camp, through which flowed a creek. The Japanese officers and guards had taken over the plantation manager's house and most of the newly arrived nurses, nuns, women and children were housed in large, poorly built *attap* huts – constructed using a type of thatched native grass – which meant continually coping with leaky roofs and walls and a muddy earthen floor. They were warned in advance that the huts were also infested with swarms of lice and fleas and the occasional rat. Once again, Captain Siki Kazue was in overall charge of the camp.

Whenever it rained, which was often, water would seep into the huts and turn the already muddy ground into a glutinous mess. They slept on native 'bali bali' beds, basically an individual platform made of bamboo with short legs, and each person was allocated 22 inches of bed space. The eighteen Charitas nuns lived in a one-room cottage, Hut 12, and ten of the fitter nurses – the hospital staff – lived nearby in Hut 13, as the camp hospital was only a five-minute walk away. Both of these huts had concrete floors and galvanised tin roofs, which meant that during the day they were like ovens.

The long wooden hut used as the camp hospital was in poor condition. It also had a mud floor, and the timber in the walls and roof was rotten. When the severe Sumatran storms hit, which was a frequent occurrence, water would gush through the roof onto the patients. Located in a hollow at the bottom of a hill, the hospital hut received no direct sunshine – not the best situation for treating the seriously ill.

Betty would consider herself fortunate to be assigned to Hut 13 after spending a day recuperating in the hospital, which, not unexpectedly, did not have any medical supplies or medicines. She would share the house and hospital duties with Sisters Jean Ashton, Vivian Bullwinkel, 'Jessie' Blanch, Iole Harper, Nesta James, Wilma Oram, Chris Oxley, Val Smith and Flo Trotter.

The three doctors who worked in the camp hospital lived in their own small hut, located at the edge of the jungle near the barbed-wire fence, and they lost many hours of sleep as they often heard tigers, wild pigs and other animals prowling nearby, coming to drink from the creek outside the wire.

According to war historian Catherine Kenny, in writing about the camp in her excellent 1986 book *Captives*:

There were no bathrooms so they used the creek in full view of the guards whom they had learnt to ignore as their clothes barely covered them anyway. The creek supplied their water but the eight tiny open-fronted lavatories were built over the creek, which became even more polluted with refuse from the kitchen and the Japanese quarters further upstream.

As it was the only source of water in the camp – apart from when it rained – any water used for cooking, washing and bathing had to be boiled beforehand.

Soon after they had settled in and established a routine, there was the devastating news that the extraordinarily gifted Margaret Dryburgh, who had given everyone so much pleasure and lifted spirits with her voice orchestra, had died after being seriously ill for some time. The hellish trip across to Loebok Linggau had just proved too much for her ailing body. As news of her death swept through the camp, it caused sadness and gloom for everyone. Many tears were shed for a proud and loving lady who deserved far better treatment in her last days on earth.

Apart from the ten Australian nurses who lived near the hospital, the rest were housed in the *attap* huts on the top of a hill, along with an estimated 600 prisoners of all ages. If they wanted water they had to climb down to the creek, fill their containers and then slowly trudge back up the slippery hill, although this laborious task was made a little easier after several women hacked out steps using a heavy chunkel. It was still hard for those in a badly weakened condition to face this task, but the biggest challenge of all was carrying food up those same sticky earthen steps after visiting the community kitchen, located at the foot of the hill near the creek, to collect the food for their hut. There was always the danger that a slip would cause the precious food to spill, but the long struggle up the slope also meant that by the time the food reached the summit, it was no longer hot.

As well, for those on the top of the hill who were ill and weak, bathing was either carried out using a tin-full of water, or by slowly and painstakingly wending their way down to the creek where they could bathe, trying to ignore the guards who watched on with interest. Despite this, Betty did have an amusing tale from that time:

There was a little creek near the hospital and we had one bed pan for the whole hospital. The only way to clean it was to go down and wade into the creek and swish the bed pan around. I was swishing it around one day and caught a fish. It was terribly funny. It was only a little fish, but I thought, 'Good-o, here's lunch!' So we saved the fish and took it home. I tried again to fish with the bedpan, but I only caught the one fish. It was a silly little thing, a little incident, but you know, everything wasn't grim all the time. We laughed. We could laugh at ourselves and the silly things that we did. I think it sort of helped keep our sanity.

Surrounded as it was by tropical trees, the camp presented yet another visual agony for the prisoners, who could see bananas, pawpaws and other delicious fruits simply rotting and falling to the ground, when they could have done so much good if eaten. Worst of all, some of these trees were growing within the barbed-wire barrier close to the huts, but anyone caught trying to pick this fruit would be subjected to severe punishment. It would have been extremely difficult to cut down the large pawpaws or a bunch of bananas without it being noticed by the guards. Nevertheless, the women were allowed to gather up banana flowers on the ground, which were very tasty when cooked in a curry. Even though the flesh of the rotten bananas they occasionally picked up from the muddy ground was deemed inedible, the skins could be dried and fried and were a nice supplement to any meal.

Within weeks, any sort of vegetation – every leaf or grass – had been pulled up and consumed, leaving the ground bare. As Jessie Simons later recalled, the nurses soon found themselves once again obsessing over food, although things were a little different in this camp:

The diet was a considerable change from the predominant rice ration with which we had become so familiar; rice supplies were reduced, but sweet potatoes and *obi kayu* [tapioca] were added, together with a much better supply of palm oil for cooking. Culinary instincts sprang to the surface under the new challenge, and for a few days we tried all sorts of experiments with chipped and fried potatoes, or baked them in the hot coals like children round a bonfire. Result – most of us suffered severe bouts of indigestion through over-indulgence in the new elements of our diet.

Those who were still strong enough began digging gardens. The nurses and nuns tried cultivating a small vegetable patch, but the heavy soil was not only difficult and exhausting to till, but the results would prove poor. They did find that planting sweet potatoes also produced a green leaf that was high in vitamin and mineral content when added to any meal. Making matters even worse was when the Japanese kept announcing that life-saving Red Cross parcels had arrived some time back and would be distributed soon, but everyone had to *nanti nanti* (wait). Their patience was growing increasingly thin, as everyone knew that the parcels were already stacked up in the guard house. It was yet another example of the bastardry that existed, and people continued to suffer and die as a result.

Having recovered sufficiently, Betty Jeffrey now worked in the two wards of the camp hospital, but the Australian nurses were so weak they could only work shifts of one or two hours. Sister Veronica Clancy later said,

There were many sick cases, and the work was very heavy. There was little we could do except to give the patients a wash, a drink of water, and rice. If they didn't eat the rice they died. And, towards the end, dying did not take long. Sheer dogged persistence in forcing down rice kept many alive. Night duty was the heaviest. 'Sister!' would be called from so many directions at once you would nearly go crazy . . . It's still ringing in my ears.

But, as Betty wrote in her diary, they did not get any special treatment – unlike some others in the camp:

Food comes in to camp alright, but it is for the workers (not nurses, they don't work – they nurse and have to live on rations). The workers are mostly Indo-Dutch and Indonesians and big boys – they get sugar, cakes, bananas, rice, corn, vegetables, extra to rations. If one works in the kitchen, one gets a dish full of rice. If one nurses, one gets nothing but insults, malaria and an empty tummy.

If the nurses complained or asked for extra rations, the Japanese would tell them, 'plenty room in cemetery', while pointing through the clouds and trees to an area in the mountains where the bodies were buried.

CONQUERING DESPAIR

Death was hardly a stranger in the camp, and visited often. The main reasons were starvation and malnutrition, a lack of water, and virulent tropical diseases. Among these were malaria, amoebic dysentery, Banka fever and beriberi. If contracted, beriberi could cause the hapless victim a lingering, excruciatingly painful death. Starting at the feet, the body would swell up, and once the swelling reached the heart that would be it; death quickly followed.

Many of the camp guards were locally recruited Javanese. They would scream and shout at the prisoners as they had been ordered, but fortunately they were generally smiling and pleasant. It seems the Japanese would only trust them so far; one of them even confessed to one of the nurses that even though they carried guns, they were not given any bullets. They never resorted to physical violence, unlike two Japanese sergeants, named Shigemura and Amana, who often slapped women across the face if they sensed disobedience. Shigemura was even known to have used a thick stick instead of his hand, and both would make women stand in the heat of the sun for up to an hour over something as trivial as not bowing in their presence – even if they had not been seen.

If there was any good news at all, it came in early May, when to everyone's surprise and joy another large batch of mail was handed over and distributed. Although there was outrage that it had been withheld for so long, it did not matter to most that the letters and cards were dated 1942 and 1943 – it still provided news of loved ones back home. Betty and Iole each received twenty letters, 'most of them containing 25 words only', and to Betty's delight three family photographs were enclosed. She would take them out every day and gaze longingly at the healthy children posing for the shot, while comparing them to the thin, ever-hungry children around her in the camp.

While there had once been different vegetables to supplement their meagre rice diet – carrots, chokoes, *brinjals*, long beans – these were mostly no longer available and starvation, as Betty recorded, had set in again. 'Very few of us have a tail to sit on these days, mostly bone, and our legs look just like bones re-covered with some skin.' She now weighed less than 6 stone (38 kilograms), and to make matters worse, their daily diet was temporarily reduced to just rice and sweet potatoes. Vegetables would sometimes become available once or twice a week, but even then they had to overcome totally unnecessary antics by the Japanese delivering the food:

> The potatoes are brought to the guard-house just outside the barrier, dumped in the nearest pool of water, and left there in the sun and rain for three or four days. When they are thoroughly bad we may take them into the camp and eat them . . . So far in this camp we have had meat, which looked like bullock, twice. A piece weighing about 5 pounds was brought in on each occasion to feed 640 people.

Things were getting worse all the time. Apart from the malaria, beriberi and other assorted illnesses, everyone was being constantly tormented by fleas and other bugs. Meat was a rarity and when it came it was always rotten and stank of decay, but the smell would vanish once it was diced and tossed into the cooking pot, and everyone ate it. There was simply no alternative if they wanted to survive.

A black market did operate in the camp, with duck eggs selling for up to 10 guilders each, and whole chickens 30 guilders. The women would barter anything they owned, particularly jewellery, and the nurses took on all manner of tasks and chores for other prisoners to earn a little money for food. They even took out binding 'loans' – to be repaid after the war.

On 14 May 1945, the nurses gave Betty a small birthday party – her fourth while in captivity. A small amount of rice had been held back for the occasion and was fried with some sweet potato leaves from their little garden next to Hut 13. Val Smith then presented her with a small, self-made gift – a small model of one of the guards they'd nicknamed 'Bully'. It was made from a small scrap of a khaki shirt worn by the Japanese that someone had found and was stuffed with other fragments of rags. It even had the correct three stars on the collar. That small doll would remain with her for the remainder of her days as a prisoner and is now on display at the Australian War Memorial in Canberra.

The nurses somehow managed to become skilful in making craft items. One of these, according to a post-war interview with Betty, was extraordinarily creative:

The men would sometimes be able to smuggle some extra food – even meat – onto the ration truck, which was greatly appreciated, so in return some of the Australian nurses decided to make them a small gift . . . We took down a rafter out of the roof (which would not be noticed) and chopped it into 144 pieces with a piece of old chisel that we had found [and] turned it into a mah-jongg set . . . We would just sit on the floor and work on it. We were alongside the cemetery and there was a tree just outside the barrier that had a sort of rough, sandpapery leaf. So we gathered these and would rub and rub and rub until we had them absolutely like white satin . . . You could put a spirit level on the pieces – absolutely spot on straight! We had Kong, the Chinese nurse, to do the Chinese characters and we made the circles and the bamboos and things.

They managed to have the mah-jongg set taken to the men's camp 'in a funny little bag that [one nurse] made out of a little piece of fishing bag that the fish ration came in' and got word back that it had caused great excitement and would be in constant use.

Now I think that was pretty clever. We made two or three mah-jongg sets. And of course we made cards, playing cards. We found photograph albums on the rubbish heaps and turned these into cards.

Every so often, something completely unexpected would occur in the camp, which would both surprise and delight the starving, malaria-infected prisoners. Such an occasion came three days after Betty's birthday, when a Japanese band came into the camp, complete with their own chairs, as there were none in the camp. It was announced that a concert would be held that afternoon on the top of the hill. Many of the nurses, including Betty, were simply too weak to attend, but promptly at 2.30 pm the Japanese interpreter known to them as 'Gold Teeth' stormed into their huts and the hospital swinging a long stick and screaming 'Lekas!' ('Hurry'). Everyone, no matter how ill or disinclined, had to clamber up the hill and become part of the large audience.

When they got to the top of the rise they were amazed at the sight of the neatly turned-out band, all 30 dressed the same, smiling as they sat down with their instruments and prepared to play. Most of the prisoners sat on the ground or on the trunks of fallen trees. No one knew quite what to expect, but then the band launched into some European overtures and waltzes they all knew, and one of the band sang a marching song they all agreed was quite lovely. When the concert finally ended, there were tears everywhere and the crowd applauded as loudly as their weak hands would allow. 'For two hours we all forgot we were prisoners,' Betty later wrote in her diary. The day after the concert, everyone was told to write and thank the band and say how much enjoyment it had brought them.

The euphoria associated with this unexpected treat did not last long, as the nurses returned to their hospital and patient duties. As if things were not bad enough, the hated *tenko* now took place twice a day, at 7 am and 5 pm. The hospital was perpetually full and the nurses could only manage to work there for about an hour at a time before they became too weak to continue. Despite the grim circumstances, Sister Nesta James was proud of the nurses she worked with, saying after the war, 'I cannot pay too high a tribute to the spirit of our girls. They never gave up. They never lost hope. They never gave the Japanese the satisfaction of seeing them beaten.'

On 26 May, some wonderful news filtered into the camp: the war with Germany was at an end. They would later learn that the surrender had actually taken place days earlier – on 8 May – but that did not concern them, it only mattered that the Allies had been victorious, and could now turn their full attention to defeating the Japanese. That could not come soon enough, they all agreed.

Five days after receiving this good news, the nurses lost another of their members when New Zealand-born Sister Gladys Hughes (2/13th AGH) from Victoria died from the effects of beriberi. Another three AANS nurses were destined to lose the fight to survive over the next three months.

As mentioned earlier, one of the less desirable tasks – a sad necessity – was digging graves for the women of all ages and nation-alities who died in ever-increasing numbers. The cemetery was located outside the wire on a hill behind the hospital. As more of their number died, the nurses had been forced to dig the graves themselves using chunkels, and had to make the holes deep enough to prevent wild pigs that roamed the hills from digging up the bodies. The graves were still marked with small wooden crosses. As Betty remarked, 'Many people go to funerals just to get firewood. Most of them come back into camp dragging dead branches of trees behind them. It does seem so awful to be forced to do this, but it is the only way to get enough wood to cook meals.'

The coffins, supplied by the Japanese, were crude, due to a shortage of materials, and were constructed using thin slats of wood, much like those in vintage fruit boxes, and the bodies within could be seen through the slats. Knowing full well that one day they might themselves be yet another statistic, the prisoners were expected to scrounge and save six nails for nailing down their own coffin lid, if death came ahead of freedom. Betty said they would line the coffins with leaves and flowers 'to hide the crudeness'.

Sister Pat Darling, suffering from malaria and beriberi, did not know how much longer she could survive. 'By the end, we were so weak that we could hardly carry the coffins. When you are that thin – I weighed only 30 kilos – you walk in a different way because you never know which way your legs are going to bend.'

There seemed to be no end to the grim processions up the mountain to dig shallow forest graves and bury the dead. Grieving mothers buried their children, who had died mostly of malnutrition, and the death rate began to amount to several prisoners every day. Although they would never willingly give up hope, most of the Australian nurses had already drawn up crude wills. As Jessie Simons later wrote, they were 'leaving to any of their friends who might survive, their pitiful pieces of personal property – a few cooking utensils, a pair of shorts, a pair of ragged boots'.

Even Betty, despite her determination to survive, had prudently written something in the event of becoming yet another losing the battle to live. Her will read:

Muntok
12.2.45
I, Agnes Betty Jeffrey, in the event of my death while interned by the
Japanese authorities,
desire all my possessions to be given to Sister Iole Harper, and I desire
that the British Commandant carry out this request.
A.B. Jeffrey
Witnesses: J. Blanch
J. Ashton

Betty and the other occupants of Hut 13 had solved the problem of being able to reheat their midday and evening meals by building a small fireplace behind their hut, made by balancing two short pieces of railway track on some bricks. While it was deemed quite effective, it still needed wood, which was in very short supply in the camp, so there was always a mad scramble when a tree branch fell on the right side of the barbed-wire fence – sometimes aided by prisoners throwing rocks at dead branches, or throwing a rope over the branch and in a combined effort hauling it down. Betty recorded one pleasant occasion on 10 June:

We are still eating peculiar things. We had deer one day about a week ago, a huge old animal, and it was excellent. A few days later we had what we thought was tiger meat, bad and very high. It was eaten because the smell left it after it was cooked. So far, no ill effects.

The carrots didn't last long and we are back to the old diet of tapioca leaves and that bitter jack fruit. Rations are still left outside in the weather for a couple of days before we get them, but we are getting used to it now. The creek has flooded again and down the stream came logs of wood, fallen trees, and other debris. As we are desperate for wood Blanchie, Flo Trotter, and I went in after a tree. We dragged it on to the bank, then got back into the stream and had a grand old swim! The water was deep and cold and it was most stimulating being rushed down with the tide. We did not allow ourselves to go far because of the rocks, now hidden. We were blue with cold when we came out, but soon warmed up – couldn't help it in this hot place.

In mid-June it was discovered that two Indonesian families had been catching, cooking and eating snakes and even rats. Both were plentiful in the camp, but after one family member suddenly became violently ill and died in hospital a few hours later, the doctors issued a camp-wide warning that consuming snakes and rats was strictly prohibited.

On 8 July, Betty reported that some more messages from home were being distributed – this time dated 1943 and 1944. Sadly for her, one of the letters contained the tragic news that her elder brother Alan had died in Queensland on 25 March 1944, at just 46 years of age. She wept for him and his widow Aimée.

There was further sadness eleven days later when Sister Winnie May Davis (2/10th AGH) died after being seriously ill for several weeks. She had turned 30 a few days earlier, on 7 July. 'I shall never forget how wonderful Win was to me during my first weeks of internment when my fingers were burnt and bandaged,' Betty wrote in her diary, 'and for so long I was so useless.'

A little more mail from home was handed out on 26 July and Betty's great friend Iole was almost inconsolable when she read that her young brother Wilfred, serving as a wireless operator/air gunner with the RAAF, was listed as 'missing over Germany'. There was little Iole could do apart from pray that he was okay, hopefully nothing worse than a prisoner of war in Europe. She would later learn that he had been killed exactly one year earlier, on 26 July 1943, when the Wellington bomber he was operating on during a raid to Essen, Germany, was shot down over the North Sea. The crew's bodies were never recovered.

'Food is coming into the camp,' Betty noted in her diary, 'but not for us who do all the nursing without a let-up. It is for the "hard workers".'

Workers belong to squads who go out of camp and chop down rubber-trees. We did it for a while, but could not last too long and had no energy at all. The first working squads in this camp had to go for quite a long walk to a main road, then they had to remove a great heap of stones from the side of the road and put them all in a heap on the other side about 20 yards further down. Next time they went out they had to put the same stones back in their original position!

We Australians have done more than our fair share of chopping trees, digging drains, and clearing roadways for the last three years and simply haven't time or strength to go out on these squads now. We are all working ourselves to a standstill nursing and doing our own chores in order to make life bearable.

9

JAPAN CAPITULATES!

IT WAS A PARTICULARLY SAD DAY for Betty when she recorded the loss of yet another nurse, this time Sister Dorothy ('Dot') Freeman. She had been Betty's senior back in her pre-war training days in Melbourne and had worked with her, Iole and Rene in the camp's bakery business, 'having lots of fun with us'. Sister Freeman had become increasingly ill with malaria, dysentery and beriberi and had to be placed in the camp hospital in a serious way. On the evening of 8 August 1945, she and Flo Trotter, who was on night duty, had been enjoying a quiet chat over a cup of tea before Sister Trotter left for a few minutes to do her rounds. On her return, she found to her dismay that Dot Freeman had passed away. She was devastated. As Betty wrote in her diary, 'We must get out of here soon, or we shall lose more of our girls.'

There would be still more sadness. Sister Pearl ('Mitz') Mittelheuser, also of the 2/10th AGH, died on 18 August, ten days after Dot Freeman. She had been a tower of strength in the different camps. In the space of just seven months, Betty had lost and buried eight good friends – four from her own unit. Sixty-five nurses had left Singapore on the *Vyner Brooke*, 12 of whom drowned in the sinking, another 21 murdered on Radji Beach. Now only 24 were still living, and if they were not liberated soon, the death count would rapidly rise, as many of them were hospitalised and critically ill.

Writing post-war, Sister (Ellen) Mavis Hannah from Perth said she knew all too well the terrible sadness associated with the loss of her nursing colleagues, which was often violent and other times so easily preventable:

By September 1945 I remained the sole surviving Sister of my unit [2/4th CCS], four were shot, two drowned and two [Gardam and Raymont] died in camp in 1945. One of these died a raving lunatic from cerebral malaria. I had begged the Commandant to give me anti-malarial medication, which they had withheld from Red Cross parcels; I was told there was plenty of room in the cemetery. He laughed, smacked my face and his guard hit me with his rifle. I bear the marks to this day.

By now they knew for certain that Germany had surrendered and the European war was finally at an end. What they did not know for some weeks was that on 6 August – just two days before Dot Freeman died, an American Boeing B-29 bomber aircraft named *Enola Gay* had flown high over the Japanese industrial city of Hiroshima at 8.15 am. From 31,060 feet (9,470 metres), the crew dropped a devastating weapon which exploded about 1,968 feet (600 metres) above the ground and levelled much of the city. In an instant, 80,000 people perished, and tens of thousands more would later succumb to their injuries or from exposure to radiation. Just three days later, on 9 August, another B-29 dropped a second atomic bomb, this time over the city of Nagasaki. An estimated 40,000 people were killed and at least 30,000 more would die by the end of the year. The Japanese government could not allow such massive destruction and loss of life to continue. The day after the bombing of Nagasaki, they capitulated, issuing a statement agreeing to accept the Allied surrender terms.

Although rumours of the war ending began to trickle through to the camp, no one allowed themselves to become excited, knowing that disappointment would crush their spirits if it turned out to be yet another false bit of gossip. Everyone carried on as before.

In mid-August, in what was seen as a curious demonstration of humanity, Captain Siki announced that he would allow the children in the camp who had male relatives in the nearby men's camp to pay them a visit. It was not all it seemed and was yet another example of completely uncompassionate behaviour as the guards read out the names of the children who could *not* go. It was in this awful way that many of the women and children in the camp found out that their husbands, fathers and brothers were no longer alive.

The story of the nurses finally realising freedom was well related in Betty Jeffrey's 1954 book *White Coolies*. In preparing a tribute booklet following the death of her wartime Matron-in-Chief, Colonel Annie Moriah ('Sammie') Sage, CBE, RRC, in April 1969, Betty decided to revisit and write once again about that joyous time and all that followed when they were finally liberated after years of Japanese captivity, retelling the story with the benefit of hindsight. Here, then, is that remarkable tale of liberation in 1945, as told in part in Betty's own reflective words:

The end of our prison camp life came very suddenly. We had been getting thoroughly fed up and, in August 1945, everybody was ill. Our camp was tatty and dirty in spite of our efforts, which were feeble at this stage. Everybody had lost much weight; legs and arms were like matchsticks – we were in fact only shadows of our former selves. But nobody had given up hope of survival. The camp hospital was full, our girls were nursing both there and in the camp huts. Everyone who could give a helping hand, did just that. At this stage we were only four, five or six stone in weight but all kept on going. Our 'clothes' were in rags.

For Betty and all those held in the camp there came a truly memorable moment on the afternoon of 24 August when the diminutive and normally belligerent camp commandant Captain Siki Kasue came from the Japanese barracks accompanied by two guards carrying a table, which they carefully set up in the centre of the compound. After being assisted onto the table, Siki stood to his full but abbreviated height and began making a speech. After a few sentences he paused while an interpreter tried to convert his words into Malay. He was doing such a poor job that one of the Dutch women shoved him aside and began interpreting in both Malay and English. In essence this is what he told his stunned audience: 'War is ended and soon we will all leave Sumatra; Americano and English will be here in a few days. Please forgive us for any mistakes we have made. We are now all friends!' He did neglect to mention just *who* had won the war, but for the inmates it was somewhat obvious by his awkward apology and uncommonly meek behaviour.

Once he had delivered his news, Siki was assisted from the table and retreated, head down, back to his barracks. After the war, he would be found guilty of brutal treatment of the inmates under his control and was sentenced to fifteen years' imprisonment. Meanwhile, there was jubilation and joyous sobbing throughout the camp, with kisses and hugs as everyone tried to comprehend the stunning news and what it now meant for them. Amid all the excitement, Betty did pause to grieve for those eight nursing colleagues who had died in captivity and were no longer alive to share in this long-anticipated day. But most – 24 in all – had somehow managed to survive, and were no longer prisoners of the Japanese.

It all seemed too good to be true, and there were still lingering doubts, knowing all too well the duplicity of their captors, so for the time being they carried on as usual. Then a young Chinese girl they knew well named Katrine ran up to Betty, who was talking to Sister Nesta James, yelling out in excitement, 'War is finished at six o'clock tonight and big gate opened!' Soon others were running up and saying the same thing. No more endless *tenko* for hours in the heat of the day, no more face-slapping, no more humiliating bowing to the lowliest Japanese guards. Someone managed to brew a huge tin of black coffee to celebrate, and despite some hesitation they were finally free to walk outside the hated barbed-wire fence and collect some firewood. Their joy knew no bounds, but it was mingled with feelings of anger and sadness for those who would never know this day.

Mavis Hannah was a staff member of the 2/4th CCS, and the only nurse from that unit to survive the *Vyner Brooke* sinking and subsequent captivity. She would later reflect on those lost years and the people who shared them with her:

We had to work on practically no food, but it was a kind of mental attitude, and your friends – there was no doubt about that – you kept each other going. The POWs have a saying: 'the spirit that kept the spirit going'. That was true; you had to have that will to live, you had to have companionship, you had to have the will to do things, you had to be able to cope.

Along with this sudden new-found freedom from *tenko*, daily chores and other drudgery came some necessary caution, which meant that Betty and several other nurses were ordered into hospital care so they could rest up before the physical exertion of starting the long journey home. It was an annoyance, but as nurses they knew it was advice they would be wise to accept, although it was hard hearing all the merriment going on outside and wanting so much to join in.

If there was great euphoria that day, it soared to new heights the day after, when some trucks arrived carrying vegetables, powdered milk and butter, among other food items. There were dozens of towels, wash basins, mosquito nets and cotton that could be torn up and made into bedsheets and even clothing. More importantly, passed down from the vehicle came box after box of medical supplies, including bandages, serums and vitamin tablets – essentials that had been cruelly kept from them throughout their captivity. These life-saving items and food withheld from Red Cross parcels were rushed straight over to the hospital.

There was some cause for added laughter when the Japanese guards tried to order one last *tenko*, but for the first time in three-and-a-half years everyone simply ignored them and went about their celebrations. The guards, bewildered, gave up and wandered off.

As well as the food, medical supplies and clothing, there were cries of joy when lipsticks were handed out – one between two women – along with small bottles of scent and Chinese hair oil. All too soon, grinning women were rushing about with red lips, laughing and experiencing a sense of female normality they hadn't felt in a long time.

Food and other supplies such as soap, tins of Australian butter and cigarettes kept pouring into the camp. While they had to be very cautious about over-indulging in all this rich food, Betty and her bed neighbour, Sister Eileen ('Shortie') Short, opened and shared a tin of butter – the first they had tasted in three-and-a-half years – which they each spooned onto a *koekje* (a small sweet biscuit). As they slowly consumed the treat, they thought they were in heaven. It was just such a good feeling, Betty explained, not to be ravenously hungry every day.

All this time the camp gates were open and people were free to come and go as they pleased. 'The only trouble was,' Betty stated, 'being in the middle of an overgrown rubber plantation, there was nowhere to go. In any case we were not going to miss being found by the "Americanos" or the English!'

While recuperating in the camp hospital, Betty was busy making notes in her diary, most of them reflecting on the fact that they would soon be heading home, perhaps within a few weeks, and this coming Christmas would be the one they had prayed for over so many years. She even heard that a Dutch doctor had performed a successful operation in a nearby house, aided by two Australian nurses – something that would not have been permitted a few days back.

Good news followed good news. Betty was told, much to her glee, that soon after Siki's announcement, one of the most hated guards named Amana had persisted in his attempts to subdue the women by ordering everyone to line up for *tenko*. He was not only ignored, but derisive comments and gestures were thrown his way, which infuriated the little man, who screamed and threatened those laughing at him. His actions were reported to one of his superior officers, and Amana was made to stand in the compound while the officer berated and humiliated him, much to everyone's delight.

On 27 August, three days after Siki's speech, Betty recorded more good news when a large group of mainly Dutch male civilian prisoners began strolling through the gates and into the women's camp, completely ignoring Siki and his bewildered guards, who simply shuffled back and allowed them to pass. The men's camp was located on the same rubber estate a mile or two down the road and they had been naturally anxious to be reunited with their wives and children. There were very few British men, but the nurses enjoyed talking with them and catching up on their news.

These men insisted on taking over all the exhausting manual and domestic chores that the women had carried out for all those years. Within hours, they had formed into working groups, fetching water and cutting down trees near the kitchen for firewood, rather than the women having to carry it for some distance back to the camp. They also scouted around for any decent food and located some carrots, which greatly supplemented the otherwise bland rice diet.

The men then ventured out with guns liberated from the Japanese, shooting deer and wild pigs, allowing the women and some of the Dutchmen to conjure up a hearty and plentiful thick stew. In the hospital, a special liver soup had been prepared for the patients, which Betty declared 'superb'. They were also treated to fresh papaya, plucked from trees just outside the camp. It tasted like heaven.

While there was frustration as they waited to be located by liberating forces, the camp's inhabitants were still in party mode. On the last day of August, the Dutch were celebrating Queen Wilhelmina's birthday, while the nurses added Sister Pat Gunther's birthday to the festivities. To mark the occasion, some local Sumatrans killed a bullock and presented it to the camp. The men cut the animal up and cooked it, with everyone sharing in their first real taste of beef in ages; something Betty said they were finally able to chew on and thoroughly enjoy after years of nothing but rice, rice and more rice. Three days later, she was well enough to leave the hospital and participate in camp life once again.

Withheld stocks of food, clothing and other essentials continued to arrive in the camp, particularly medicines they had continually asked for but were always denied. By the time the camp was liberated, 237 women and children had died needlessly, including the eight Australian nurses.

On 7 September, some more clothing arrived – mostly Japanese military shirts and shorts, which fitted just fine. The best issue, however, was a large supply of boots, some of which were black army issue and the rest were solid leather and hobnailed. They were heavy and certainly inelegant, but the women didn't care, as they were perfect for navigating the muddy ground in and around the camp.

Later that day came a long-anticipated moment for everyone. Betty's narrative continued:

After two weeks of camp freedom we were found by two young Dutch soldiers and a Chinese military man – advance guard of the Army of Occupation. It was these two young Dutch men who made the Japanese guards open up their store houses and bring *all* the contents to the men's and women's camps. This consisted of food, medical supplies, cotton materials and mosquito nets – things that would have saved many lives. But before we were actually rescued from the camp, we were still having a bad time in the hospital where people were dying each day. Help had come too late for them.

While this was going on, desperate efforts were being made to locate and liberate all the Japanese camps, known and unknown, in the region. One of the principals in this operation was Major Gideon Jacobs of the Royal Marines, who would later write a book, *Prelude to the Monsoon*, in which he revealed that while interviewing some Japanese commanders they only named some camps, but Jacobs knew from intelligence previously gathered that they were not being completely truthful. Eventually they admitted they had been mistaken and there were indeed other prison camps.

One of these was the camp at Loebok Linggau. In his book, Jacobs said he drove to the camp, and even at first look he saw it was in what he described as a 'deplorable condition'. After touring the camp and talking to many of the prisoners, including the nurses, he sent an urgent message to Intelligence Headquarters of the South-East Asia Command in Colombo, Ceylon, which read:

Have encountered among 250 repeat 250 British female internees in Loebok Linggau camp Sister Nesta James and 23 other surviving members of the Australian Army Nursing Services remnants of contingent AANS evacuated from Malaya in Vyner Brooke stop In view of their precarious health suggest you endeavour arrange air transport direct to Australia from here soonest stop Am collecting particulars massacre of members AANS on Bangka Island for later transmission.

As Betty wrote in her diary on 11 September, there were 'cheers and more cheers':

We have been discovered by two young Australian paratroops who visited our camp today and came straight past everybody until they landed on the doorstep of our Hut 13. Viv, who is usually unmoved and very quiet, came rushing in, face positively crimson, and panted, 'Australians are here!' They were about five yards behind her. To see that rising sun badge on a beret again! It did us more good than anything we have experienced so far.

The two youthful-looking soldiers were made to sit down as the nurses eagerly surrounded these men from home, peppering them with questions about things back in Australia: who was our prime minister; had the Japanese managed to reach Australian shores; what were the latest songs; who had won the Melbourne Cup the past three years, and the results of the Aussie Rules football finals. There were also questions about whether Winston Churchill and the royal family were safe.

The men were able to answer these and other questions quite easily, but most interest was centred on just how the war against Japan had ended, and if they were fully defeated. It was then that they learned about massive bombs that had been dropped on two major Japanese cities, instantly killing tens of thousands of people and leading to a complete and unconditional surrender.

JAPAN CAPITULATES!

Betty's account continues:

About three weeks after we had been told of the end of the war, we were rescued from the camp late one night. We were all asleep when Mrs [Gertrude] Hinch, our Camp Commandant, quietly called to Sister [Nesta] James and told her that we were to be ready to leave at 4 am as we were to be flown to Singapore! This was news we had waited three and a half years to hear!

The air was electric. We were all off our sleeping bench and wide awake in a minute. A supper party was organised, we gave away all our newly acquired food and belongings, then made our farewells to our friends of three-and-a-half years.

At 10 pm, Sister James was told she was *wanted on the phone*! Nobody had seen or heard a telephone since leaving Singapore in February 1942. However, she was taken to the guard house where she spoke with Flying Officer [Ken] Brown of the RAAF. He told her of arrangements he and an Australian War Correspondent, Mr Hayden Lennard, had made to get us to the aerodrome at Lahat, about 100 miles away. We were to be driven in trucks to a railway station then travel by train to Lahat.

Hayden Lennard, a journalist and senior Far East war correspondent with the Australian Broadcasting Commission (as well as the BBC), was another of those who had been instrumental in locating the Loebok Linggau camp and its internees. Following the Japanese surrender on 15 August, he had begun searching for the 65 missing nurses, flying into the area with two airmen, Squadron Leader Fred Madsen, DFC, and Flying Officer Ken Brown, both of the RAAF. They finally found the camp on 14 September by flying into the tiny Lahat airfield and following a number of leads from local villagers.

Ken Brown later stated that, although he didn't visit the nurses' barracks,

> the smell of the camp area was an indication of the conditions under which they had to live. I also met the Camp Commandant who had been master and I have never set eyes on a more ruthless man. Needless to say we were the most welcome guests these poor souls had seen for many a day and they did not fail to show it.

Hayden Lennard reported that he was shocked when he learned how few of the nurses had survived, believing beforehand that the Japanese would have respected who they were and taken good care of them. When the surviving nurses were ready to leave the camp, Lennard and Brown escorted them in the train to Lahat, from where they would be flown back to Singapore. They had already organised for the train to be fitted with mattresses, sheets, pillows and blankets for the four-hour journey.

Following a tearful farewell dinner, the Dutch nuns serenaded the nurses with some songs, and the nurses reciprocated before the Dutch women began to pack up, ready to leave the camp for ever and heading home. In anticipation of doing likewise – without the enticement of going home – Betty and the stronger nurses began tidying up their hut and giving away to the local villagers anything they could not take with them – including all their remaining food and items of clothing.

The one regret Betty had was that she had been busy with Jean Ashton making a cotton dress and, after many hours using a rusty needle and drawn threads for cotton, it was almost ready to wear. But they were told they would be restricted in what they could take with them, so with great reluctance she gave it away as well. To the men in the nearby camp they gave all their remaining Japanese shirts, shorts and boots, which they could in turn trade with the local people for needed items until they were also evacuated.

Betty's narrative continues as they walked out through the open gates, leaving the hell camp and memories both good and terrible behind them:

> We dressed in our tattered old army uniform dresses we had saved all through the prison camp years to wear home if and when we were rescued and left the camp in pouring rain on a pitch dark night. We arrived at the station after a ghastly ride in the open trucks as the sun came up.

Hayden Lennard and Ken Brown were delighted to see that the nurses, for the most part, were travelling on the first leg of their journey home wearing their nurse's uniforms, even though some outfits were quite tatty and frankly malodorous. But it was more their physical appearance that Lennard would later recall:

> Some were suffering badly from beri-beri. Their knees and legs were hopelessly swollen (a sure sign of beri-beri), and all they could do was shuffle towards the carriages. Their bloated knees just wouldn't move and if they did make an effort to walk normally the pain from beri-beri would be intense. Some were little more than skeletons. One had lost six stone in weight. Their skin was yellow. Yet their determination to get onto the train without help was silently evident,

or, so I felt – they smiled at me in appreciation . . . You started to go forward to help them . . . and suddenly stopped. You felt that even that small assistance might be resented . . . that they could manage. Hadn't they done so for four years . . . in a filthy Jap POW camp?

The train that would transport them to Lahat was waiting at the platform. To the annoyance of the nurses and a number of British prisoners, they boarded the train expecting it to depart as soon as everyone was aboard and accounted for. However the Indonesian train driver just sat still, refusing to fire up the engine despite everyone's shouted protests. The British men remonstrated with him, using signals and train noises to indicate they wanted to be under way. It was later explained that the man had been driving the train to Lahat for many years and he never left the station on his regular run before 8 am. Even though this was far from a regular service, he simply refused to move. Finally he consulted his watch and was satisfied it was the scheduled departure time and the train pulled out of the station to a chorus of cheers and whistles. When it finally arrived at Lahat station around noon, everyone disembarked, ready for the next phase of their rescue:

From there we were again transported in trucks to a tiny unused aerodrome where we waited for what seemed hours (and many false alarms) for our plane to arrive. We sat in the shade of an old shed or by bushes wondering if that plane would ever appear.

I can distinctly see it now – 25 years later. It was about 4 pm. I was lying on the ground in the shade of the shed and watching the clear blue sky. For ages I did this, then at last I saw what looked like a splinter just above the horizon – it got larger so I yelled 'Here it is!'

We all came alive again and stood up in a pathetic little group and waved as it got nearer and nearer. It *was* an aeroplane and it was *our* aeroplane. It circled to have a good look at the tiny airfield, then came in and made a perfect landing. What a relief! The field could have been mined.

The engines stopped, there was complete silence, nobody spoke, and we just stared in silence. Then a door opened and out stepped two women who smiled and waved to us. This was completely unexpected; who were they? Both were dressed in the same good old army grey we knew so well and were then wearing – not skirts as before, but *slacks*! This was a new thing but it made us feel shabbier than ever in our patched-up old grey dresses. As they came closer we knew it must be [Colonel] Matron Sage, our Matron-in-Chief, followed by Sister [Jean] Floyd, one of our 2/10 AGH nurses who had miraculously made it home from Singapore in March 1942 with another group of nurses.

This was an incredible sight; we could hardly believe our eyes. We tried to hurry forward to greet them but our legs wouldn't carry us; we seemed to be stuck to the spot. Matron Sage tried to smile as she came closer, but she couldn't; she suddenly became distressed just looking at us, her mouth and chin were working away and she could not speak. It was a dramatic moment, like a tableau, nobody moving or speaking for a minute.

Suddenly, we all started talking and laughing together, with Matron trying to talk with each one of us at once. She kept saying, 'I am the mother of you all' – and we liked it.

'Where are all the others?' she asked. Poor Sister James, we let her do the talking.

'This is all,' she said simply. 'There are 24 of us.'

The rescue team had arrived aboard a Dakota C-47 aircraft hoping to locate all 65 missing nurses, and they too were shocked to discover that nearly two-thirds of that number had died – most while in Japanese hands – and would never return home. Accompanying Colonel Sage on the rescue flight was an Australian Army doctor, Major Harry Windsor (who years later would perform Australia's first heart transplant), and (as mentioned by Betty) Sister Jean Floyd, originally from the 2/10th AGH and later the 2/13th. Sister Floyd had managed to safely evacuate in time from Singapore aboard the *Empire Star*.

When he heard of the Japanese atrocities inflicted on the nurses, the way they had been so brutally treated over the years and the inexcusable death toll, Major Windsor would later recommend – officially – that any of the Japanese found to be involved 'be forthwith slowly and painfully butchered'.

Betty's account continues:

About 30 other people – all British – had been brought out of the camp with us to Lahat for repatriation to Singapore in our plane, but as it was only a small one, the pilot suggested he take the 24 Australian nurses on this trip to Singapore and return for the second group the next morning. This group of people were not at the aerodrome with us but had been taken to a large building or hall for the time being.

Our wonderful Matron, who told us that she would not have returned to Australia without finding us and taking us home, then did a great thing. The place was still full of Japanese everywhere, but she and Sister Floyd arranged to stay there in Lahat for the night to look after the British group, many of whom were sick, saying she would fly to Singapore next day on the second plane trip. Nobody but us would ever realise what a risky and brave action this was. We hated waving goodbye to her and flying off in *her* aeroplane, but this we did – still in a daze and not believing any part of it.

In a letter sent from Singapore to her parents in Longreach, Queensland, which was published in the *Longreach Leader* newspaper on 13 October 1945, Sister Beryl Chandler of the RAAF Nursing Service gave a description of the rescue of the Australian nurses who had been held prisoner by the Japanese. In her letter she wrote:

I have just finished the most epic of all flights I have ever made. You have undoubtedly heard I played a small part in the rescue of the Australian Army nurses who were interned in Sumatra. It is a very long, sad, story, and I can't take time to tell you all.

When we ([Hayden Lennard], ABC radio reporter; Major Windsor, an AIF doctor and our air crew) left Singapore for Palembang, in Sumatra, we had one aim fixed in our minds – the finding and rescue of these girls who were last heard of at Palembang over three years ago. We had been told before leaving here that they had been moved from that area, but nobody knew where they had been sent. There was only one thing to do, and that was to find out.

We had been told that the Japanese at Palembang were still armed, and did not know what sort of a reception we would get. Also, we did not know if we could land our plane when we did get there, as it was thought generally the airstrip was unfit to land on. Once again there was only one thing to do: find out. So, with our very small party on board, and some medical equipment we set off for Palembang. We arrived there after two hours' flying. Our arrival and stay in Palembang and our efforts to locate our nurses will take too long to write, so I'll miss that, and continue with a little more of the actual rescue.

Our co-pilot and [Hayden Lennard] set out by truck with some Japanese from Palembang to drive to Schat, about 200 miles away, to see if they were there, and to check up on an old Japanese airstrip as to its serviceability for landing our Douglas. They went from Schat to Kublick Tunga, another 50 miles, before ultimately finding the nurses. They helped to get them ready, and Ken Brown, the co-pilot, with his knowledge of airstrips, knew we could make it.

In the meantime, back at Palembang, I had visited a prisoner of war camp and several hospitals. And arranged for 30 very sick prisoners to be taken back to Singapore. The pilot took off without his co-pilot – quite an effort in a Douglas transport – and left me behind with Major Windsor in Palembang. While Major visited the prisoners of war and hospitals, I endeavoured to find out from the Japanese the condition of the airstrip at Schat. After sitting up and waiting nearly all night, word came through that the airstrip was considered dangerous, but we might be able to get in. They also said there were several Australian civilians there, approximately 26, who may be nurses. That was enough for us.

Next day, Fred [Madsen], our pilot, arrived back at Palembang with Miss Sage, the matron-in-chief of the Australian Army Nursing Service, and another AIF sister. Fred still had to fly on his own. On arrival at Palembang the aircraft developed a flat tyre, and it took the Japs considerable time to fix it. However, that was managed, and at three o'clock in the afternoon we set off for Schat, hoping that we could land OK, and that the two boys had discovered the nurses and got them down to the strip. We arrived at Schat 45 minutes after leaving Palembang. Fred made an excellent landing and there they were, 24 of them; all terribly sick and tired, but waiting with smiles and laughter for us. Five of the girls I had trained with at the Brisbane General. They knew I was coming for them, because I gave Hayden a letter for them. There were seven, but two had died. We hugged and kissed and talked about the silliest things.

Our arrival in Singapore is indescribable. Batteries of photographers and news reporters were everywhere. This was really news. There are a hundred and one interesting stories attached to this flight which I will have to tell you when I see you.

On Monday, 17 September, the aircraft containing the 24 nurses touched down at Singapore's Kallang airfield. Applause and cheers rang out within the cabin as they made ready to disembark. It did not matter one bit that the uniforms some wore were in a threadbare condition, with obvious signs they had been repaired. Others were wearing straw hats, and simple native slippers on their feet. Once the engines had been silenced and the door opened, helpers were immediately on hand to assist the still-frail nurses down the steep steps and onto the tarmac, where they hugged each other, crying tears of joy and laughing at the same time. They were finally free.

A small squad of Red Cross workers gently walked the nurses to the field's canteen, where they had organised cups of tea. Many of the nurses would ask for more than one refill of the much-missed beverage, especially with the added luxury of milk and sugar. It was the perfect welcome back to civilisation.

Following their reception and tea service at Kallang airfield, the nurses were escorted to a number of ambulances, which carried them straight to the familiar St Patrick's College, now administered by the 2/14th AGH. The AIF patients already being tended in the hospital were told that a group of nurses would be arriving and that they had been prisoners of the Japanese for more than three years. As the nurses shuffled up the stairs and were being assisted into the hospital by orderlies, it was reported that the Australian soldiers were both shocked and infuriated when they saw the gaunt, skeletal appearance of the nurses and became hysterical with rage, jumping from their beds and shouting, 'Give us guns. Let us out and get at those dirty bastards!'

10

HOMEWARD BOUND

IT WAS THE MORNING OF 4 October 1945 as the great orange disc of the sun stole into a streaky sky over a war-shattered Singapore. For the first time in three-and-a-half years the freed nurses had been sleeping between sheets on real beds in the 2/14th Australian General Hospital, which had been set up in the familiar surroundings of St Patrick's College to assist in the repatriation of Australian prisoners of war.

On their arrival in Singapore in mid-September, the hospital's Commanding Officer, Colonel William Langford, was apologetic but had been unable to tell them when they would be leaving for Australia. He did tell representatives of the Australian press, 'In a week you won't know them. In a fortnight or three weeks they should all be pretty fit.' It was an overly optimistic forecast; apart from malnutrition, many of those rescued were extremely ill and even close to death, while others had debilitating diseases such as malaria and scabies, on top of poorly treated injuries that would affect them for the rest of their lives.

As Sister Flo Trotter recalled,

We were all so tired and were longing for a bath and bed. When we arrived in Singapore, however, cameras and reporters took precedence. Red Cross helpers from England and Australia were there to greet us with cups of tea and biscuits. All [of us] felt so dirty, shabby and untidy. The Red Cross people were wonderful and helped us with our few miserable belongings. Soon we were in the hospital surrounded by the familiar faces of nurses we knew so well.

As the still-overwhelmed nurses arrived at the hospital, a reporter from the Brisbane *Telegraph* stopped Betty and said, 'Well, you are free!' Her reaction was to laugh gaily and wave her hands around. 'Free!' she exclaimed. 'I have been free for three weeks. I am free forever!' She then proceeded to tell the reporter how thrilling it was to realise that they were really alive again, with friends and the prospect of home and health and the 'good old way' of living.

Apart from this clamorous welcome, the nurses were given a warm and sympathetic greeting by the doctors and nursing staff. They were escorted to rooms decorated with flowers and offered the luxury of a warm bath before the still-bewildered nurses were assisted to bed. 'We bathed and put on the very pretty nighties these girls had given us,' Sister Trotter continued. 'When we finally got into bed we hardly slept a wink all night because it was too comfortable!' In fact many of them climbed out of bed and opted to sleep on the hard floor.

While they were understandably keen to go home, they were still nurses and understood that many of them remained in precarious health. Any voyage home, however appealing, would have to be delayed until their physical condition had improved. They were well looked after in a private ward in the hospital, had small, high-protein meals at regular times, were given vitamin tablets, physiotherapy on their wasted muscles and received priority dental treatment.

It was all like a dream, as Betty recalled:

The next day Matron Sage arrived at the hospital in Singapore where we greeted her properly. This time we were clean and wearing clean pyjamas and sitting up in large white beds. She was indeed like a mother to us all. She brought us up to date with as much news as she could, telling us a little more each day until she had to leave Singapore for home.

The good matron had also instigated one of the greatest morale boosters for the nurses. As early as the previous year, she had begun preparing for the hopeful return, recovery and rehabilitation of the missing Australian nurses and she was now able to provide each of them with one of the greatest aids to their well-being when they were presented with a collection of cosmetics. Their glee was infectious and they were soon putting on lipstick and other make-up essentials and preening themselves in hand-held mirrors. Now they were *really* ready to go home!

Over the next few days, their meals slowly increased in content following the starvation diet of the past few years, allowing their stomachs to slowly become used to unfamiliar quantities and the richness of this sudden intake of food. Soon they were waking up to a breakfast consisting of small portions of porridge, sausages, duck eggs, toast and coffee. *Real* coffee.

While spending most of their day in bed, several took the opportunity to discuss recipes many of them had exchanged and managed to jot down in the camps, hoping to be able to try them out one day. Sylvia Muir said she had collected around 500 recipes, and Flo Trotter stated that 'The hungrier we got, the more we talked recipes.' Betty had written a long list of suggestions for breakfast, lunch and dinner in one of her diaries, headed in bold red ink with the notation: 'What I want Millie [her mother] to make for me in case I forget.'

Three weeks after arriving in Singapore, on Thursday, 4 October, many of the nurses woke early filled with excitement over what the day would bring. Despite skies which threatened an afternoon thunderstorm, they knew their long and brutal ordeal of suffering over the past three years was coming to an end. Tomorrow, they would be boarding the Adelaide Steamship Company's white-painted motor vessel *Manunda* on the first leg of their journey home, with Fremantle the first Australian port of call. There was packing to do.

When news of the nurses embarking on *Manunda* for the voyage became known, there was an immediate surge of interest from civilians who suddenly found they had business to attend to in Australia. However, the authorities were unrelenting, stating that the ship would carry only sick or convalescing patients and some former prisoners, including the nurses – no one else.

The past three weeks had been joyous, even though five of the nurses were so weak they would remain in hospital. The rest were in good spirits, strolling around the less-ruined parts of Singapore, doing a little shopping, and buying up Chinese silks of all descriptions, although for safety reasons they had been restricted to daytime activities only.

On Monday, 1 October, they travelled to Changi, where a POW Reception Centre had been established at the former residence of Japanese Major-General Masatoshi Saito. Lady Mountbatten dropped by for a chat and they were entertained with a concert exclusively staged for liberated Australian prisoners by the highly popular English singer and comedian Gracie Fields and her husband Monty Banks, the debonair Italian-born comedian and actor. The nurses were delighted to be part of the audience, and their applause was long and heartfelt. According to Betty, 'She was wonderful and had us all in fits of laughter. We loved listening to her pianist, too; we haven't heard a piano played like that for years.'

The next day, 2 October, they held a party for the nurses to thank all those who had aided their recovery. The hospital's medical staff and nursing sisters were invited, as well as the special guests of honour, Squadron Leader Fred Madsen, DFC, of the RAAF and the crew of his Dakota aircraft who had brought the sisters out two weeks earlier, and Sister Beryl Chandler, the flying nurse from Longreach with the RAAFNS, who had accompanied Madsen on the reconnaissance flight during which they managed to locate the prison camp at Loebok Linggau.

Named after an Aboriginal word for 'a place near water', the twin-screw, diesel-powered 430-foot MV *Manunda* arrived in Singapore harbour the following day from Labuan Island carrying 428 British ex-POWs and civilian internees. Once docked, it was being repaired and provisioned for the expected two-week journey to Australia. Commissioned and converted as a hospital ship in July 1940, it was under the command of Captain James Garden.

On 19 February 1942, *Manunda* had been severely damaged while berthed in Darwin harbour, which had suffered an unexpected attack carried out in two deadly waves by around 240 dive bombers and Zero fighters of the Imperial Japanese Navy, launched from four aircraft carriers. Despite displaying very distinctive Red Cross markings, bombs rained down on the defenceless ship. Eight of the 47 ships at berth there that day, including the American destroyer USS *Peary*, had been sunk, with another beached.

In the aftermath of the attack it was found that twelve of those on *Manunda* had been killed. One of the nurses on board, 26-year-old Sister Margaret Auguste De Mestre from Bellingen, New South Wales, had received shrapnel wounds to her back and abdomen and died during the second attack. She was the first AIF nurse ever to be killed in action within Australia. Another 18 people on board were seriously wounded, with around 40 others sustaining minor wounds. The ship itself had been badly damaged by bombs and shells, while a fierce blaze caused extensive damage to the medical and nursing staff quarters. Despite this, the ship served as a casualty clearing station for the injured transferred from other ships.

Fortunately the ship's engines still operated – albeit minimally. In case of further attacks and carrying as many of the injured as possible, *Manunda* limped out of Darwin harbour, heading for Fremantle. The journey took eight days under the most trying of circumstances, and would result in Captain Garden being awarded an OBE for his sustained seamanship in delivering the crippled ship, its crew, hospital staff and the injured safely to port.

Adding to the excitement felt by the nurses as they waited to board their 'freedom ship' was the news that dozens of new uniforms had been supplied for their use. Happy cries filled the air as they eagerly picked out the items that would come closest to fitting their gaunt bodies. Forgotten for the time being was the fact they were now so close to going home; for now the familiar uniforms had their full attention.

As Betty recalled, 'At the moment we are flat out trying on borrowed grey safari jackets and slacks, army shoes and hats.' They quickly realised how heavy and constricting these clothes felt. 'We feel as if we have an awful lot of clothes on after wearing shorts and sun-tops for so long,' she added, having taken great delight in seeing the familiar army grey once again, 'but *slacks* in place of skirts!' They would soon realise that many things had changed during their absence.

Prior to leaving Singapore on Friday, 5 October, 394 Australians – former prisoners of the Japanese including the 24 nurses – eagerly embarked on the good ship *Manunda*. The numbers bound for each state were eight soldiers and two nurses from Western Australia; 19 soldiers and two nurses from South Australia; 98 soldiers and five nurses from Victoria; 52 soldiers and one nurse from Tasmania; 141 soldiers and five nurses from New South Wales; and 52 soldiers and nine nurses from Queensland. They were on board and ready to go, but it would be three frustrating days before the ship was fully prepared to set off on the journey home.

Although everyone was anxious to get under way, there was some compensation, as Betty stated: 'All the things we have been wanting for so long we had in the first two days on board – lamb's fry, steak, Irish stew, oxtail, fresh apples.' They had to exercise a degree of caution, however, as their shrunken stomachs were still not used to the unlimited quantity or richness of such food.

On 8 October, *Manunda* slowly eased out of Singapore harbour. Most of those able to do so lined the deck railings, not just to farewell the island nation but also to offer a silent prayer for those brave colleagues and friends they had left behind, who would never have this chance to return home to their loved ones. Two days later, the ship was carefully guided through the dangerous, mined Malacca Straits by Japanese Navy escort vessels as far as the north-west tip of Sumatra at Aceh. Having successfully negotiated their path through the mined waters, the escort ships peeled away, the *Manunda* cruised into the Indian Ocean and Captain Garden set a course south, bound for Fremantle, a little over two weeks away if all went well and if the faulty engine continued to operate.

On Thursday, 18 October, the excitement on board *Manunda* was palpable, and that afternoon, around 3 pm, hundreds on board lined the deck railings, eyes glued to the horizon. Loud cries began to erupt, 'There it is! Land ho!' Soon everyone could make out a sliver of land on the port side of the ship. Fingers pointed, there was a happy babble of voices and not a few tears as *Manunda* slowly turned towards Fremantle harbour.

As Betty recorded in *White Coolies*, their initial excitement soon gave way to a near eerie silence as they all watched Fremantle drawing closer, with anticipation in their hearts. Betty knew that only two of the 24 nurses would be leaving them here: Ada Syer and Iole Harper, both of whom had shared so many experiences with her over the past three-and-a-half years. Iole especially had become a dear friend throughout their many ordeals. 'You will be home tonight,' Betty managed to say to Iole. 'How does it feel?' Iole was caught unawares, still feeling like she was living a dream, and her mind was elsewhere. 'I wonder if my family will be on the wharf,' was her vague response.

It was just on six o'clock as *Manunda* gently moved into its berth at Fremantle and, as the ropes were secured to bollards on the wharf, laughter broke out when the dinner gong sounded. There would be little appetite for a meal at that time. Sister Pat Darling would later comment, 'Arriving at Fremantle in the mid-afternoon of 18th October, we were confronted with a transport drivers' strike, so we knew we were in Australia!'

The Western Command Band struck up the popular tune 'Nursie'. This acted as a musical cue for the excited, cheering crowd to surge forward through the barriers, crying out to those they recognised lining the deck, mingled with shouts of 'Coo-ee!' Hundreds of servicemen dressed in khaki uniforms or hospital blues waved and shouted back, but in their midst stood the nurses, easily distinguishable in their brand-new tropical uniform of grey army tunic and slacks. Standing on the wharf, also waving, was a beaming Colonel Annie Sage.

As Betty later wrote, the sight of Colonel Sage waiting there to greet them filled her with renewed emotion and gratitude for all this remarkable woman had done for them:

> There were hundreds of Perth people waiting on the wharf cheering
> and waving, excitement everywhere, and in the middle of this crowd
> was our wonderful Matron-in-Chief, Colonel Sage – waving away
> to us. She had arranged to bring us back to Australia and home.
> We will never cease to thank her.

Iole Harper's parents were indeed on the wharf, waiting patiently for a glimpse of their daughter. Tears filled their eyes when they saw her waving back to them. As Betty recalled, Iole then rushed downstairs to her cabin and started to pack again. 'I might add she had been packing all day!'

According to the *West Australian* newspaper the following day, the honour of being first aboard *Manunda* went to the small red-headed son of one of the returning servicemen, who was passed up to his father by a sailor. The first official to proceed up the gangway was the GOC (General Officer Commanding) Western Command, Major-General Allan J. Boase, followed by Matron Colonel Sage, and then the Principal Matron in Western Australia, Lieutenant-Colonel Eileen V. Joubert. Next to board was an eager contingent of Red Cross workers, their arms laden with baskets of sweet-scented flowers and fruit for the nurses and comfort items for the men. When Sister Flo Trotter of the 2/10th AGH was asked what it was like coming home, the Queenslander replied, 'It is like a dream, being in Australia at last. Even on the trip home we expected to wake up and find ourselves back in Sumatra.'

Eventually it was time to disembark, and as the group of nurses made their way down the gangway they were treated to an even more tumultuous round of hearty cheers. As each nurse set foot on the wharf she turned and waved to the crowd. Some had a huge smile of joy on their face, while tears of pure joy filled the eyes of many. The only 'casualty' noted by the press that day was Sister Joyce Tweddell, who had her arm in a sling after falling down the ship's companionway the previous day, injuring her wrist. Iole Harper rushed into the arms of her family, hugged them tightly, then slipped her arm through her mother's and would not let her go. She was truly home again.

There was still a medical formality to be conducted. Once the nurses and freed servicemen could be extricated from the welcoming crowd, they were transported to the Hollywood Military Hospital in Perth, where most would spend the night. Once there, they received another overwhelming reception, underwent a brief medical examination and were presented with more brand-new uniforms.

As Betty recalled of that evening, the reception rooms were filled to overflowing with flowers. 'Flowers were everywhere, even on the ceilings; such arrangement of flowers we had never seen before, mostly, red, white, and blue. Apparently they had broadcast [on radio] for flowers and they came from every garden in Perth and kept on coming.' One special addition to the floral arrangements was a posy from the garden of Sister Peggy Farmaner (2/4th CCS), one of those killed by the Japanese on Radji Beach. The flowers were delivered to the hospital by her mother.

Another feature of their arrival home was having to respond to the eager questions of newspaper reporters. To Betty's relief, she was 'just another' of the returned nurses and was not singled out for any particular reason. In fact the majority of the questions were directed to Vivian Bullwinkel, as the reporters had come armed with information concerning the massacre of the nurses on Banka Island and were anxious to hear her account as the sole survivor of the brutal shooting.

That night, Betty was invited to the home of Iole and her family, where one of her favourite recollections was enjoying a long, languid hot bath in a real bathroom. 'The baths on the ship were cold salt-water ones, so this was the real thing at last,' she later commented.

The following day Betty was back on board *Manunda* for the final leg of the journey home to Melbourne. She remembered some of her Sydney friends joking with her as they left Fremantle, betting that it would be raining in the southern capital when they got there. And it was!

On the evening of 24 October 1945, *Manunda* slipped into Melbourne at 6 pm. As a final, closing reflection in her best-selling 1954 book, *White Coolies*, Betty wrote wryly of the weather on arrival, saying that, 'it is wet and cold, visibility nil; my Sydney friends are grinning all over their faces. They expected it . . . Well, here it is, and I'm proud of it.' Her book might have ended on that humorous note, but a whole new chapter of devotion would soon blossom for Agnes Betty Jeffrey.

On arrival in Port Melbourne the remaining 22 nurses disembarked, along with 188 servicemen – the recovered prisoners of war. As everyone waited for *Manunda* to dock, they could hardly believe that so many people had turned out to welcome the big white ship and heartily cheer its passengers, but they were doing so with persistent rain spattering their faces. Lady Dugan, wife of the Governor of Victoria, Sir Winston Dugan, was standing on the pier sheltering beneath an umbrella, waving at the nurses on board as she stood next to recently arrived Colonel Annie Sage, as well as the Principal Matron for Victoria, Lieutenant-Colonel Edith Shaw, and the Deputy Director of Medical Services, Major-General Sir Samuel Burston. A band had assembled on the pier, and they were playing the melancholic Great War tribute song to nurses, 'The Rose of No Man's Land'.

As reported by Melbourne's *Age* newspaper the following day:

When the ship berthed Lady Dugan went on board and chatted with the girls, each of whom was presented with a bouquet and a shoulder spray. The sisters passed through a guard of honour of

cheering members of the AANS and were rushed by five members of
the same unit who were in Malaya with them but who had escaped.

While crowds of people lined the pier, continuing to cheer and
applaud, the nurses boarded two buses – one from the Heidelberg
No. 115 Military Hospital and the other from the Women's Officers'
Club – as the first vehicles in a procession of buses carrying the
former prisoners of the Japanese to Heidelberg Repatriation Hospital
for an official reception. Altogether there were 188 on the buses from
Victoria, South Australia and Tasmania.

The buses made their way to the Melbourne Town Hall for a brief
ceremony of welcome conducted in the rain by the Lord Mayor,
Sir Thomas Nettlefold, before going on to Heidelberg Repatriation
Hospital. Here the nine Victorian nurses were finally able to meet
and talk with their relatives. Vivian Bullwinkel had received many
bouquets of flowers, but she was happy to hand them over on arrival;
she was far more interested in catching up with her mother, who had
travelled from Adelaide to greet her.

As each nurse entered the hospital, they were presented with yet
another box of flowers as well as a welcome-home message and a
book from Victorian members of the AANS. Later in the proceedings they were given complimentary vouchers for shops in their
various states by the sisters on the staff at the hospital. Following
another brief reception and responding to some questions posed by
news reporters, the nurses were finally able to travel by car to their
homes, courtesy of Red Cross volunteer drivers.

Somewhat ironically, the hospital ship *Manunda* would be
decommissioned and refitted a year after the war, following which
it resumed carrying passengers around Australia before being sold

to a Japanese company in 1956. The ship that had proudly carried Australian troops and nurses to and from the war was renamed *Hakone Maru* and there were plans for it to join the Okadagumi Line. However, those plans fell through and the ship was broken up and sold as scrap in Osaka in June 1957.

On 14 October 1946, a year after the nurses had returned home, fifteen Australians, all former prisoners of war, set sail for Tokyo aboard the converted passenger ship HMAS *Kanimbla*. They were to give evidence before the International War Crimes Tribunal of Japanese atrocities at Ambon, Borneo, Outram Road Gaol and Changi in Singapore, the Burma–Thailand railway and other camps in Java, Japan, Formosa, Manchuria and Malaya. Two of the fifteen were Sisters Vivian Bullwinkel and Nesta James, the latter the senior nurse in the Sumatran prison camps.

Vivian in particular would give a graphic account of the massacre of her fellow nurses on Radji Beach in February 1942. Both women had earlier given witness accounts before the Australian Board of Inquiry into War Crimes on 29 October 1945, chaired by Sir William Webb, Chief Justice of Queensland. Their testimony was so compelling that both women were asked to travel to Tokyo for the tribunal a year later, although procedural delays at the tribunal meant they did not give their evidence until December 1946.

The Japanese Captain who ordered the killings on Radji Beach would later be identified as the sadistic Captain Masaru Orita of the 229th Regiment of the 38th Japanese Division. According to Ian Shaw in his authoritative book *On Radji Beach*, Orita was captured while fighting on the Manchurian front against the Russians and held in the Soviet Union before being extradited to Tokyo, where he was placed in Sugamo prison awaiting trial as a war criminal. It was there that he committed suicide in September 1948. Others implicated in the Radji Beach killings and tried as war criminals were Sergeant Major Taro Kato and Lieutenant Masayuki Takeuchi. Kato was captured in New Guinea, while Takeuchi was identified in a POW stockade and sent to Taiping gaol in northern Malaya.

Sukero Shibayama was also detained in May 1947 and held for questioning by the Australian war crimes unit. He was the paymaster for the Japanese unit that committed the massacre on Radji Beach. It was not known at the time if he could be directly implicated in the killings, but if not then it was felt that he could indicate which individuals were responsible and their whereabouts. Any punishment meted out to Kato, Takeuchi and Shibayama for their part in the beach massacre is unknown.

11

BACK HOME AGAIN

FOR BETTY JEFFREY, DESPITE HER recurring illness and greatly weakened condition, the return to her home, family and friends was a tonic above all others – an occasion for tremendous joy, reunion and reflection. As reported by the Melbourne *Herald* on 25 October 1945,

> Last night, the Jeffrey family in Ailsa Avenue, East Malvern, listened to her until 1.30 am. Then they lifted the dozens of presents from her bed, and she fell into it. The house today looks as if all their Christmases had come at once. There are hundreds of telegrams, letters, presents, and flowers in all the rooms.

She may have been thrilled to be home again, but those three-and-a-half years in a Sumatran hell had taken a severe toll on Betty's health. Despite eating decent food once again (she told her family to never, ever give her rice in her meals), she was still quite ill, weighing just 66 pounds (30 kilograms) when she came home suffering from severe pulmonary tuberculosis. She would spend the next two years recovering in and out of Heidelberg Hospital, receiving regular injections of cortisone, but would never regain full fitness or health.

She was only just well enough to leave the hospital and celebrate her parents' golden wedding anniversary on Sunday, 8 September 1946. With their son Lieutenant Rex Jeffrey serving overseas, and Betty one of a group of AANS nurses being held in prison camps by the Japanese in Sumatra, with precious little news about her, the past few years had been quite dramatic and worrying for Will and Millie. So the celebration of 50 years of marriage surrounded by family was one of the happiest occasions they had known since the beginning of the war six years earlier.

Betty's friend Wilma Oram was 29 when she left Australia. Beyond the welcome-home cheers and family reunions, she was also puzzled at certain reactions to her years of imprisonment. 'The strange thing was a lot of people here were not interested in what we did. They wanted to talk about how they passed the war in Australia. How they had to buy things with coupons and how they didn't have enough cigarettes!'

According to Betty,

The thing that brought me back to normal life, from POW to home life, was that I was allowed to go home the first night . . . In the morning I got up and we'd all been given a gorgeous pale blue box of face make-up . . . it was marvellous. I was putting it on, well I hadn't played with cosmetics for five years. I'd put some powder on my nose and spilled a bit on the dressing table. I went straight out to the kitchen to the cupboard where Mum used to keep the dusters and there were the dusters . . . I thought that's right, I'm home. Both my parents were there, my home was there and the duster was in the right cupboard!

There were some precious souvenirs she managed to carry back with her as a reminder of those lost years she spent as a prisoner of the Japanese. Among these was a small china bowl, which Betty had found and kept soon after arriving in the 'coolie lines' at Muntok. Throughout the time she was a prisoner, she ate and drank from this precious bowl. Then there was her spoon, a heavy one made of silver, which was a thank-you gift left to her by a Dutch nurse whom she had tended for several days before the woman died.

Betty had also kept a soft doll representing the ill-tempered Japanese guard nicknamed 'Bully' that her fellow nurses had made and presented to her on her 36th birthday in May 1944.

One of her greatest treasures from that time, however, were the three blue-covered exercise books she had used as diaries, which she had secretly kept while under Japanese captivity in Sumatra. She would one day convert them into a best-selling book detailing those years of despair, defiance and deprivation in Muntok, Palembang, and Belalau (Loebok Linggau).

When Betty first began her diary, it was mostly to satisfy herself and keep a record of all that had happened to her and other people, and where they had been held. She had absolutely no idea it would ever be published; in fact, as she slowly and meticulously filled the small books' pages, she did not even know if she would ever see Australia and her family again. Her first entries were written on blank pages taken from mostly Dutch novels she had found in the first camp. The books had been left there by the residents when they were forcibly evicted by the Japanese. The looters who moved in afterwards to seize whatever they could obviously had no interest in reading, so there were plentiful numbers of books – some in English, which traded hands often – and each of them contained several blank pages.

Betty wrote in near-microscopic script in order to set out as much as possible on each page. Later she managed to acquire a small exercise book – the first of three she would 'borrow' from a Japanese hut – and placed those loose pages in the front.

I wanted to write a diary. So many things were happening to us and I thought when I get home, I'm going to forget all this, I must get it written down. Also I didn't want my brain to rust. I wanted to keep remembering how to read and write, but there was nothing to write on. I found a pencil and thought, well I'm getting started, but no paper. And on a working party one day, going through the guard-house I saw this little exercise booklet and thought that's exactly what I want. I hope it's still there when I come back in, and it was!

She noticed that the guard was distracted, talking to someone, so she seized the opportunity. 'I slipped it inside my clothing as I passed the hut, hoe in hand. I knew it was dangerous, I had to keep it hidden. Quite often for weeks on end I couldn't write anything in it.'

These days her diary notes are a treasured possession of the Australian War Memorial in Canberra, presented to them in 1954 along with her nurse's uniform and a watch she had worn throughout her ordeal, although the Japanese had made her remove the hands so she would be unable to tell the time. The tattered little collection of diary pages, with writing so small that even she had difficulty reading her words, was carried back home with her and re-examined while she was in hospital after returning to Australia. Betty recalled:

> At the end of the war when we were rescued and finally got to Singapore, they wanted to fumigate us and fumigate everything we had . . . Well, they could fumigate me and the clothes I had on, but I didn't let them fumigate my music or my diary. So my diary had finally arrived home safely and [was] eventually turned into a little book.

During the eighteen months she spent convalescing in hospital, Betty painstakingly typed out an edited version of her diary, but this was mostly for her own satisfaction. She had no plans at all to submit it for publication.

Recognition of what they had endured during the war continued. Late in December 1945, the CWO (Catholic Welfare Organisation) Younger Set held a Victory Ball at the Earl's Court ballroom in St Kilda, with a special welcome extended to six of the Sumatran nurses: Vivian Bullwinkel, Wilma Oram, Beryl Woodbridge, Ada Syer, Nesta James and Betty Jeffrey. They arrived dressed in their white uniforms and scarlet capes and entered the ballroom through an honour guard of Younger Set members, before each was presented with a bouquet of flowers. On leaving, they were also given a gift package.

Ever so gradually, with thanks to the caring staff at the Heidelberg Hospital, Betty regained her health sufficiently to be independent once again. Meanwhile, she and Vivian Bullwinkel had stayed in contact and were determined to do something to honour the memory of nurses who gave their lives in war, and especially those who never made it back home. As Vivian stated while looking back in 1991, their plans were

> . . . the result of an idea, born nearly fifty years ago in a Japanese prisoner of war camp, germinated by the wish to keep alive the memory of our young Australian nurses who were murdered on Radji Beach, Banka Island, and the endurance, tenacity, initiative and sense of humour of the nurses who later died in the prisoner of war camps and in the sinking of the hospital ship *Centaur*.

In 1988, in response to a question during an interview with Jennifer Williams, who was writing a history of the Australian Nurses Memorial Centre in Melbourne, Betty Jeffrey revealed – like Vivian – that the origin of the centre began quite simply as a conversation in the steamy jungles of wartime Sumatra. One day in 1943 – the date was not recorded in her secret diary – she was sitting outside a prison camp hut with Vivian Bullwinkel, Jean Ashton and Beryl Woodbridge, discussing ways in which to honour the nurses who had been massacred on Radji Beach. They were all determined that should they get back to Australia (all four did) they would have to do something worthwhile and lasting so those women would never be forgotten. As Williams later wrote:

> Again, as their numbers dwindled towards the end of the war, they discussed how they could commemorate the lost nurses. They didn't want a shrine. They wanted something that would live, because the nurses had not. Sixty-five of their young colleagues left Singapore, but only 24 returned to Australia after the war. They didn't know it then, but as the group talked in the camp, moves

were taking place in Melbourne which laid the foundation for their dream of a 'living' memorial to become a reality.

With the end of the war and the return of the surviving nurses, those plans were not forgotten; on the contrary, their commitment to realising the idea had grown even stronger, as Vivian outlined:

With the assistance of senior members of the nursing profession, 'the idea' began to take shape, and with the help of some great Australian men, whose support, encouragement and expertise made the project feasible, and then finally with the generous financial support of the Victorian and Riverina public, it became a reality.

One person who supported that 'idea' in Australia did so not knowing of those plans hatched in a squalid camp in Sumatra, to be carried out once – if – the originators returned. Edith Hughes-Jones was a dedicated civilian nurse who through hard work and enterprise had become Matron and owner of the 'Windermere' Private Hospital in Prahran, Victoria, in 1938. It was Edith, with her entrepreneurial and financial skills, who was responsible for the establishment of the Centaur Memorial Trust following the tragic sinking of the hospital ship *Centaur* in May 1943. She took on the role of honorary secretary of the trust that year. Her dedication to doing more in the ongoing recruitment and support of nurses was further fuelled by her earlier association with many of the nurses who died as a result of the war. To this end, when she learned that Betty Jeffrey and Vivian Bullwinkel had returned home with plans to establish a memorial centre for those lost nurses, she asked to become part of their fledgling team, and would play a significant role in the later establishment of what was then called the War Nurses Memorial Centre in St Kilda.

Edith Hughes-Jones was never one to rest on her laurels; she would also help in establishing another trust from which the Annie M. Sage Memorial Nurses' Scholarship was awarded. As well, as foundation honorary secretary (1946–75) of the Florence Nightingale Committee of Australia, she devoted several years to promoting postgraduate education for nurses. Continuing her work, Edith was one of the founders and a fellow of the College of Nursing, Australia, serving as its honorary secretary from 1950 to 1955, and president the following year. In 1957 she was awarded the OBE and later appointed president of the (Royal) Victorian College of Nursing, also becoming a member of the Victorian Nursing Council. In 1973, she set up the Windermere Hospital Foundation to provide funds for charitable organisations and nursing education. Edith Hughes-Jones, OBE, FRCNA, passed away in April 1976 after an amazing life of dedication to the nursing profession.

On 6 November 1946, the official papers 'For Termination of an Officer's Appointment' were signed, showing that Lieutenant Agnes Betty Jeffrey, VFX 53059, of the 2/10th AGH had completed her AIF service after 2038 days, of which 378 were served in Australia and 1616 on 'overseas duty'. She would never go back into active nursing.

Despite still recuperating from their shared three-and-a-half-year ordeal, Betty and Vivian Bullwinkel were not content to simply form committees and fundraise from behind an office desk. They wanted to be positioned right at the front line again, fully hands-on and resolving to do whatever it took to realise this very special dream.

To aid them in spreading the word and fundraising, they would set out on a long, state-wide crusade, utilising a wonderful gift presented to Betty for this purpose following her discharge from the Heidelberg Repatriation Hospital. It came in the form of a brand-new car donated by the Austin Motor Company. As Jennifer Williams noted, the company 'broke all the rules to have the new car ready in time for the start of the tour. They even put in the back seat. This was something in those early post-war days when the back seat was generally left out to save manufacturing costs and petrol, which was still rationed.'

With the support of their nursing colleagues Wilma Oram (later Young), Colonel Annie Sage, Edith Hughes-Jones and others, Betty and Vivian toured Victoria in that little Austin car to raise funds for the establishment of the goal they now had firmly in mind – a fully funded nurses memorial centre. To this end, despite the fact that neither of them had ever been involved in public speaking, they gave their presentations to packed audiences and visited every hospital in the state containing more than twenty beds.

As well as discussing their wartime experiences, they explained to nursing colleagues how they hoped to make their vision of a living memorial a reality – a memorial not just to remember the loss of all the fallen nurses, but to continue the ongoing recruitment and professional development of nurses through education. Of all the fundraising activities undertaken, this would prove to be the most successful appeal ever launched in Victoria at the time.

Their very first stop was Ballarat on Armistice Day, 11 November 1947, speaking at a girls' grammar school before meeting a number of dignitaries and family members of two of the Sumatra nurses – William, the father of Beth Cuthbertson (killed on Radji Beach), and the sister of surviving nurse Beryl Woodbridge. From there, over the next three days, they travelled to Ararat, then Stawell and Horsham, and took a great deal of pleasure speaking to groups of nurses and doctors.

They did make one crucial stop at the small Bush Nursing Hospital in Dimboola, home town of Matron Olive Paschke, as well as the town's Memorial High School, where her life and sacrifice is remembered by the students every year around Anzac Day. On these solemn annual occasions a school pupil tells an assembly of students the story of Matron Paschke's life. Since 1949, a memorial sundial has been situated on the school grounds, fitted with a bronze plaque inscribed to her memory.

As Betty and Vivian picked up momentum, moving from town to town, together with the support of fellow nurse Wilma Oram, people were eager to hear their story and money for the planned nurses' centre began flowing in. They were able to present their case for the centre on some local radio stations and it was not unknown for Betty and some helpers to stand outside Melbourne's Flinders Street Station encouraging people to throw any loose change into a blanket.

At the same time, Sister Vera Haughton (later a founder member of the centre), who had served as a bush nurse across Australia during the war years, was similarly touring the eastern half of Victoria, encouraging participation in a parallel fundraising venture for the proposed centre called the 'Queen' contest, a brainchild of Betty and Vivian, which entailed each hospital across the state nominating a fundraising 'Queen'. The total amount raised by each of these Queens would take into consideration the daily bed average of the hospital they represented so that all hospitals, irrespective of size, would begin the campaign on an equal footing.

What all the travelling nurses proposed to their audiences was the establishment of a memorial centre somewhere in Melbourne at an estimated cost of around a quarter of a million pounds. Once operational, this centre would provide excellent facilities for city and country and interstate nurses living away from home, even those on holiday, and by members of the profession awaiting or returning from hospitalisation. Social facilities, where nurses could entertain friends and repay hospitality extended to them, would be incorporated, and postgraduate courses could also be conducted.

They explained that a number of Australian nurses were then in England completing these courses, and on their return they would be asked to establish a similar course in the centre. This would mean that many more nurses would be able to undertake the course in their own country, significantly raising the standard of nursing in Australia.

A sizeable hall would be incorporated within the centre, which could be used by nurses doing final examinations or attending conferences, as well as offices of the various branches of the profession, at that time scattered all over Melbourne. An offer had already been made on a suitable, furnished building on St Kilda Road in hopeful anticipation of a purchase. This had provided further incentive for the launching of the appeal, as it might be several years before an alternative, purpose-built building could be constructed and opened.

As Betty and Vivian pointed out in their fundraising talks, when the appeal was first launched it was said by many to have been overly ambitious, but they did not agree. Nothing, they declared, could ever replace the nurses who were lost during the war. They had known 45 of them and understood just what amazing women they were. In discussing their years of captivity and many of the episodes and people they recalled from that time, their audiences would be stunned and horrified at what they had been through. The two nursing sisters spoke of the extraordinary leadership of women like Matron Paschke of Dimboola and Matron Irene Drummond, who, like Vivian, had come from Broken Hill. They had helped, mentored and protected the nurses who served overseas, and the selfless manner in which they always had their hospitals ready to take on patients was an inspiration to all.

Betty and Vivian told how Matron Paschke, who could not swim, issued orders to her nurses after their ship *Vyner Brooke* had been bombed and was sinking. This gallant matron had reminded them in the midst of the tumult that their first duty was to ensure that all civilians were safe. Once this had been carried out, she told them in such an authoritative manner to jump overboard that no one hesitated. She had been lost, later presumed drowned, in the aftermath.

Then there was Matron Drummond, who, following the sinking of the *Vyner Brooke*, had helped another woman ashore, having endured ten hours in the water herself, and quickly took charge of the surviving nurses, civilian men, women and children and injured servicemen on Radji Beach. Tragically and undeservedly, she had died when all 22 nurses were marched into the water by a squad of Japanese soldiers and machine-gunned from behind, with badly wounded Vivian Bullwinkel the sole survivor of the terrible massacre.

Following one speech they gave in the city of Ballarat, an elderly man came up and gave them a donation, thanking them for what they had said and explained that he was the father of Sister Beth Cuthbertson, who had died on Radji Beach. Some years later, in 2004, Beth's sister Joan was still residing in Ballarat and told a local reporter that the family had only learned of her death while listening to a radio interview given by Vivian Bullwinkel after she had returned home, during which she read out a list of the names of the nurses who had died on that tragic day.

In finalising their talks during the long, exhausting journey around Victoria, Betty and Vivian would always express their thanks to those who had gathered to hear their stories and for the welcome extended to them, saying that those who had known the nurses who did not return were very proud of them and felt it their duty to tell people something about them. They explained that the most poignant part was that many of the young nurses with whom they shared those years of deprivation and torment had died towards the end of the war and within weeks of subsequent liberation. As related by Jennifer Williams, 'Having overcome incredible difficulties and survived ordeals so terrible that they sounded fantastic in the telling, the Sisters accepted no excuse, large or small, in their quest for support for the big scheme.'

On 6 April 1948, at Melbourne Town Hall, the selected hospital nursing 'Queens' from across the state had assembled for an announcement by the Lord Mayor of the winners in the different categories. Betty and Vivian were honoured guests at the ceremony, at which it was announced that an amazing total of £121,000 had been raised for the War Nurses Memorial Centre appeal, of which £78,000 had been collected by competition nurses across the state. The centre could now become a reality, thanks to the generosity of many. This was at a time of post-war frugality for most citizens, when many things were still rationed or in short supply and money was tight. The biggest individual amount was raised by Sister Ruth Anderson from the Queen Victoria Hospital, collecting a massive £5,607.

The War Nurses Memorial Centre was eventually established in the elegant Victorian mansion 'Madowla', located at 431 St Kilda Road, Melbourne. Originally a private house of eighteen rooms, standing in spacious grounds, it was being used as a guest house before being purchased for the centre. The Memorial Committee paid £22,500 for the property, which would need a considerable amount of renovation before all its facilities became available.

The centre's doors opened on 14 May 1949 (coincidentally Betty's birthday), and it would become a permanent 'living' memorial to the heroism and sacrifice of all Australian nurses at war. On 19 February 1950, the centre was officially opened by the Governor of Victoria, Sir Dallas Brooks, in front of a large gathering of returned service sisters, as well as civilian sisters and trainee nurses from metropolitan hospitals. In his address, Sir Dallas said he dedicated the centre 'to the glory of God, and in memory of those sisters who lost their lives in the war'. General Sir Thomas Blamey, chairman of the centre committee, said there was hardly a fighting soldier who had not at some time experienced the care and devotion to duty of the service sisters. Matron-in-Chief Annie Sage then pointed out that the ceremony marked a stage towards the goal of a nurses' centre 'from which there can be no turning back'. A delighted Betty Jeffrey would be formally announced as its first administrator, following which she helped serve tea to the visiting nurses.

For a time, out of convenience, Betty lived at the centre, finding immense satisfaction in tackling such a demanding position. She was said to have done a truly wonderful job in the centre's infancy, when there was much to establish and try to fund at a time when money was tight. The hours were long and tiring – often involving working from 9 am until 10.30 pm. Among other projects she would also establish the Betty Jeffrey Auxiliary, formed to raise additional funds, enabling the purchase of much-needed equipment for the centre.

As Vivian Bullwinkel later wrote, 'In the post-war years, the nursing profession was stirring and becoming restless. The Nurses Memorial Centre gave them cohesion and an identity that had been lacking.' Additionally, Australia's Royal College of Nursing was set up within the centre to provide education for nurses, as well as the Nurses Board of Victoria and what would become the Australian Nursing Federation. Within just a few years the centre had become the focal point for the enormous growth of professional nursing organisations in Australia. A cherished dream born in Sumatra had become an outstanding reality.

One great friend and supporter of Betty and the centre was Ethel Marian Casey (known to her friends as Maie), wife of the future Governor-General Lord Casey. She would often impose on her many influential friends to assist in some way in the finances and other needs of the centre. She would call Betty every day to discuss any ways in which she could help. Prior to the opening of the centre, Ethel Casey was concerned for Betty, living all alone in such a huge house while it was being converted, and for Christmas 1949 presented her friend with a small dachshund named Robbie. Betty loved the little dog, as did everyone who worked in or visited the centre. The following year she also decided that a permanent nurse should be employed in the residence to look after Betty's health and welfare. The nurse appointed was Gay Mole, who had served with the 2/4th AGH in the Middle East, and she became what Betty described as a 'great joy and help'.

As detailed by centre historian Jennifer Williams, Betty and Gay were working in one of the large reception rooms one Saturday morning when an obviously agitated Robbie appeared in the doorway, running around in circles and barking loudly, so they crossed the floor to see what was wrong. 'As they left the room,' Williams wrote, 'large, heavy pieces of cement from the ceiling fell to the floor where they had been standing. The pieces were so large and heavy that they had to be taken away in a wheelbarrow.' Little Robbie, through some innate animal instinct of danger, had saved the day and quite possibly a life or two.

In May 1950, although still suffering poor health, Betty took a leave of absence from the Nurses Memorial Centre in order to travel to England with Vivian, appointing Margaret Cuthbert as Relieving Administrator while she was abroad. The two women intended staying in England for two years while Vivian undertook post-graduate courses in modern blood bank methods, as well as the two of them engaging in a little sightseeing and catching up with a number of people and dignitaries. They also had the names and addresses of ten nurses who were in the camps with them in Sumatra and were repatriated after the defeat of Japan. Both were keen to renew friend-ships with them under far more pleasant conditions. They sailed out of Melbourne in September 1950 aboard the liner *Arawa*.

Once they had arrived and settled in, the invitations flowed. They were enjoying London and the experiences it brought, and their excitement knew no bounds when they received a letter dated 15 November from Cynthia Colville, Lady-in-Waiting to Queen Mary, the mother of Edward VIII and George VI and grandmother of Princesses Elizabeth and Margaret. The letter extended an invitation to a meeting with Queen Mary at Marlborough House in London. They eagerly accepted and while waiting for a response they both took up temporary positions at St Mary's Hospital in Paddington and moved into a small flat in Kensington. They also purchased bicycles and went on long sightseeing trips that took them far and wide around Britain, with a special fondness for the Lake District in Cumbria with its breathtaking rugged fell mountains and glacial ribbon lakes.

The letter had explained that Queen Mary was currently suffering from a 'particularly tiresome and obstinate cold' but would love to meet them when she was feeling better. It actually took much longer than they had anticipated, but the following February they were informed that Queen Mary was over her cold and would be pleased to meet them. It still took another three months.

In the meantime, they accepted another royal invitation to meet with Princess Alice, Duchess of Gloucester, on 16 March 1951, at York House, St James's Palace. Finally, in May, Betty and Vivian were presented to King George VI and Queen Elizabeth in the throne room at Buckingham Palace. They were also received by Her Majesty Queen Mary in her comfortable sitting room in Marlborough House, which overlooked The Mall. They were invited to sit down, and Her Majesty sat between them. Betty later said this was a truly unforgettable and quite wonderful experience.

Queen Mary, who had been appointed patron of the War Nurses Memorial Centre, wanted to hear about the work being carried out there and was interested in learning a little of its history. They were both astounded, Betty said, 'when she asked how the nurses had raised the money for it; she mentioned the exact sum – not even an approximate amount'. When they told Queen Mary about a couple of the more amusing ways in which the nurses had raised some of the money she had laughed, 'a lovely infectious laugh; a low, soft chuckle'.

Insofar as asking about their years as prisoners in Sumatra, Betty was quite astonished. 'Queen Mary knew everything about us,' she later stated, 'and showed an amazing interest in the details of our years with the Japanese.' The Queen asked each of them questions no one had asked before, and finally put a pointed question to Betty: 'Do you hate the Japanese?' Betty hesitated, looked at Vivian, and replied: 'Certainly.' At that, the Queen smiled and simply said, 'I'm not surprised.'

In a lighter vein, they told Queen Mary about their skiing holiday in Switzerland and the bruises they had collected, at which the Queen said, 'Show me them.' The two women thought it the most natural thing in the world to show royalty their bruises. 'Queen Mary's eyes are so blue and clear; her hair is so pretty,' Betty remarked after the meeting. 'She really is the loveliest old lady I have ever seen.' The meeting went for 45 minutes, which seemed to pass very quickly. Just before they left, the Queen gave each of them a photograph of herself, signed 'Mary R., 1951'. Another signed photograph was sent to the nurses' centre in Melbourne.

Another highlight for Betty and Vivian was an invitation to attend the Albert Hall Armistice Day gathering of 7000, which could be attended only once in an individual's lifetime, by roster. Despite being the undoubted trip of a lifetime, it was also tiring, and after eighteen months abroad, Betty was growing increasingly fatigued. She decided to return home. On 19 March 1952, Betty disembarked from RMS *Mooltan* in Melbourne. The following year, in March 1953, she was saddened to hear that the 85-year-old Queen Mary had died shortly before the coronation of her granddaughter Elizabeth.

While Betty now took on the responsibility for taking care of her elderly parents, Vivian had elected to stay on, now working as a nurse receptionist at Australia House in London. Towards the end of her time in England, she was delighted to meet the famed George Medal winner and war heroine Odette Churchill, who had worked for the French Resistance before being captured and tortured by the Gestapo in Paris. 'We had tea together and did not talk much about the war,' she later recalled of the meeting.

On her return voyage home aboard SS *Oronsay*, the captain of the ocean liner heard that Vivian was on board and upgraded her from a tourist-class cabin to a first-class suite. She arrived in Fremantle on 26 September 1953 and made her way to South Australia to spend time with her mother before returning to Melbourne and resuming her duties on the staff at the Heidelberg Repatriation Hospital.

In 1951, while they were travelling around England, the mews at the rear of the 'Madowla' house had been converted and now became the new College of Nursing, Australia, which allowed postgraduate studies in nursing administration, teaching and ward management. Prior to this, any such studies had to be undertaken in England.

While 1954 may have been a poor one health-wise, there was a tremendous pickup on its way for Betty when someone suggested sending her edited, typed diary notes to a publisher. Thinking nothing would come of it, she submitted the manuscript to a couple of publishers, including Angus & Robertson in Melbourne. The publishing company's head man Arthur Smith initially rejected the book, even though he stood in admiration of the author. 'Never mind, Betty,' he is reported as saying to her. 'It *will* be published one day. And when it is, I'm going to take you to dinner at the [Hotel] Australia every time there's a new edition.'

Eventually the decision was made by their editorial board to publish *White Coolies* (changing the title from Betty's original working title, 'A Diary of a White Coolie'), and the first edition was released in 1954, immediately garnering huge public interest – so much so that it was reproduced in full over several issues of syndicated Australian newspapers.

Quite to Betty's surprise and delight, copies of her book began flying off the shelves. In less than two months, 10,000 had been printed and within ten days supplies were dwindling. An order for a further 5000 copies was lodged, but the entire second edition was sold out, on orders, before it even reached the booksellers. At the time, publishers Angus & Robertson said the book had been their best seller every day since it landed on the market. Within two years, it had topped the 80,000 sales mark for the delighted publishers and Arthur Smith laughingly regretted his earlier promise, as it had already cost him eleven dinners.

The drawings at the head of each chapter in *White Coolies* were the work of Jan Pieter Lodewijk Kickhefer (also known as Kick). He was a commercial artist born in the Netherlands who had moved to the Dutch East Indies in 1932, and was himself held prisoner in Japanese internment camps. During this time he drew evocative sketches of life in both the men's and women's camps. Jan migrated to Australia in 1948, where he passed away in Sydney in 1965.

The book proved so popular with the public that it was scripted into a radio serial of 52 weekly episodes. About the time the serial first went to air, Betty commented to a newspaper that her book had already enjoyed six reprints (by the year 2000 it had been published in nineteen editions). The serial helped to popularise the book even more, and Betty became something of a sought-after celebrity, even though she was still undergoing treatment for the severe tuberculosis suffered and mostly untreated during her time in Sumatra, and was generally reluctant to talk about her experiences.

Radio historian Ian Grieve later said of the broadcast series:

'White Coolies' was also a game changer in Australian radio production. The producer, Fifi Banvard, scriptwriter Gwen Friend, and all the lead actors were women. This was a first. A big deal in Australia in 1955. Yes, there were some men involved in the production. The announcer and the actors playing the Japanese guards were the only men involved.

The part of Betty Jeffrey fell to Ruth Cracknell (they would become great friends) and, according to Grieve, the part of Matron Olive Paschke was said to have been read by Vivian Bullwinkel herself.

Following her return from England, as well as caring for her parents Betty had settled back into her former administrative job at the Memorial Centre, while Margaret Cuthbert reverted to her previous role of Assistant Administrator. Ill-health continued to wear Betty down and affect the work she loved carrying out at the centre and throughout 1954 she was in and out of Heidelberg Repatriation

Hospital, often for several weeks at a time. The publication of *White Coolies* and the sudden acclaim it brought her was both a tonic and a hindrance to her health.

There was no getting around this ongoing illness, and she was strongly but respectfully advised by the medical team that she should consider retiring from her position at the Nurses Memorial Centre for the sake of her health. It was a heart-breaking decision, but one that she knew in her heart was best for her. Betty announced her resignation for health reasons at the annual meeting of the council of the centre on 23 July 1954. The chairman of the centre, Sir Clive Steele, paid tribute to her outstanding work, saying it was chiefly through her efforts and those of Vivian Bullwinkel that the facility, which provided a meeting ground for nurses from all over the country, was first established. The ties were still strong, however, and from 1986 until 2000 Betty served as Patron of the Memorial Centre.

In retirement, she still took on voluntary work supporting former prisoners of war and for relaxation was often seen strolling the greens playing competitive golf at the Huntingdale Golf Club, where she had signed on and become a member in 1947. Betty's interest in the sport took on a whole different direction in the 1960s, when she also became involved in first-class golf as a caddy for Victorian champion Burtta Cheney, an old and dear friend of hers, as well as the renowned soprano, Dame Joan Hammond, who also played at Huntingdale. The three woman would forge a lasting friendship.

One could say it was almost inevitable that golf would become a major part of Burtta Cheney's life. She was named after her maternal grandmother, who lived in the Kingdom of Fife, widely known as Scotland's traditional 'home of golf'. Her parents had joined the Eastern Golf Club in Yering, Victoria, and arranged for her to attend the final round of the 1930 Australian Ladies Championship being held at the Commonwealth Golf Club in Oakleigh South. At fourteen years of age, she was determined to become a part of that world. She first came to prominence in 1937 as runner-up in the Ladies Amateur Championship of Australia. When war erupted in 1939 she voluntarily joined the Red Cross in Melbourne, transporting wounded servicemen from hospitals to rehabilitation units, while ferrying blood and other needed supplies to medical facilities.

When peace finally came in 1945 she resumed her burgeoning golfing career, reaching domestic and international status. Over pre- and post-war years Burtta was a member of the Victorian team on fifteen occasions, played in Australian teams six times between 1937 and 1963 and captained the Australian team in 1956, 1958 and 1963.

Golf had been a major influence for Burtta in her early years, and she was determined to offer other young girls the same opportunity. In 1966, along with Audrey McLaren, she set up the first junior girls' golf camp at Anglesea Golf Club, through which a number of young women would become familiar names at golfing tournaments across Australia and overseas. The major junior girls' interstate series was later named the Burtta Cheney Cup in her honour.

In her later years she was presented with the inaugural Lifetime Achievement Award by Women's Golf Australia, and was named as one of the first six members of Victoria's Golfing Hall of Fame, and in 1976 she was awarded an MBE for her 'valuable and untiring services to the Australian and Victorian Ladies' Golf Union'. Burtta Cheney, MBE, a true legend and champion of Australian golf and its administration, passed away in September 2012, just a month short of her 96th birthday. It is hardly surprising that Betty Jeffrey always admired and looked up to this amazing, inspirational woman.

Dame Joan Hammond was another dedicated golfer who often joined Betty on the lush green links at Huntingdale. Born in New Zealand in 1912, her family moved to Sydney, where, in 1929, aged seventeen, she won the New South Wales Junior Golf Championship and took out the state women's golf championships in 1932, 1933 and 1935, later representing Australia in the inaugural Tasman Cup against New Zealand at the Victoria Golf Club in Melbourne.

Harbouring a deep desire to become a musician, Joan spent three years with the Sydney Philharmonic Orchestra studying the violin. Then her life took a dramatic turn after she suffered a badly broken arm in a car accident, forcing her to reassess her ambition. In 1936, Joan travelled to Vienna to study opera singing as a soprano, making her stage debut in London in 1938, and the following year performed at the Royal Albert Hall. Success followed success, and she often returned to Australia on sold-out concert tours. She finally returned home in 1965, became artistic director of the Victoria Opera Company, was decorated four times by the Queen, and was honoured in receiving the title of Dame Joan Hammond in 1974.

For relaxation, she had joined and played golf at Yarra Yarra Golf Club and later at Huntingdale. Dame Joan had a holiday house at Anglesea. When the week-long Anglesea Golf Club clinics for young girls were being held, Burtta Cheney, Helen Gadsden, Alison Searle and Betty Jeffrey would often stay with her. One annual treat was when Dame Joan would host New Year's Eve celebrations for the women golfers at Anglesea. As nephew Antony Jeffrey recalled:

I remember from my own interactions with Betty how much she enjoyed these gatherings and so much admired Joan Hammond and regarded it as a great privilege to be her friend. My feeling is that Betty was never happier than in the company of those women and their gatherings and parties.

Sadly, both Dame Joan and Burtta Cheney lost their houses during the Ash Wednesday bushfires that swept through Anglesea and Airey's Inlet on 16 February 1983. Dame Joan Hammond, DBE, CMG, a glorious soprano, a great character and sportswoman, well-liked and respected by all who knew her, died on 26 November 1996.

Post-war, the game and its associated exercise had helped significantly in restoring much of Betty's former fitness, and today the Betty Jeffrey Perpetual Trophy is still awarded annually at the Huntingdale Golf Club. The event is normally held around Anzac Day in recognition of her distinguished war career.

Huntingdale member Olga Mackenzie recalls playing golf 'infrequently' with Betty, whom she remembered as 'reserved, quiet and well mannered'. Betty was a regular player on Tuesdays, so they did not often meet up, but when she and Olga did play together it was usually in company with Burtta Cheney, Alison Searle and Dora O'Sullivan, from Toorak. Dora, like Burtta, had served as a volunteer in the Red Cross during the war, rising to Assistant Commandant for Transport. Burrta and Dora would remain great friends for the rest of their lives. Olga also remembered Betty often acting as caddy for Burtta, but only domestically; Alison Searle was the champion's international caddy.

Another long-serving club member, Jill Elrick, spoke about when the Huntingdale social secretary came up with the concept of a

Betty Jeffrey Trophy, to be played over two days and 36 holes, as a way of honouring their eminent member. Betty would obviously not play in this tournament, but travelled around the course in a golf buggy along with the social secretary and other committee members. She also attended the presentations and associates' dinners.

Jill recalled that while Betty was recuperating post-war at the Heidelberg Repatriation Hospital, Burtta Cheney would often pick up Betty and one or two other patients – some still in their night attire – and drive them to the Huntingdale Golf Club. Thus a lifelong golfing friendship was forged between the two women. Jill said Betty was 'easy to speak with, and a much-loved and well-respected member of the club', and she was thrilled to have once won the Betty Jeffrey Trophy.

Yet another club member, Elizabeth Randall, found Betty 'very humble, but had an aura about her'. They would often share a post-game lunch at the club, although she would find Betty a little reserved in their conversations about her wartime experiences, saying Betty 'was often teetering on telling more, but she had borders, and then an "I am Betty Jeffrey" attitude would kick in and she would only say what she wanted to say.'

As well as golf, Betty thrived on attending other sports fixtures, in particular first-class cricket games, astounding everyone with her extensive knowledge of the rules and players of the game. As her surgeon nephew Dr Tim Gale recalled, 'She was phenomenally interested in sport and used to go to the MCG [Melbourne Cricket Ground] a lot. I'd see her there and she always knew who was bowling, what they were bowling and how well they were bowling. Knowing what she had been through, my admiration for her grew all the time.'

Once Tim's wife Elaine got to know Betty, she also found her 'an inspiration of course. She was so independent and I always found her interesting and fascinating, and for her part she always found anything her family was up to of great interest to her. She was fiercely loyal, not only to her family, but to her "cobbers". She would always refer to her friends as her "cobbers".'

In 1967, despite harbouring feelings of great uncertainty, Betty paid a visit to Japan 'to get the hate out of my system'. She found she actually she enjoyed touring the country for five weeks, and when she returned home it was with a better understanding and far less hatred of the Japanese people. Understandably, and not uncommonly for those who had once experienced their cruelty as prisoners, there would always be so much that she could never forgive nor forget. She told one interviewer:

Yes I went to Japan, privately of course. I wanted to get it all out of my system. It was still around and I thought there's only one way to get it out – that was to go to Japan. So, with a friend, I did that and I just loved the place. I thought it was marvellous! I still didn't like the men much but I thought the women and the children were and Japan itself, absolutely fantastic! So interesting – how they pack so many people into such a small place. And everybody seemed to get everywhere and everybody was spotlessly clean and you didn't see washing on the line! I loved it!

I was there for nearly five weeks and when I came home I was a different person. I've been a different person ever since. I'll never forget it, I suppose, but the hatred and the horror has gone from me and as far as camp life is concerned, I can only remember the good parts of it, the good friendships, the music we had. There was quite a lot of good that came out of it. That's what I remember now when people say, 'Tell me about life in camp.'

For years, people wanted to know all about it and I had to go around . . . I was a guest speaker. We [the nurses] have all had to do that and I think, like me, everybody was fed up with it. So no more of it. I've had enough of that, having done it for all that time. I think it's time to stop. After all, it's nearly 40 years since it happened and we look forward and not backward.

There were often times when she was openly critical of any pro-Japanese thing, such as on her annual holidays to the Gold Coast, south of Brisbane, when she would gripe about the numerous tourist signs displayed around town in both English and Japanese. As well, she always refused to ride in a Japanese-made car.

Those annual trips to the Gold Coast became a significant part of Betty's later life, as recalled by Tim Gale:

For over 20 years, Betty greatly enjoyed escaping the Melbourne weather by spending about three months on the Queensland Gold Coast at a holiday home owned by Helen Gadsden, one of her close golf associates from Melbourne. Invariably, for much of this time, she would be accompanied by one or two of her widowed sisters.

Betty's sisters would also travel there for shorter stays, and for Betty those relaxing visits would be recalled with great fondness, harking back to the times she spent at her brother Alan's beachside holiday cottage, 'Breffney', which she enjoyed so much before going off to war, and even the idyllic family days of her youth, swimming and playing at Kingston, south of Hobart.

'I really don't know what they did,' Tim added,

other than sitting on the veranda watching the surf! But it was also an opportunity for Betty and her sisters to spend some time with Aimée, the widow of their eldest brother Alan. She had later married for a second time to Steven King, a Brisbane solicitor with whom she had ultimately retired to their home on the Nerang River near the Gold Coast's Southport. She would remain in close contact with the Jeffrey family all her life, dying at the grand age of 95 in 2003.

Whenever they could arrange it, Betty would get together with Wilma (Oram) Young and Beryl Woodbridge as members of the Returned Nurses' Club in Anzac House, Melbourne. Throughout their years of captivity they had found comfort and friendship in each other's company. 'We are just like a family,' Wilma once stated. Betty agreed:

We are all wonderful friends – those of us who survived. We are all in different states, but when we get together it is magic! We have a reunion once a year. A magnificent bond of friendship [exists] between us all. I think it kept our sanity that we were used to group living – used to living in a nurses' home in a hospital before we ever left Malaya to get onto the *Vyner Brooke*. We were used to living in one great big ward. We were a team. I think that's why it was easier for us to assimilate quicker than the others, the civilian people, because they left their husbands and families and suddenly they were put into a confined space with somebody they didn't know with 22 inches space each – somebody lying alongside you that you probably didn't even like. That must have been terribly hard for them. But we just took it in our stride as it were.

Of the 24 nurses who survived those traumatic years in Sumatra, one-third would never marry. Many were also treated poorly by their own government; unmarried army nurses did not receive the home loans granted to Australian soldiers until 1972. As Beryl Woodbridge told one inquisitive reporter, 'You can't help what the war did to you. I am glad to be alive, to be living as I am. Perhaps if we had stayed in Australia we would have been married; we would have had a married life, but it is your own choice.'

12

A FULL LIFE OF STRENGTH AND HONOUR

THE CREATION OF WHAT WOULD one day be the Nurses Memorial Centre, which meant so much to Betty Jeffrey in her post-war life, had its origins in two tragic massacres at sea, which cost the lives of young Australian nurses, killed in the wartime service of their nation.

The first, as related earlier in this book, was the merciless bombing, strafing and sinking of the rescue steamship *Vyner Brooke* on 14 February 1942. The second tragedy at sea occurred on Friday, 14 May 1943. This involved the callous sinking of the 2/3rd Australian Hospital Ship (AHS) *Centaur*. When the ship departed Brisbane, bound for Port Moresby via Cairns to pick up casualties from the Buna–Gona–Sanananda battle, it was carrying 332 people, including twelve AANS nurses. The attack occurred off Stradbroke Island. As detailed in the article, 'Survival at Sea' from the magazine *Grey and Scarlet* (published by the Royal Australian Army Nursing Corps), that final voyage of the *Centaur* would prove catastrophic in many ways.

The *Centaur* was ablaze with floodlights, which clearly showed the traditional red crosses of a hospital ship painted on her hull, deck and funnel. Therefore, there was no doubt as to the nature of the target, when at 4.10 am on the morning of May 14th, a torpedo hit the *Centaur* just forward of amidships. A blinding blue flash lit up the vessel as the explosion practically ripped her in two, and fire from ignited oil raged through the ship. In just over three minutes the *Centaur* had sunk, taking with her most of those on board.

The sole surviving nurse of the cowardly Japanese submarine attack was Lieutenant Eleanor (Ellen) Savage from Quirindi, New South Wales. In August 1944, for her courageous actions during and after the sinking, she was awarded the George Medal – only the second Australian woman to ever receive this honour, after Sister Margaret Anderson on the *Empire Star*. Lieutenant Savage's award citation stated that,

> although suffering from severe injuries received as a result of the explosion and immersion in the sea, she displayed great heroism during the period while she and some male members of the ship's staff were floating on a raft, to which they clung for about 34 hours before being rescued by a US destroyer. She gave conspicuous service while on the raft in attending to wounds and burns suffered by other survivors. Her courage and fortitude did much to maintain the morale of her companions.

In her own words, while recovering from her experience at a Queensland army hospital, Ellen Savage told how she had been awakened by a massive explosion and a cry of 'On deck, Savage!'

from her best friend, Sister Evelyn King, who was in the next cabin. She quickly grabbed her lifebelt and a set of rosary beads she always kept at her bedside. The two nurses were forced to make their way to the top deck of the *Centaur* by means of a usable staircase, as the main companionway was blocked. Evelyn King could not swim and Ellen yelled that she would look after her, but suddenly her friend disappeared from sight and she never saw her again. Dressed only in her silk pyjamas, Ellen jumped overboard into the black, oil-covered water. There was one thing to be thankful for; the fractured ship sank so rapidly that the thick oil floating on the water did not ignite from the burning fuel tanks. Had it done so, the death toll from those struggling in the cold water would have been far higher. Many who did make it into the water were unable to swim clear of the overwhelming suction as the *Centaur* sank and were dragged down with the ship. Others were terribly burnt and died in the water, while several were taken by shoals of sharks attracted to the sudden, bloody melee. As she later described the sinking, Ellen was one of the fortunate ones.

> I could see the bridge aflame and I knew the ship was sinking. I jumped and the suction dragged me down and down – it seemed for fathoms. I thought I'd lose consciousness because a piece of wreckage hit me on the head and I became entangled in ropes and more wreckage, but I suddenly shot to the surface beside a man. I was in the water for two hours before men dragged me onto a raft.

Given the speed at which the *Centaur* was sinking, the ship's crew did not have a chance to send out a wireless SOS or launch any undamaged lifeboats. Within just three minutes, the doomed ship had capsized, sinking bow first.

Ellen stated that, although she never saw the Japanese submarine, she had a distinct memory of what they discovered was a cruel ruse by the crew:

We heard the drone of the engine suddenly near to us and voices calling 'Cooee'. Near me was a man who had been in Rabaul and he said quickly and suddenly: 'Don't answer. They're Japs. Remember sailors never say "Cooee"– they say "Ahoy".' So we kept very quiet and all we could see was a small green light. I felt tense because I knew they were Japs and I thought I might finish up in Tokyo.

Although badly hurt, suffering a broken jaw, several broken ribs, deep bruising, cuts and a black eye, Ellen ignored her own injuries and set about helping other survivors. She tried to ignore the terrifying sight of sharks circling the raft, and even organised a sing-along while waiting to be seen from the air and rescued. She also said a prayer for a man who succumbed to his burns and had to be buried at sea, where those vicious sharks made short work of his body.

We had no first aid equipment so we couldn't do much for the injured except bathe their burns with salt water. One man's feet we massaged to keep the circulation going. The men were all marvellous. They talked to each other and to me and we made plans for spending the hours until we were picked up. We saw one plane and lit flares but it went the other way. Anyway that day passed and at 2.30 next afternoon we saw a plane flying very low – our rescue plane signalling to the ship that picked us up.

As a result of this ruthless sinking of an unarmed and clearly marked hospital vessel, supposedly protected under the Hague Convention, 268 of the 322 on board were lost. This number included nurses, doctors, field ambulance officers and crew members. Only 54 managed to survive their burns, the ingested oil, the circling sharks and the 34 hours of hell while waiting to be rescued. The eleven nurses who lost their lives were: Sister Evelyn Veronica King, Sister Helen Frances Haultain, Sister Myrtle Moston, Sister Edna Alice Shaw, Sister Doris Joyce Wyllie, Sister Margaret Lamont Adams, Matron Sarah Anne Jewell, Sister Alice Margaret O'Donnell, Sister Eileen Mary Rutherford, Sister Wendy Jenny Walker, Sister Mary Hamilton McFarlane.

At the end of World War II, Sister Ellen Savage was awarded a Florence Nightingale scholarship and subsequently attended the Royal College of Nursing in London to study nursing administration. She later became matron of the Rankin Park Chest Hospital in New Lambton, New South Wales, until her retirement in 1967. She was also actively involved in a fundraising campaign that helped establish Centaur House in Brisbane.

The Centaur Memorial Fund for Nurses was established in 1948 as a memorial to those who perished in the sinking of AHS *Centaur*, and as a tribute to the nurses of Queensland who served the state during and between two world wars, both on the home and military fronts. The fund initially fulfilled its tribute to the profession by providing a centre for nurses, with educational, recreational and accommodation facilities. Since the 1980s, the fund has focused on providing financial support to nurses and midwives undertaking postgraduate studies and recognising excellence in undergraduate nursing studies.

On 25 April 1985, aged 72, Ellen Savage, GM, collapsed and died outside Sydney Hospital after attending an Anzac Day reunion. She lies at rest in Sydney's Northern Suburbs Cemetery.

After moving to live in Victoria, Vivian Bullwinkel transferred from the army and took a position at the Heidelberg Repatriation Hospital for the next fourteen years, firstly as a charge sister, and in the last five years as assistant matron. She then took up the position of Director of Nursing at Fairfield Infectious Diseases Hospital, Melbourne, for the next seventeen years before retiring.

For her services to nursing during and after the war, Vivian became one of the few Australians to hold the Florence Nightingale Medal (FNM), awarded in 1947 by the International Red Cross committee. She was presented with the MBE in 1973 for her services to nursing, became an Associate of the Order of the Royal Red Cross (ARRC), and in 1993 made an Officer of the Order of Australia Medal (AO). The citation on her AO reads: 'Her heroism, courage and humanitarian achievements are unique.'

She even travelled to Vietnam in 1975 to evacuate orphaned children from that war-torn country to Australia in a charitable program called Operation Babylift. In early 1977, she was being widely tipped as a possible replacement for then Governor of South Australia, Sir Douglas Nicholls, but there was soon to be a major change in her life, and she would have politely declined the honour if offered.

On 16 September 1977, Vivian married Colonel Frank Statham, OBE, in a quiet wedding at St Margaret's Church, Nedlands, a western suburb of Perth. The wedding had been kept secret and was attended by only a few close friends. The couple had known each other for several years, having met during Statham's Citizen Military Forces (CMF) work in Victoria after the war, during which he had served in North Africa with Headquarters 9th Division and in New Guinea with Headquarters 1st Army Corps. He was demobilised from the AIF on 29 October 1945, having attained the rank of lieutenant-colonel. A widower with two children, he had become director of the Commonwealth Department of Construction in Western Australia and honorary commandant of the Royal Australian Electrical and Mechanical Engineers in Perth.

Following the wedding, the new Mrs Statham paid a visit to Adelaide for a national reunion of prisoners of war before returning to Melbourne and relinquishing her positions at the Heidelberg Repatriation and Fairfield hospitals. She then announced she was looking forward to being 'just a housewife' with her husband in Perth.

Despite her somewhat frail condition, Vivian continued in her tireless commitment to the community in many volunteer and service organisations, even after being disabled by a stroke in the early 1990s.

Fifty years after the appalling tragedy at Radji Beach, in preparation for an upcoming commemoration marking the loss of the nurses in 1942, Vivian and Frank Statham travelled to Banka Island. Disappointment was in store when she was unable to locate the exact place where the nurses had been killed. 'We couldn't find the beach,' she later lamented.

We went down to a beach near Muntok but it wasn't the one I recalled. There was only a jungle track down to the beach, and the track led to a village. Apparently, when Private Kingsley and I gave ourselves up, the village people became rather frightened because the women had helped me. They felt that they would be tortured by the Japanese, so they abandoned their village and went into the town. They never went back.

Instead, Vivian agreed to select a beach site near a lighthouse situated at the northern end of Banka Island. 'That lighthouse was a beacon for lots of the girls when they were out at sea,' she added. 'It's a nice spot, and the Indonesians have been very generous in allowing us to have that area.'

In early 1993, although far from well at the time, Vivian accepted an invitation extended to her by the Australian Department of Veterans' Affairs to join a return pilgrimage to Banka Island, where a commemorative war memorial plaque was to be placed on the selected seafront near Muntok on 2 March. She said she simply had to attend 'because of those girls who did not come back'. Betty Jeffrey was also invited and desperately wanted to go, but as the time grew near she knew she would be unable to attend due to a severe illness. As well as Vivian and six other surviving prisoner nurses – Pat Gunther, Florence (Trotter) Syer, Jenny Ashton, Mavis (Hannah) Allgrove, Wilma Oram and Joyce Tweddell, the official party included representatives from the Australian and Indonesian governments, the Repatriation Commission, Australian Defence Force and the Returned and Services League, as well as the head of the Australian Army Nursing Corps, Colonel Coralie Gerrard, and her team of support personnel.

(Vivian would never know, but some years later Radji Beach was formally identified in a near-inaccessible cove. Plans were then put in place to remove and transplant the tribute plaques to what had now been correctly identified as Radji Beach.)

Unfortunately the trip exhausted Vivian and exacerbated her illness. She returned home to Perth in poor condition, and would never enjoy fully good health from that time onward. When her husband Frank suffered a massive heart attack and died in December 1999, it was another cruel blow in life for Vivian.

Meanwhile, life went on for Betty Jeffrey. Helen Pickering from the ANMC remembers meeting her for the first time at a luncheon held for the somewhat reluctant nonagenarian at ANZAC House, Melbourne, on the occasion of Betty's 90th birthday in May 1998. 'I was a somewhat surprised at how well she looked. Tanned, fit; I couldn't imagine she was a lady who'd been through all those privations.' Betty was surrounded by many old friends, and one of the highlights of the day was when she cut into a massive birthday cake made, she was told, with 24 eggs. According to her family, one of her chief delights at this time was sitting quietly in her small flat playing her collection of 78-rpm classical records on a vintage gramophone equipped with a horn.

Robert Malone, married to Betty's niece Jane, recalls that she always maintained a lifelong friendship with Ken Brown, the pilot who had flown her and the other nurses out of Sumatra after their liberation from Japanese captivity. He would call her every Sunday night to check on her welfare. She also had a ritual of calling her younger sister Mary some evenings, while arming herself with a scotch and water and Mary a brandy and soda. They would say 'Cheers!' and clink their glasses against the phone in a toast to each other.

Around this time Betty had a severe fright that her family said caused her great anxiety. She had gone out to tend and water her little garden through the back door of her Lido Court flat, as always leaving the front door locked. Somehow a burglar managed to slip into her flat and grab her purse, but then he heard her coming back inside and ducked into her bathroom, hiding behind the shower curtain. He waited for his best chance of escape and ran to the front door, opening it and running off down the street with her handbag. Fortunately he didn't hurt her, but she lost her wallet and many other personal items in her purse.

On 3 July 2000, Lieutenant Colonel Vivian Statham, Matron, AO, MBE, ARRC, ED, FNM, FRCNA, passed away at Perth's Hollywood Hospital after suffering a heart attack while recovering from leg surgery. She was 84 years old. A state funeral was held a week later at St George's Cathedral, which was filled to capacity. During the service, the President of the Victorian RSL, Bruce Ruxton, remarked that 'her bravery was extraordinary. Death was no stranger to her; she confronted death so many times. I've lost a great friend.'

Bruce Scott, Minister for Veterans' Affairs, in representing the Prime Minister, said the nation had lost 'a great Australian', adding, 'her courage and endurance while a prisoner of the Japanese exemplified the bravery of Australian Service nurses who have faced injury, capture and death in times of war.' He went on to say that while Vivian was humble about her part in Australia's wartime history, she was an inspiration to all who knew her.

On Friday, 18 December 2015, Vivian's medals and awards were presented to the Australian War Memorial by her nephew, John Bullwinkel, on the day she would have turned 100 had she lived.

In 1991, a history of the Nurses Memorial Centre (1948–1990) was published. Titled *Victoria's Living Memorial*, it was researched and written by author Jennifer Williams. A delighted Betty Jeffrey was asked to pen a short retrospective view of the centre. In part, looking back over more than four decades, she wrote:

> We have come a long way from our years in the beautiful old mansion 'Madowla' which was always busy with nurses coming in and out of the various nursing organisations housed there, including the many students doing their postgraduate courses at the then College of Nursing, Australia. Busy days indeed for everybody working at 431 St Kilda Road. Now these nursing organisations have outgrown the Centre and gone elsewhere. It still works very actively assisting in many ways, including grants given to nurses to help them further their studies and bring their knowledge back to Victoria to the betterment of all the different kinds of nursing care . . . These days I can do so little to help, but it comforts me to know the Nurses Memorial Centre is in good hands and is appreciated by so many members of the nursing world.

In October 2018, a resolution was passed at the Annual General Meeting of the Nurses Memorial Centre, officially changing their name to The Australian Nurses Memorial Centre. The resolution was proposed as the centre was the only remaining organisation of its kind in Australia, with all other organisations having ceased operations. Further, the centre's scholarships were made available to any Australian nurse. In this way, according to centre manager Elizabeth Allwood, the centre would also recognise and memorialise those Australian nurses who lost their lives in the Banka Island massacre.

Today, the Australian Nurses Memorial Centre is still situated at the same longstanding address on St Kilda Road, but the venerable old 'Madowla' mansion is long gone, replaced by the modern Fawkner Towers. The ANMC is situated at Suite 11 within the office and residential building. As the centre's president, Arlene Bennett, recently observed, while the organisation doesn't look the same as it did seven decades ago, its sense of purpose remains as strong as ever. 'We now only own a small piece of 431 St Kilda Road, but the spirit of the centre lives on,' she emphasised.

Betty's nephew, Antony Jeffrey (son of Alan and Aimée), believes that what his Aunt Betty went through during the war eventually led to some noticeable shifts in her personality:

In her later years, Betty changed quite a lot, no doubt from her terrible war experiences. The Nurses Memorial Centre I'm sure she felt was her most important achievement, even greater than the finishing, publication and reception of *White Coolies*. But in subsequent years, as she moved into and beyond middle-age, she became more querulous, at least within the family. This was almost certainly due to loneliness and no doubt to a gradual loss of the entertainment and friendships from what you might call the Joan Hammond set she loved belonging to.

Continuing her many charitable and service roles despite recurring illnesses, Betty was the patron and life member of the Victorian Ex-Prisoners of War Association, president of the Warwick Old Girls Association, and a member of the Returned and Services Nurses Club. During this latter period of her life, Betty had also worked on the Ex-Prisoners of War and Nurses Memorial Centre committees. During the 1970s and 1980s, she frequently spoke to various groups on ex-servicemen and women and prisoner of war subjects. She was also patron and member of the Ex-POW and Relatives Association and a committee member, and then later became the association's vice-president for many years.

White Coolies kept her busy during this time, writing many articles about it and answering hundreds of letters about POWs. In 1987, Betty received the Medal of the Order of Australia (OAM) for her services to ex-servicemen and women. In June 2000, the Victorian branch of the Returned Services League (RSL) awarded Betty with a life membership, presented to her by RSL President Bruce Ruxton and Major General Peter Cosgrove.

On 13 September 2000, just two days before Sydney hosted the Olympic Games and two months after her close friend Vivian Bullwinkel had died, we also lost Lieutenant Agnes Betty Jeffrey, OAM, RN, when she died of a heart attack in Melbourne's Cresthaven Aged Care Facility in Malvern East, aged 92. She had never married and lived alone in her East Malvern home before entering the nursing home just two months before her death.

As her nephew Tim Gale's wife Elaine commented,

In her later years she had remarkably good health considering her history. She did have regular check-ups at Heidelberg Repat as an outpatient. She was just becoming frail due to old age. She often said she was tired of life. Betty was fiercely independent until the end. She only needed housekeeping help, shopping, cooking, cleaning, clothes washing and so forth, but no nursing care. In fact, she fought the decision to leave her flat for some time but sadly there seemed to be no alternative. I think she was only in Cresthaven for two to three weeks. She hated going there and having to go to the dining room with the other residents and her loss of independence and privacy. The day she died they had let her stay in bed for the day at Cresthaven, which was not encouraged, but she was still settling in. She had persuaded them she was extra-tired. Our family feel certain it was then she got her wish to die.

Betty's niece Sara Renshaw said at the time that 'the POWs were her family – her other family. The Australian airman [Ken Brown] who flew in to rescue them after the war became a lifelong friend of Betty's. They forged a close bond and spoke every week until he died. I guess he was her saviour.' She added that one thing which often caused her aunt distress was when Japanese students would contact Betty. 'They used to call her up to find out what really happened during the war. They never got the full story in Japan and so they were searching for answers, I guess. Betty always spoke to them.'

Robert Malone said that Betty had enjoyed her post-war association with the nurses' centre and was always a little self-effacing about the recognition and awards lavished upon her. 'She was very determined but very humble about it. She didn't talk too much about her experiences. They were pretty painful memories.'

Robert and Jane's daughter Emily has always held a great affection and admiration for her great-aunt, and offered some recollections on behalf of all Betty's great-nieces and nephews:

Aunty Bett was a very generous person – generous with her time and with gifts and always giving us a good laugh when she wrote funny little ditties and poems in our birthday cards, with hilarious little sketches. But on the other hand, when we – the great-nieces and nephews – asked Aunty Bett about her wartime experiences, she would say she did not want to spend time talking about it, that there were much happier things to talk about and that we could read about it in *White Coolies*. She would then quickly change the topic and ask questions about how we were going at school or playing sport or our other interests.

It was only when I became older and was completing a Year 9 English project (writing a biography on my favourite great-aunt), that Aunty Bett began to share her thoughts with me and was happy to answer interview questions I had prepared about her wartime experience. She then spent time showing me her treasured wartime and post-war possessions, including telegrams, letters, newspaper articles, photographs, sketches and copies of music from the vocal orchestra, all which was kept inside an old brown suitcase in her little flat, which of course, I pored over!

It was from that moment I was completely hooked. I couldn't believe my great-aunt had lived through this experience and then led such an amazing life in her post-war years. She had met royalty, had famous friends and was a celebrity of sorts. I immediately wanted to know more about Aunty Bett and the nurses' story, and so began my research and subsequent involvement with the ANMC and other organisations and attendance at memorial services for the nurses and POWs.

Eulogy to Betty Jeffrey given by Wilma (Oram) Young, AM, at St Peter's Anglican Church, Eastern Hill, Melbourne, on 20 September 2000

It is with sadness at parting and a sense of joy that I had the privilege of a long and special friendship with Betty. She was known affectionately by her colleagues as 'Jeff' and by other people in the prison camp as Sister Jeff.

When she was in London some years after the war she was greatly surprised to hear herself hailed as 'Sister Jeff! – Sister Jeff!' by a mother and her daughter with whom we had shared living space in camp.

Betty and I were in different hospital units and met on the ship as we were being evacuated from Singapore. When our ship sank in Banka Strait we were all, if we survived, scattered in the water and had to struggle to get to land as best we could.

Betty and Iole Harper found themselves together and had to struggle for three days in the water, resting occasionally in mangrove swamps. They were eventually picked up by two Malay fishermen who took them to their village where they were well received. Here they were given food and water and a little first aid and they were then advised to give themselves up to the Japanese. Betty and Iole arrived in our camp sunburnt, tired, hungry and covered in bites and sores. The nurses who were already prisoners were overjoyed to see them and we couldn't stop talking. They were looked after as well as possible, a space was found for them on the cement floor and they lay down without any bedding and slept for three days.

Sixty-five nurses had left Singapore and there were 31 survivors until Vivian Bullwinkel joined us – making 32 nurses now in captivity. Taking a great risk, Betty was to record almost every day of our captivity in her diary. This later became the book *White Coolies*, which became the factual basis for radio, television and film about women in captivity under the Japanese.

Betty's wonderful sense of humour and her adjustment to our situation helped us all. During our imprisonment she never lost hope of eventually finding Matron Paschke and her friends. During our three-and-a-half years of incarceration she was ever helpful and inspiring – full of fun when things were grim. I recall on one Melbourne Cup day in the camp, Betty found an old bag, slung it over her shoulder and called the odds. A lovely, light-hearted moment when we were all hungry.

She was a familiar figure around the camp as she took part in all our chores, looking after the sick and the hygiene of the camp. Betty helped with the sharing out of the food and extra materials that were allowed into the camp.

With our meagre ration of rice and vegetables Betty was innovative and imaginative, dressing up the rice with a little oil or *kangkong*, which grows prolifically and resembles our spinach. In our sordid surroundings, Betty would always strive to make things as attractive and civilised as possible. Sometimes it was possible to borrow or buy a spoon or a bowl from the Dutch internees who brought their belongings into the camp with them.

Betty took her turn at the unpleasant jobs such as cleaning drains and emptying the toilets with good humour and grace. She was a member of the camp choir which has been immortalised in the film *Paradise Road*. The choir brought untold pleasures for the prisoners and Betty loved her part in it. As our captivity continued, the number of very ill grew to an alarming degree. Betty, though ill herself, always took her turn on the hospital roster, working under appalling conditions with great skill and compassion.

On our return home in October 1945, Betty was found to be suffering from severe tuberculosis and spent nearly two years in isolation receiving treatment for this condition. When the time came for her discharge from the AANS, she was to travel from the Heidelberg Repatriation Hospital to Royal Park Barracks for the formalities. The day was cold and, not having a greatcoat, Betty was offered the use of a colonel's coat for protection against the elements. This was most fortuitous for, on arrival at the barracks, the queues awaiting their processing for discharge were enormous. Noticing the insignias of her rank, Betty was ceremoniously ushered to the head of the line amidst calls of, *'Make way for the Colonel! Make way for the Colonel!'* With a mischievous twinkle in those blue eyes she acted out her role and was later to admit that it was the first time that she really enjoyed pulling rank.

Betty was a much loved and valued member of our camp life and a true friend since we were released. Since arriving home, Betty has had concern for the families of the nurses who lost their lives and has been active in keeping their memory alive. She has always mourned her friends – we spoke of them often.

In November 1947 Betty set out with Vivian Bullwinkel to fulfil an idea which was born in one of our camps. This was to establish a memorial in memory of our young nurses who were massacred at Radji Beach on Banka Island, or were lost at sea, and to those who

301

later died in the camps. The nurses who died on the *Centaur* were also to be remembered. Together, Betty and Vivian were to make two trips around the State of Victoria in Betty's little car to raise monies for the establishment of a Nurses Memorial Centre. By March 1948 they had raised £822/3/- towards the project. The next two years saw countless fundraising activities and by April 1949 a magnificent single-storeyed Victorian mansion was purchased for £22,500 at 431 St Kilda Road, Melbourne.

Once the centre was open, it was necessary to find someone who could manage it and Betty was appointed Administrator with a salary of 400 (Australian) pounds per year, plus board and residence. She really didn't want to take on the job, as she was so terribly tired after all her efforts at fundraising, and her war-related illnesses required many weeks of hospitalisation each year. Even before she took up this new position, she had to spend nearly a month in the Repatriation Hospital.

Betty also wanted to go overseas and after getting the centre up and running, in September 1950, she and Vivian were to travel together to the United Kingdom. Here they were to be presented to King George VI and Queen Elizabeth; to Queen Mary, the Queen Mother, and to the Duchess of Gloucester. A signed photograph of Queen Mary was to become one of her most treasured possessions.

Leaving Vivian behind in England, Betty returned to Australia at the end of 1951 to continue her work at the Nurses Memorial Centre. She held the position of Administrator until her continuing ill-health forced her retirement in 1954. These years at the centre were to cement the lasting friendship with Maie Casey, who later became Lady Casey, Baroness of Berwick and the City of Westminster.

A FULL LIFE OF STRENGTH AND HONOUR

Lady Casey worried about Betty often being alone in such a big mansion, so she gave her a little dog, Robbie, for company. Everyone at the Centre knew and loved Robbie and Betty still spoke of his escapades right up until the time of her death.

But her Administrator's duties did not always go according to the book, and Betty loved to recall the hot summer's day when she received a telephone call from Sir Clive Steele, the then president of the centre. He had rung to tell her that some men were coming to erect a small, temporary, wax model of the proposed Canberra American War Memorial in the shadiest part of the centre's gardens. In her own words: '*At about 2 pm I went out to see how it looked and was horrified to notice that the hot weather – about 103 degrees that day – was softening the wax a little. I rang and told Sir Clive, who was to arrive at about 5 pm with a small group of American men to see their model. He told me to 'keep an eye on it', which I did. At 3 pm it was beginning to look droopy, so I hosed it for a while to cool it down. At 4 pm the wings were really melting – more hosing. Finally I rang Sir Clive and suggested that they come as soon as they could. I was asked to keep hosing. When the American group finally arrived the Eagle's wings were so soft, they were almost folded – a depressing sight and water everywhere!*'

Despite the mess the Americans must have liked what they saw, for that eagle now soars majestically above Canberra.

Betty's retirement did not stop her love of people and challenges. She now had more time to pursue a number of interests: competitive golf at Huntingdale Golf Club; weekends away with golfing friends such as Dame Joan Hammond; card games with Girlie, Simmy, Dulcie and other friends from the Returned Nurses' Club; club luncheons and other activities, as well as her strong support for the (then) newly established RAANC and later the Corps Association. She was unstinting in her loyalties and, despite her poor health, seemed tireless in her activities. She attended many reunions with both her POW friends and her 8th Division colleagues.

Betty kept in contact with her many overseas friends from camp days as well as her friends locally. Her letters were always a joy to receive and were very entertaining.

I know of one of our friends from camp who lives in England and has a grandchild with a disability. Betty wrote bright and charming letters for some years to the mother of that child. This is a measure of her compassion.

Betty was much loved. We have lost a gifted and sincere friend. My personal loss is very great and in the words of Margaret Dryburgh: '*How silent is this place . . . a hush enfolds me, deep as I have known.*'

I want to express my sincere sympathy to Mary and her family. Betty, we must continue without you but you will live on in all our hearts. Farewell my friend. *Salamat Jalan.*

Much earlier, Wilma had recalled that in the last weeks before liberation, Betty was desperately ill in the Belalau, Loebok Linggau, camp hospital with a number of life-threatening ailments. Wilma had done what she could for her friend, scrounging up whatever medicines she could from the very few available. One onerous part of her duty was to assess who might die that day and make the necessary preparations. 'We had coffins lined up ready, leaning against the wall of the hospital,' she told historian Barbara Angell. 'Then we had to have graves dug.' One day, Betty was coherent enough to know why Wilma was standing at the end of her bed space. She was there to see if she should dig a grave for Betty that day. Betty looked up and said: 'On you go. I'm not dying today.'

She was not to know for some time after that Wilma had already – and reluctantly – dug a grave for Betty in the camp cemetery. When Betty had recovered most of her strength soon after the war ended, she was surprised when Wilma confessed this to her. She said with a smile on her face, 'I'll never forgive you for that.' Wilma returned the smile, saying, 'Somebody had to dig it, Jeff.' As it turned out, the grave was eventually filled by someone else, but for the rest of her days Betty would always laughingly call Wilma 'That wretched girl who dug my grave!'

In an interview she gave in her final years, Betty was asked what perspective her years as a prisoner gave to her, and how this might be passed on to a younger generation.

I think I came alive. I have always said it wasn't a prisoner of war camp, it was the University of Southern Sumatra. I have always called my prison days as my life at the University of Southern Sumatra because I learnt so much. It was a wonderful experience if you survived. Wasn't too good if you didn't! I gained more tolerance. You stop and you listen. You can always learn. We are better people for it. There is no doubt about it.

And her advice for those young people?

Keep doing things. Keep earning. Help everybody. Be interested. For goodness sake, don't have any wars. Make the peace. Try for peace first before going to war. Don't get hot headed and think 'Right-o, let's get into them.' Don't do that! They are human beings too. Whoever they are. And have a good time. This is a wonderful land of ours and we are part of a pretty wonderful world. Be part of it!

Betty Jeffrey's final resting place is a rose garden within the Springvale Botanical Cemetery, alongside her parents William (1870–1951) and Amelia Matilda (Cooley) Jeffrey (1875–1960) and sisters Frances Amy Gale (1907–1989) and Gwenyth Mary Denny (1911–2013). She rests in eternal peace beside her beloved Will and Millie, Mickey and Mary.

During World War II, around 3500 nurses served with the Australian Army Nursing Service. When that conflict broke out in 1939, the AANS was the only service in which women could actively participate, but due to a desperate need for further nurses this led to the formation of the Royal Australian Air Force Nursing Service (RAAFNS) in 1940 and the Royal Australian Navy Nursing Service (RANNS) two years later. Their courage and fortitude, caring and compassion, is reflected in today's nurses, who selflessly protect the weak, the aged, the sick and those most vulnerable in today's society. Most would know and acknowledge the inspiration and example set by many of those named in this book, particularly Sisters Betty Jeffrey and Vivian Bullwinkel, as well as the dedication and sacrifice of those such as Matrons Irene Drummond and Olive Paschke.

Although she witnessed and experienced the very worst of evils and inhumanity that war and a deplorable unaccountability can often and brutally inflict on the innocent, Betty Jeffrey and her fellow nurses always stood tall and resolute in their devotion to their patients. This would never waver, despite their own personal pain and suffering, and Betty always took care to acknowledge her pride and admiration for those with whom she served. When life seemed at its lowest ebb, they were always there, ready to reach out and hold the hands of the grievously ill or injured, while constantly despairing at the almost total lack of life-saving medicines, equipment and materials that could have saved so many lost lives. These women knew how to protect and comfort others, but the sheer callousness of their captors deprived them of even those fundamentals of medicine and decent food.

There is a stoic dignity that lives on in today's nursing fraternity. They can look back with pride at those colleagues who have served and often suffered in times of war. They stand in the light of the candle that has shone on such early pioneers of care as Florence Nightingale, Edith Cavell and Australian nurse Nellie Gould, who served overseas during the Boer War and World War I.

Famed author Louisa May Alcott saw service as a battlefield nurse during the American Civil War, spending each wearying day, according to biographer Rachel Williams, in

a tiring whirlwind of dressing wounds, cleaning and sewing bandages, supervising convalescent assistants, fetching bed linens, water, and pillows, assisting during surgical procedures, sponging filthy, broken bodies (a shocking experience for an unmarried lady!), writing letters on behalf of the sick and injured, and feeding those too weak to feed themselves.

Betty Jeffrey would surely have agreed that little has changed since then. We should all sincerely thank and remember her and all those fellow nurses – civilian and military – in Australia and around the world for their service in tumultuous times of war, disaster and need, and for creating a truly mighty legacy of selfless caring that not only continues unabated to this day, but will forever endure.

Appendix 1

NURSES WHO DIED FOLLOWING THE ATTACK ON SS *VYNER BROOKE*

Sister Louvinia Mary Isabella **Bates** (32), 2/13 AGH, WFX11169, Fremantle, Western Australia

Nurse Ellenor (Nell) **Calnan** (29), 2/10 AGH, QFX19072, Culcairn, New South Wales

Nurse Mary Dorothea **Clarke** (30), 2/10 AGH, NFX70938, Rylstone, New South Wales

Senior Nurse Millicent Hulda (Millie) **Dorsch** (29), 2/4 CCS, SFX10597, Brighton, South Australia

Sister Caroline Mary **Ennis** (28), 2/10 AGH, VFX38751, Swan Hill, Victoria

Sister Kathleen (Kit) **Kinsella** (37), 2/4 CCS, VFX61126, South Yarra, Victoria

Sister Gladys Myrtle **McDonald** (32), 2/13 AGH, QFX22815, Ashgrove, Queensland

Matron Olive Dorothy **Paschke** (36), 2/10 AGH, VFX38812, Dimboola, Victoria

Sister Lavinia Jean **Russell** (32), 2/10 AGH, NFX70571, Hurstville, New South Wales

Sister Marjorie (Shule) **Schuman** (31), 2/10 AGH, NFX70520, Inverell, New South Wales

Sister Annie (Merle) **Trenerry** (32), 2/13 AGH, SFX13419, Moonta, South Australia

Sister Mona Margaret **Wilton** (28), 2/13 AGH, VFX61225, Willaura, Victoria

- *AGH: Army General Hospital*
- *CCS: Casualty Clearing Station*

Appendix 2

NURSES MURDERED BY JAPANESE SOLDIERS ON BANKA ISLAND

Sister Elaine Lenore **Balfour-Ogilvy** (30), 2/4 CCS, SFX10596

Sister Alma May **Beard** (29), 2/13 AGH, WFX11175

Sister Ada Joyce **Bridge** (34), 2/13 AGH, NFX76284

Sister Florence Rebecca **Casson** (38), 2/13 AGH, SFX13418

Sister Mary Elizabeth **Cuthbertson** (31), 2/10 AGH, VFX38746

Matron (midwife) Irene Melville **Drummond** (36), 2/13 AGH, SFX10594

Sister Dorothy Gwendoline Howard **Elmes** (28), 2/10 AGH, NFX70526

Sister Lorna Florence **Fairweather** (29), 2/13 AGH, SFX13431

Sister Peggy Everett **Farmaner** (28), 2/4 CCS, WFX3438

Sister Clarice Isobel **Halligan** (37), 2/10 AGH, VFX47776

Sister Nancy **Harris** (31), 2/13 AGH, NFX76285

Sister Minnie Ivy **Hodgson** (33), 2/13 AGH, WFX11174

Sister Ellen Louisa **Keats** (26), 2/10 AGH, SFX11647

Sister Janet **Kerr** (31), 2/13 AGH, NFX76279

Sister Mary Eleanor **McGlade** (38), 2/13 AGH, NFX76275

Sister Kathleen Margaret **Neuss** (30), 2/10 AGH, NFX70527
Sister Florence Aubin **Salmon** (26), 2/10 AGH, NFX70991
Sister Esther Sarah Jean **Stewart** (37), 2/10 AGH, NFX70936
Sister Mona Margaret Anderson **Tait** (27), 2/13 AGH, NFX76281
Sister Rosetta Joan **Wight** (33), 2/13 AGH, VFX61329
Sister Bessie **Wilmott** (28), 2/4 CCS, WFX3439

Note: There was also a British civilian, Carrie Rose Faraday Betteridge, among the victims. She had chosen to stay with her husband of 50 years, Thomas, and was present when he was butchered by Japanese soldiers. She bravely walked into the water with the nurses, knowing her fate.

Appendix 3

NURSES WHO WERE PRISONERS OF THE JAPANESE IN SUMATRA

Died in Sumatra

Winnie May (Win) **Davis** (2/10 AGH), Rubina Dorothy (Dot) **Freeman** (2/10 AGH), Dora Shirley **Gardam** (2/4 CCS), Pauline (Blanche) **Hempstead** (113 AGH), Gladys Laura **Hughes** (2/13 AGH), Pearl Beatrice (Mitz) **Mittelheuser** (2/10 AGH), Wilhelmina Rosalie (Mina/Ray) **Raymont** (2/4 CCS), Irene Ada (Rene) **Singleton** (2/4 CCS)

Returned to Australia in 1945

Jean C. **Ashton** (2/13 AGH), K.C. (Pat) **Blake** (2/10 AGH), Jessie J. (Blanchie) **Blanch** (2/10 AGH), Vivian (Viv) **Bullwinkel** (2/13 AGH), Veronica R. **Clancy** (2/13 AGH), Cecilia E.M. (Del) **Delforce** (2/10 AGH), Jess G. **Doyle** (2/10 AGH), Jean (Jennie) **Greer** (2/13 AGH), Janet P. (Pat) **Gunther** (2/10 AGH), E. Mavis **Hannah** (2/4 CCS), Iole **Harper** (2/13 AGH), Nesta **James** (2/10 AGH), A. Betty **Jeffrey** (2/10 AGH), Violet I. (Vi) **McElnea** (2/13 AGH), Sylvia J. **Muir** (2/10 AGH), Wilma E.F. **Oram** (2/13 AGH),

Christian S.M. (Chris) **Oxley** (2/10 AGH), Eileen M. (Shortie) **Short** (2/13 AGH), Jessie E. **Simons** (2/13 AGH), Valerie E. (Val) **Smith** (2/13 AGH), Ada C. (Mickey) **Syer** (2/10 AGH), Florence E. (Flo) **Trotter** (2/10 AGH), Joyce (Tweedie) **Tweddell** (2/10 AGH), Beryl (Woodie) **Woodbridge** (1/10 AGH)

Appendix 4

THE NURSES WE HAVE LOST TO ALL WARS

BOER WAR
HINES, Sister Frances Emma

WORLD WAR I
BERRIE, Sister Charlotte
BICKNELL, Sister Louisa Annie
BRENNAN, Sister Kathleen Adele
CLARE, Sister Emily
DICKINSON, Sister Ruby
HENNESSY, Sister May
HOBBES, Sister Florence Narrelle Jessie
KNOX, Sister Hilda Mary
McPHAIL, Sister Irene
MILES-WALKER, Matron Jean Nellie
MOORHOUSE, Sister Edith Anne
MORETON, Sister Letitia Gladys
MOWBRAY, Sister Norma Violet

MUNRO, Sister Gertrude Evelyn

NUGENT, Sister Lily

O'GRADY, Sister Amy Veda

O'KANE, Sister Rosa

PORTER, Sister Katherine Agnes Lawrence

POWER, Sister Kathleen

RIDGWAY, Sister Doris Alice

RIGGALL, Sister Louisa Blanche

ROTHERY, Sister Elizabeth

STAFFORD, Sister Mary Florence

THOMPSON, Sister Ada Mildred

TYSON, Sister Fanny Isobel Catherine

WATSON, Sister Beatrice Middleton

WILLIAMS, Sister Blodwyn Elizabeth

WILSON, Sister Myrtle Elizabeth

WORLD WAR II
(Army and WRAAF)

ADAMS, Captain Margaret Lamont

ATKINSON, Sister Marguerite May

BALFOUR-OGILVY, Sister Elaine Lenore

BATES, Sister Louvinia Mary Isabella

BEARD, Sister Alma May

BRIDGE, Sister Ada Joyce

CALNAN, Sister Ellenor

CASSON, Sister Florence Rebecca

CLARKE, Sister Mary Dorothea

CONNELL, Sister Joan

COX, Captain Florence Adelaide

CRAIG, Sister Marie Eileen

CUTHBERTSON, Sister Mary Elizabeth

DAVIS, Captain Winnie May

De MESTRE, Sister Margaret Augusta

DOIDGE, Lieutenant Doris Eileen

DONOHUE, Captain Ellen

DORSCH, Sister Hilda Millicent Maria

DRUMMOND, Matron Irene Melville

ELMES, Sister Dorothy Gwendoline Howard

ENNIS, Sister Caroline Mary

EUNSON, Sister Marion Watt

FAIRWEATHER, Sister Lorna Florence

FARMANER, Sister Peggy Everett

FINCH, Staff Nurse Nancy Mary

FOULKES, Lieutenant Francesca Mary

FREEMAN, Sister Rubina Dorothy

GARDAM, Sister Dora Shirley

GAY, Staff Nurse Jean Margaret

HALLIGAN, Sister Clarice Isobel

HARRIS, Sister Nancy

HAULTAIN, Sister Helen Frances Jane Cynthia

HEMPSTED, Captain Pauline Blanche

HODGSON, Sister Minnie Ivy

HUGHES, Lieutenant Gladys Laura

JACKSON, Sister Margaret Lawrence

JEWELL, Matron Sarah Anne

KEATS, Sister Ellen Louisa

KERR, Sister Janet

KING, Sister Evelyn Veronica

KINSELLA, Sister Kathleen

LONG, Sister Sheila Mary

MITTELHEUSER, Captain Pearl Beatrice

MORTON, Staff Nurse Edith Mary

MOSTON, Captain Myrtle

McDONALD, Sister Gladys Myrtle

McFARLANE, Sister Mary Hamilton

McGLADE, Sister Mary Eleanor

McMAHON, Lieutenant Bernadine Theresa

McPHAIL, Sister Lilian Elaine

NEUSS, Sister Kathleen Margaret

O'DONNELL, Sister Alice Margaret

PASCHKE, Matron Olive Dorothy

PRIDEAUX, Lieutenant Nita Alice

RAYMONT, Lieutenant Wilhelmina Rosalie

ROBERTSON, Sister Gwendoline Hope

RUTHERFORD. Captain Eileen Mary

RUSSELL, Sister Lavinia Joan

SALMON, Sister Florence Annin

SCHUMAN, Sister Marjorie

SHAW, Sister Edna Alice

SHEAH, Sister Verdun Bernice

SINGLETON, Lieutenant Irene Ada

SMITH, Lieutenant Lillian Winifred

STEWART, Sister Esther Sarah Jean

STEVENSON, Lieutenant Frances Amy

STEVENSON, Lieutenant Heather Lillian

TAIT, Sister Mona Margaret Anderson

THIEDEKE, Sister Cynthia Mabel

THOMAS, Matron Gladys Margaret

TRENERRY, Sister Annie Merle

WALKER, Sister Wendy Jenny

WIGHT, Sister Rosetta Joan

WILMOTT, Sister Bessie

WILTON, Sister Mona Margaret

WYLLIE, Sister Doris Joyce

VIETNAM

BLACK, Captain Barbara Frances

Appendix 5

AUSTRALIAN ARMY NURSING SERVICE (AANS) PLEDGE OF SERVICE

I pledge myself loyally to service King and Country and to maintain the honour and efficiency of the Australian Army Nursing Service. I will do all in my power to alleviate the suffering of the sick and wounded, sparing no effort to bring them comfort of body and peace of mind. I will work in unity and comradeship with my fellow nurses. I will be ready to give assistance to those in need of my help and will abstain from any action which may bring sorrow and suffering to others. At all times I will endeavour to uphold the highest traditions of Womanhood and of the Profession of which I am Part.

Map 1: Route taken by SS *Vyner Brooke*

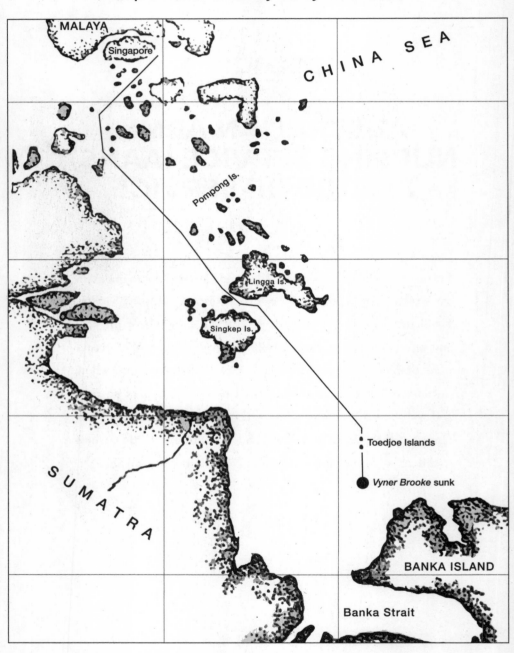

The ship was sunk off the northern tip of Banka Island

Map 2: Routes taken by the nurses when changing camps

Source: Muntok Peace Museum

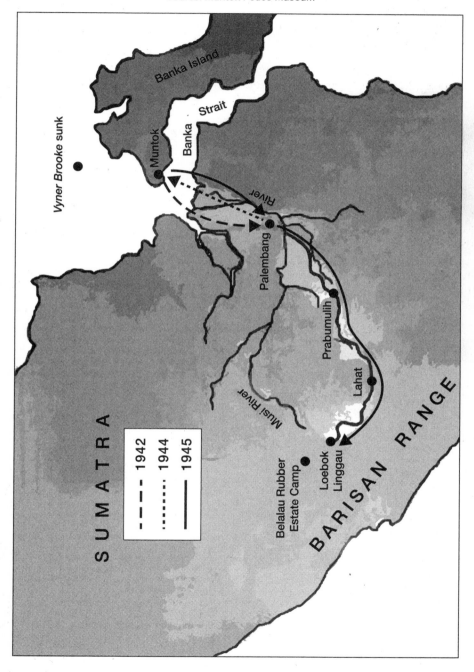

ABBREVIATIONS AND ACRONYMS

AAMC	Australian Army Medical Corps
AANS	Australian Army Nursing Service
ABC	Australian Broadcasting Corporation
AGH	Australian General Hospital
AHS	Australian Hospital Ship
AIF	Australian Imperial Force
AM	Member of the Order of Australia
ANMC	Australian Nurses Memorial Centre
ANSR	Army Nurses Service Reserve
AO	Order of Australia
ARRC	Associate Royal Red Cross
BBC	British Broadcasting Commission
CBE	Commander of the Order of the British Empire
CCS	Casualty Clearing Station
CMF	Commonwealth Military Forces
CWO	Catholic Welfare Organisation
DADMS	Deputy Assistant Director Medical Services

DBE	Dame of the British Empire
ED	Efficiency Decoration
FCNA	Fellow of the College of Nursing Australia
FNM	Florence Nightingale Medal
FRCNA	Fellow of the Royal College of Nursing Australia
GM	George Medal
GOC	General Officer Commanding
GPO	General Post Office
HMAS	His Majesty's Australian Ship
HMAHS	His Majesty's Australian Hospital Ship
HMAT	His Majesty's Australian Transport
HMS	His Majesty's Ship
MBE	Member of the Order of the British Empire
MV	Motor Vessel
OAM	Order of Australia
OBE	Order of the British Empire
POW	Prisoner of War
QARANC	Queen Alexandra's Royal Army Nursing Corps
RAF	Royal Air Force
RAAF	Royal Australian Air Force
RAAFNS	Royal Australian Air Force Nursing Service
RAANC	Royal Australian Army Nursing Corps
RAMC	Royal Army Medical Corps
RAN	Royal Australian Navy
RANNS	Royal Australian Navy Nursing Service
RN	Royal Navy
RN	Registered Nurse
RNR	Registered Nurse, Retired
RRC	Royal Red Cross

ABBREVIATIONS AND ACRONYMS

RSL	Returned Services League
SS	Steamship
TSMV	Twin Screw Motor Vessel
USS	United States Ship
YWCA	Young Women's Christian Association

SELECT BIBLIOGRAPHY

Adam-Smith, Patsy, *Prisoners of War: From Gallipoli to Korea*, Penguin Books, 1997

Angell, Barbara, *A Woman's War: The Exceptional Life of Wilma Oram Young, AM*, New Holland Publishers, 2003

Armstrong, Ralph E.H., *Short Cruise on the Vyner Brooke*, George Mann Books, 2003

Ashton, Jill, *Jean's Diary: A POW Diary 1942–1945* (transcribed by Joyce Ashton), privately published, 2003

Bassett, Jan, *Guns and Brooches*, Oxford University Press, 1992

Colijn, Helen, *Song of Survival*, White Cloud Press, 1997

Darling, Pat, *Portrait of a Nurse*, Don Wall Books, 2001

De Vries, Susanna, *Heroic Australian Women in War*, HarperCollins, 2004

Dixon, Jim and Bob Goodwin, *Medicos and Memories: Further Recollections of the 2/10th Field Regiment*, Birkdale, 2000

Henning, Peter, *Veils and Tin Hats: Tasmanian Nurses in the Second World War*, BookPOD, 2013

Jeffrey, Antony, *The Poinciana Tree*, Connor Court Publishing, 2022

Jeffrey, Betty, *Matron A.M. Sage: 'Sammie'*, privately published, c. 1970

Jeffrey, Betty, *White Coolies*, Angus & Robertson, 1954

Kenny, Catherine, *Captives: Australian Army Nurses in Japanese Prison Camps*, University of Queensland Press, 1986

Kirkland, Ian, *Blanchie: Alstonville's Inspirational World War II Nurse*, Alstonville Plateau Historical Society, 2012

Mann, A.J., *One Jump Ahead: Escape on the Vyner Brooke*, Harry Nicholson, 2020

Manners, Norman G., *Bullwinkel*, Hesperian Press, 1999

McDougall, William H., Jr., *By Eastern Windows: The Story of a Battle of Souls and Minds in the Prison Camps of Sumatra*, Charles Scriber's Sons, 1949

Nelson, Hank, *Prisoners of War: Australians Under Nippon*, ABC Books, 2001

Shaw, Ian W., *On Radji Beach*, Macmillan Australia, 2010

Silver, Lynette, *Angels of Mercy: Far West & Far East*, Sally Milner Publishing, 2019

Simons, Jessie Elizabeth, *While History Passed*, William Heinemann, 1954

Smyth, Sir John, *The Will to Live: The Story of Dame Margot Turner, DBE, RRC*, Cassell & Co., 1970

Twomey, Christina, *Australia's Forgotten Prisoners*, Cambridge University Press, 2007

Warner, Lavinia and John Sandilands, *Women Beyond the Wire*, Michael Joseph, 1982

SELECT BIBLIOGRAPHY

Williams, Jennifer, *Victoria's Living Memorial: History of the Nurses Memorial Centre 1948-1880*, Nurses Memorial Centre Publication, 1991

'Survival at Sea' (author not listed), *Grey and Scarlet*, annual magazine of the Royal Australian Army Nursing Corps (RAANC), 1980 issue

Website: The Muntok Memorial Peace Museum: https://muntokpeacemuseum.org

INDEX OF NAMES

INDEX OF NAMES

ABOUT THE AUTHOR

COLIN BURGESS WAS BORN IN suburban Sydney, Australia, in 1947. He joined Qantas Airways as a passenger handling agent in 1970, later transferring to become a flight attendant. He subsequently flew as cabin crew management with the airline for 30 years. During this time he was also the editor of two Qantas monthly publications, and for one of these wrote a well-received series of articles on famous Australian aviators.

His first book, *The Diggers of Colditz* (co-authored with Colditz veteran Jack Champ), was published in 1985. It told the stories of Australian officers who were held in the notorious German castle prison of Oflag IVC, Colditz. While writing another book on 168 Australian and Allied airmen who were illegally held in Buchenwald concentration camp (*Destination Buchenwald*), he was also commissioned to write two children's books on Australian aviation and the story of human space flight. Since then, he has had numerous non-fiction books published on a wide variety of subjects, mostly on the Australian prisoner-of-war experience, aviation humour and the history of human space exploration, with more than 40 published books to his name.

In 2002, after 32 years' total service with Qantas Airways, Colin took an early retirement in order to concentrate on his writing career. In 2003, he was appointed Series Editor for a set of books published by the University of Nebraska Press under the series title of *Outward Odyssey*, detailing the entire history of space exploration. To date, there are 21 published books in the series.

Colin lives in Sydney with his wife Pat; they have two adult sons and three grandchildren.